TALKING BACK TO THE BIBLE:

A Historian's Approach to Bible Study

by

Edward G. Simmons, Ph.D.

DORRANCE
PUBLISHING CO
EST. 1920
PITTSBURGH, PENNSYLVANIA 15238

Dorrance Publishing Co
585 Alpha Drive
Suite 103
Pittsburgh, PA 15238
Visit our website at *www.dorrancebookstore.com*

ISBN: 978-1-4809-2709-4
eISBN: 978-1-4809-2847-3

"Being Christian ... is about a deepening relationship with the God to whom the Bible points...."

"[T]he biblical canon names the primary collection of ancient documents with which Christians are to be in continuing dialogue. This continuing conversation is definitive and constitutive of Christian identity. ... Thus the authority of the Bible is its status as our primary ancient conversational partner."

Marcus Borg
Reading the Bible Again for the First Time

CONTENTS

PREFACE

This work brings to completion the efforts of many years, yet it is more of a beginning than an ending. Having just reached my seventy-first birthday, I feel that a medium has been found through which I can express the thoughts of a lifetime in a way that will be useful and interesting to a reading public.

Over many years, I began several writing projects to share what was learned through pleasurable study and contemplation. Teaching has always come naturally as a way of communicating, yet putting the same thoughts in writing led to dissatisfaction with one approach after another. In my sixties, I became determined to follow through and complete a major writing project. In the last three years there were several outlines of a major project followed by writing the first fifty pages. Each time, the scope would shift in my thinking to include more and more material so that it became necessary to start again in order to lay the proper foundation. My friend Ben Jordan at Vanderbilt was patient as he read over several drafts that he doubted would find a readership in today's publishing market.

Through the years I have always found it easy to express myself in short pieces of just a few pages. Many of them were shared with Ben. Early last spring, he looked over the most extensive manuscript yet produced, which had been rewritten to become more autobiographical than before. About that time I also sent him a short piece I had written on a related topic. He came back with a suggestion to recast the book into what he called vignettes that put autobiographical content with scholarship. At first I resisted the thought, but it settled deep within and began to emerge as five or six short pieces were written. Within two weeks a projected table of contents was written that changed very little as the book progressed. In the grips of inspiration and rushes of adrenalin, I wrote half the book in about a month. The years of thought and rewriting material found its shape and burst onto the page.

This work consists of a series of short reflections. Ben calls them vignettes. They could be called mini-lectures, short essays, or sometimes sermons. The pieces are separate topics, but there is a progression without an effort at developing a central argument. We begin with Jesus, organizing topics to reflect the course of his career through crucifixion and resurrection. Attention then turns to topics that survey the scope of Old Testament themes, jumping from the apocalyptic section of Daniel to Revelation at the end. Relationship with God is the underlying theme of the book and the point toward which the conversations point. Within this arrangement there are clusters of pieces on similar themes, just as a concerto or symphony have separate movements that develop a theme into individual yet related musical personalities.

The completed product has less history and more autobiography than originally anticipated. This may be the first of many collections of short pieces on religion, history, and education as the insights of a career that was far broader in experience than I ever anticipated are put into writing. At this point in life, I am blessed with health, energy, and opportunities that are bringing things together.

God blesses us through the influence of others in our lives. I am grateful for a community of faith at the First Presbyterian Church in Gainesville, Georgia, for welcoming me into a spiritual home that was lacking for a long time. Brenau University in Gainesville and Georgia Gwinnett College in Lawrenceville, Georgia, have made it possible for me to share love of scholarship and life experiences with young students and retirees. I am especially grateful to Kathy Amos at the Brenau Center for Lifetime Study for helping to pave the way for my involvement at two institutions of higher learning. There was also another friend whose generosity and networking ability pointed the way to opening doors that had been shut. My wife and I enjoy the benefit of those realized opportunities and recognize how much we owe to the thoughtful assistance I received.

When I first arrived on campus at Mercer University, I met four people within a few days who became lifelong influences. First was Rev. Thomas J. Holmes, the alumni director whose efforts helped me find employment that paid my tuition. We became friends, but it was three years before I met his daughter and soon after made the Holmes family my family. Even through divorce, they have remained my family of preference as friendship was maintained over the years.

Next I met Dr. Willis B. Glover, a native of Mississippi who earned a Harvard doctorate. Having the good fortune to strike up a conversation with him just before going into registration, I saw him rearrange all my classes so that I would be in his class. He became a mentor and then a second father who made a lasting impression. Through him I realized that I wanted to be a college professor.

I took only two courses the first quarter—history under Glover and introduction to New Testament under his neighbor Professor Ray Brewster. I soon learned the meaning of community on a small college campus as each class turned into an ongoing friendly rivalry between next-door neighbors and good friends. To know one was to get to know the other. Through a long life, Ray Brewster has continued to exert loving influence on several generations of Mercer students.

That first quarter I shared both classes with Ben Jordan and I soon joined the coterie of guys who gathered in his room. Charisma made his friendship very sought after. At first he irritated many who frequented his room by tolerating me, but eventually we became close friends. Similar interests and the friendship of our wives has continued over the decades since then and has brought many valuable friends gained through his ability to relate to people.

Finally, I am grateful at this point in life to have found partnership, trustworthiness, and love that have not been matched in previous relationships. How wonderful it is to share so much with such a loving wife as Vickie.

Introduction

Conversation and Historical Awareness

One of the greatest pleasures in my life has been listening to people talk. This became a notable pattern early in life and continued through college and professional careers.

When I was seven years old, my maternal uncles let me move from the children's table to eat with the men. They told the most wonderful stories and their wives served everyone and then sat together to talk among themselves. At the end of the meal, the women would sit near the men and join in their stories over dessert. My aunts and uncles talked about the misadventures of their youth, of the sternness of my grandparents when they found out what their kids were doing, and how many people helped them stay on track in spite of their mischievous ways. They laughed and talked and talked. It was always hard to break up those family times and I wanted to be there to hear every golden word.

At the age of twelve, I lived six blocks from the public library and spent every Friday morning during the summers listening to someone read stories to a room full of children. This was also the age of radio drama when stories were acted over the air. My imagination loved to play with images by word of mouth before the world was taken over by television.

As a child I was also taught to listen to the Bible. It was read in Sunday school and morning worship services. When you listen to the Bible, you are trying to hear God speaking for today. Usually you were to listen to the commands and eternal truths to be learned. Talking back was not good manners for children or an accepted practice when reading the Bible. Listening was to lead to obedience without questioning authority.

Growing into an adult, I learned the importance of conversation. Some people, like ministers, thought they were good at conversation because they talked so much and people seemed to listen. But a valuable lesson for me was that keen listening was necessary for meaningful conversation—and conversation worked best when you could speak back to authority.

Many people will say that I talked an awful lot in my adult life, especially since a lot of time was spent teaching. But listening has been a key to what was accomplished professionally. Much of my time was spent as a consultant and mediator. Those roles involved getting other people to talk and playing referee to keep it within productive boundaries. It is important to set rules to be followed in the conversation. For example, a key rule is to take responsibility for oneself rather than blaming others. When someone says "you make me so angry when you attack me in these ways," that person is expressing blame. The better approach is to say "when you do these things, I feel these ways and then I behave in specific ways that I later regret." The last example has the person taking responsibility for reactions and doesn't blame others.

When you set parameters and police them gently but firmly, positive conversation can occur. Then as a consultant or mediator, you have to listen carefully to the words and feelings behind the words in order to ask questions that keep the conversation flowing in constructive ways. This is what Socrates described as being like a midwife assisting in the birth of real communication between people. Anytime you want to get people talking, you have to know how to ask questions and then listen carefully to know how to channel the resulting flow of words in the right direction.

I think most of us have had experiences when many people kept trying to talk at the same time, leading to general frustration because no one could get themselves heard. To have productive conversation, there must be active, intensive listening as well as talking. Good listening is not just absorbing and memorizing what is heard. It means taking statements in with active mental processing that leads to questions that take the communication to deeper levels of understanding.

All my life I have heard that we should listen to God as heard in the Bible. Too often that meant listening in order to parrot back correct answers or simply obey commands. Why shouldn't we listen to the Bible interactively, raising questions that probe for deeper levels of communication? There are groups of Christians that become very upset when they think you are putting skeptical questions to the Bible as if it didn't represent eternal truth.

I have many close friends from college, and we have talked of how we learned as much from our bull sessions as from the classes we attended. Three groups were important in college. The least important of them was a social organization that allowed me to live on a dormitory floor with congenial people who had parties, dances, and other organized functions. The other two groups did more to shape my thoughts and lifelong friendships. One group was made up of guys who took history and religion courses together, so that our wide-ranging, late-night conversations tended to focus on those topics. The last group was people who were on the staff of the university newspaper. Our talk was most often on politics, literature, and philosophy.

In college I learned a new meaning for the word argument. Ordinarily, argument was a disagreement in which people were emotional and did a lot of shouting because they were angry. Many times they were almost fistfights. Arguments were considered a bad thing in high school and would get you sent to the principal's office. But in college we argued all the time. In this situation making an argument was stating a case for a position and standing your ground as many people attacked it vehemently. There was a lot of shouting and sometimes it got emotional, but always in good fun. Your position was turned inside out and upside down to see if it had strength. Shouting went with the pursuit of logic in a passionate way and seldom involved losing one's temper or getting personal in a negative way. This was real conversation full of energy. Listening and participating in these exchanges was what I lived for when I hung out with my favorite groups.

Interacting with the Bible can be that invigorating. In the course of these student discussions, we developed close attachments that have lasted through the years. Our passionate arguments over the Bible led many of us to have the same feelings about the Bible as well. Many parents were always worried that questioning articles of faith would lead us astray. Perhaps that did happen to some people, but that has not been my experience. Vigorous conversation with the Bible led to a more vital relationship with God for me and many of my friends.

Really listening can bring insights many people find threatening. For example, prayer, like Bible study, has been considered a pious activity during which praise and earnest supplication are most appropriate. The idea that prayers should complain or bitterly accuse God was not part of my upbringing.

The notion of actually including curses in a prayer definitely was out of place. Yet, when really listening to the book of Psalms, you find that one of the most used formats for Jewish prayer and poetry was the lament, a complaint. Look at Psalm 22:1–2 with fresh eyes and you can't avoid hearing the outright criticism in the words:

> My God, my God, why have you forsaken me?
> Why are you so far from helping me, from the words of my groaning?
> O my God, I cry by day, but you do not answer; and by night, but find no rest.

There is no piety or meekness to be seen in those demanding words. Look at the pathos and agony of Psalm 137 as Jews complain about being asked to sing one of the hymns from the temple in a foreign land beside the rivers of Babylon. The beginning of this psalm is often quoted, but how many people notice the irreverent concluding words:

> O daughter of Babylon, you devastator!
> Happy shall they be who pay you back what you have done to us!
> Happy shall they be who take your little ones and dash them against the rock! (137:8-9)

This is a prayer that ends by calling down a curse on their victorious enemies.

To me prayer and Bible reading are part of a relationship with God. As with all relationships, there must be room for expressing a wide variety of emotions, some of them not very presentable, without fear of one side breaking off the relationship. That is why apologizing and making up are a regular feature of most enduring relationships. Handling the Bible and God with kid gloves is out of step with the demanding tone of much of the poetry and prophecy in the Old Testament.

Looking ahead, a good friend told me I should state the purpose of this book in just a few sentences and why anyone should want to read it. That is what I will do in the balance of this introduction, looking first at purpose and then suggesting who might want to read it and why. Next comes more information about why a historian should be presenting Bible studies from a historian's point of view. Finally, I will explain key elements of a historian's approach to studying Jesus.

What you will find in this collection are examples of how to question and listen to the Bible from the perspective of a historian who is also a Christian. The pieces in this collection do not teach about Bible study but illustrate it through examination of thirty-eight separate yet connected themes. The idea is to produce real conversations with the Bible and a basis for relationship with God that does not use theology to interpret history. The result will be Bible studies that I hope are inspirational as well as provocative and insightful. This is a way to do Bible study that takes off the blinders that come with a devotional approach as it brings in the results of modern scholarship while also recognizing the shortcomings of traditional scholarship representing theological approaches. These studies represent a new twist to the historical approach to biblical studies and a confessional rather than devotional emphasis as a personal relationship with God is the bottom line, not just historical information.

The first part of the book examines themes concerning Jesus as found in the gospels. Then it turns to examining themes that cover a significant part of the Old Testament. No effort is made to present a sequential story of the historical Jesus or of the development of the Old Testament. These are discussions of separate but related themes without trying to offer a comprehensive view. The Bible, and the life of Jesus in particular, is too rich to be encompassed in a single rational and sequential presentation—although N.T. Wright and John P. Meier have attempted to do just that, each of them in volumes totaling over two thousand pages all together.[1]

The audience, I hope, will be anyone who enjoys studying the Bible and prefers seeking new and challenging insights rather than devotional rehashing of traditional messages. Pastors, scholars, students, and anyone in quest of spiritual insight through Bible study should find these conversations entertaining, challenging, and inspirational. My hopes would be met if such readers found the insights presented here did indeed promote a stronger sense of relationship with God.

Why should a historian write Bible studies? Books that study the Bible and seek to clarify "the historical Jesus" claim to use historical methods, but they have come from ministers, Bible scholars, or theological professors connected to churches, seminaries, or religion departments rather than history departments in universities. Archaeologists have also contributed to biblical studies, bringing the results of their fieldwork and interpretations, which result in historical interpretations. All of these scholars may criticize my background and approach to biblical study because I lack specialized qualifications such as knowledge of Hebrew, Greek, and similar biblical languages as well as the specialized training in biblical interpretation or in archaeological methods.

Let me go a step further. Biblical scholars have been known for applying historical, critical methods to understand Jesus and the entire Bible by placing them in their historical context. These scholars have made claims of historical accomplishments, yet they have not been historians. Their training has been in biblical languages and theological specialties. Their devotion, too often, has been to history in the service of theology or philosophy. Among those who have exposed these flaws was Albert Schweitzer, who took pride in German scholarship on the historical Jesus while exposing the biases of the researchers who found a Jesus in line with their personal philosophies.[2] More recently, Geza Vermes[3] and Amy-Jill Levine[4] have been among those pointing to misconceptions of Jewish practices and beliefs in the New Testament that continued into modern scholarship. Richard Horsley has also declared that biblical scholars have used methods such as form criticism and "synthetic scholarly constructs" derived from application of theological methods and biases to distort history. Horsley goes on to argue that study of the historical Jesus has especially suffered from theological bias:

> The study of the historical Jesus developed as a subfield of New Testament studies, which in turn developed as a branch of theological studies in modern Western European culture. Those who investigate and write about Jesus are academically trained in and teach in theological schools or in university religious/theological studies departments, not in the field of history and history departments. Not surprisingly, the standard assumptions, procedures, and conceptual apparatus of historical Jesus studies have been heavily influenced or determined by modern Western Christian theology. Even the understanding of history, the most basic understanding of Jesus, and the key issues to be investigated have been determined by Christian theology.[5]

What are my qualifications? I am a historian who started teaching European history and became waylaid by the draft during the Vietnam War. Being unable to complete my dissertation while in military service, I found it necessary to seek another career in what I first thought would be a temporary detour. Upon completing the degree, I was earning too much in my role as a consultant to top managers in a large state agency to begin at the bottom in university teaching, so I taught as adjunct faculty from time to time in various universities as my busy calendar and travel schedule permitted.

While pursuing a career in organization development and management training, I continued to keep up with my first love of history and my keen interest in biblical studies, both of which have been lifelong pursuits. Running a close third was interest in popular scientific literature. Being a historian means that one knows how to do research. I especially kept up with historical Jesus research over the years and shared that knowledge over decades as an adult Sunday school teacher in Presbyterian churches.

I also worked with public relations people a great deal in my professional career, making me aware of the importance of communicating in nontechnical language. What you will see in this book is the application of ordinary life and professional experiences in communicating specialized information from historical, biblical, archaeological, and scientific sources in what I hope will be seen as down-to-earth writing.

My method will use parameters that may be uncomfortable to conservative Christians and those versed in historical criticism of the Bible. Two of the bedrocks of my life, along with belief in God, are science combined with historical awareness. Science is not infallible, but it is as close to certainty as human beings can come. There will be no nonsense about doubting evolution and other demonstrated knowledge. Yes, evolution has been verified in the laboratory through genetics, which is quickly becoming more and more important in our lives.[6]

You may wonder what is meant by using historical awareness as a parameter. This involves the recognition that humanity, like everything in the universe, is caught in the flow of ever-changing time. Humans evolve like all other forms of life. But humans have cultures that evolve and mutate faster than physical processes. The Bible is the product of earlier cultures that we can understand but must be careful in relating to our contemporary life in order to be true to the self-understanding of the earlier time. Everything that is a product of time will become dated in some way—there is no such thing as eternal truth to be found within this time-bound universe.

The conversations in this work talk back to the Bible and to conservative and liberal biblical research from the viewpoint of history in association with science. This does not imply disrespect for the Bible or biblical scholarship, for respect, in my opinion, does not mean blind acceptance or unquestioning obedience. Displacing the priority of theology means that matters of belief based on historical events depend on historical verification for their truthfulness. Statements claiming Jesus of course could do various wonderful things because he was God must be verifiable in order to be relied upon.

Jesus, rather than Christ, will be our focus as we examine the gospels. Scholars have often distinguished between the Jesus of history and the Christ of faith. This is a way of saying that Jesus was the person who was baptized by John, performed wonders, taught in parables, and was crucified in Jerusalem, while Christ is what Jesus became at the resurrection and afterward in the experience of his followers. The distinction is also between the proper use of history versus the proper use of theology. The gospels are theological works that tell of the historical Jesus, making them useful as sources. The role of Christ in relationship to God and history leads mostly to theology, especially in the form of doctrines like atonement, incarnation, and the trinity. The ways in which claims of the leadership of Christ have influenced historical events is a matter for historical study, but that is not the key interest of those who want to emphasize the importance of knowing Jesus as the Christ.

Christians have historically struggled with the relationship of Jesus and Christ. Orthodox doctrine teaches that Jesus was fully human and fully God. Explanations of this combination run into problems when one asks if Jesus was a sinner like other human beings. He was baptized by John and taught in the temple, which means that in both cases he went through purification processes like other normal Jews who believed they were sinners. Looking away from history and toward theological issues can twist authentic memories to conform to "the way it must have been" in order to fit current orthodoxy.

Historians operate differently. By focusing on Jesus, we will treat him as an ordinary human being who felt a special sense of mission and relationship with God. Whether he was divine is something that historians can neither verify nor deny with certainty. As we deal with the humanity of Jesus, we will recognize how that leads to different beliefs from those traditionally associated with his divinity; but whether Jesus ever was or became divine or semi-divine at any point is beyond the scope of historical study.

Judaism and Christianity have always claimed to be rooted in history. Therefore, claims based on faith cannot be maintained independent of historical verification. Historical knowledge is ever changing and never completely certain, so it is not equivalent to a scientific laboratory demonstration. Nevertheless, the best historical knowledge we can achieve through archaeology, historical criticism, and numerous other historical approaches must be respected as a reasonable check on theological flights of fancy. That is why these conversations will respect historical and scientific studies but use them with the understanding that all knowledge, no matter how certain it may seem now, will become dated as newer methods and viewpoints emerge.

You will see that dogmatic or ideological viewpoints are discouraged. Many of the opinions expressed may seem irreverent, but they are made from within a confessional perspective, for I see myself as Christian no matter whether others agree. You will also see a respect for Judaism and for many Jewish contributions to contemporary culture. In stating these views, I intend to recognize that historians do not approach their subjects without their own values and preferences, which can influence interpretation. Using historical procedure does not mean achieving objectivity and complete impartiality, rather it involves the honest recognition of the historian's preferences, which naturally shape the presentation of information and interpretation.

The purpose of conversation is to reach interpersonal depths by listening as well as talking. Real give and take is involved. Stating views candidly does not imply disrespect for the rights of others to have their own perspectives. Taking a historical approach that displaces the role of theology is not intended as disrespect for theology, merely recognition that they are different forms of knowledge with their own inner integrity. As a historian I will emphasize history. Yet I am also a person brought up in Christian traditions, which will color my interpretations. I will write from a confessional viewpoint that seeks to develop relationship with God and not just historical and scientific information about the Bible and Jesus. History and science in themselves provide no answer to the question of whether God exists. It is my belief in God that makes my interpretation confessional, but focusing on history and science in our method keeps the interpretation from becoming overtly theological.

It is not possible to have a relationship with the Bible as with a person; however, an interactive relationship with the Bible can lead to a more vital relationship with God. Although God is far above human comprehension, I definitely believe God has relationships with people and that the meaning of life is wrapped up in trying to develop that relationship through the roller-coaster ride that is our very short time on this planet.

The pieces in this collection are intended as examples of conversations with the Bible. They will include some criticism and even complaint. They will also provide examples of how to study and interact with the Bible in ways that most pastors don't have the courage to do from the pulpit. They are the product of one person's scholarly and religious journey and are intended to support the religious journeys of others who respect the Judeo-Christian tradition.

CHAPTER ONE

WHAT THE BIBLE SAYS

I have always respected Billy Graham. When I grew up in Savannah, Georgia in the 1950s, my Baptist church would gather with many other churches at least one Sunday afternoon each spring in the City Auditorium to watch a Billy Graham movie. Young people were especially encouraged to attend these events, which always featured a movie with a few personal stories that culminated with the people going to one of Billy Graham's crusades. There was a sermon and the invitation, which brought on a crisis of decision for the people in the story. And of course those of us watching were also invited to make a life-changing decision. A great many young people did respond to the call each time and thereafter could tell of their personal salvation experience.

To most of my contemporaries, Billy Graham is an icon. He was a man of unquestioned integrity who was consulted by many presidents. I can see him now standing away from the pulpit, holding the Bible open in one hand and gesturing authoritatively with the other, as he said the words everyone expected him to say: "The Bible says . . . ."

I can't tell you how common that expression has been in sermons I have heard over the years. It always conveys that the authority of what someone is about to say comes from the Bible. It carries the stamp of God. The people I heard using that phrase, in addition to Billy Graham, were often ministers of fundamentalist evangelical churches; but I often heard very educated ministers say it who were known for being more liberal and supporting modern biblical criticism. It has become one of those mindless phrases people use when making

1

a reference to the Bible. I say mindless because people rarely stop to think of what they are actually saying—and because the phrase is in fact nonsense.

Yes, I am serious. It is nonsense. Would anyone ever think of appealing to authority by saying "the downtown public library says?" That would indeed be silly. The library is full of books that say lots of different things. Anyone can say just about anything and claim it bears the authority of the downtown public library because one of the books in it is bound to say something along those lines.

The same principle applies to the Bible. It is a library. In fact the very word from which Bible derives means a collection of books. It contains a series of books that were written or compiled by a wide variety of people over many centuries. Therefore, the Bible is not a book that speaks with a unified voice. It contains many viewpoints, some of which are contradictory.

Why do people who should know better use a phrase that just a little thought reveals to be nonsense? It is used very often in sermons and is intended to present something with the authority of God behind it. Most of the Old Testament prophets spoke in oracles, which was a form of poetry that began with something equivalent to "Here's what God says" or "Here's what God told me." The phrase "the Bible says" is a modern appeal to the authority of God to support something because of a statement somewhere in the Bible. And of course many Christians would immediately follow up by saying the Bible is the authoritative "Word of God" and should not be questioned. So appealing to the Bible on a subject is a way of saying something comes straight from God——an updated and slightly more modest claim of "Here is what God is saying now!"

There is no denying that Jews and Christians over the ages believe they have experienced God through the Bible. Reading the Bible is a spiritual discipline along with prayer and worship that anchors the spiritual lives of many believing communities. Indeed there is great value in the Bible as a spiritual tool. However, statements in the Bible are frequently bad guidelines for decisions today for at least three reasons.

First of all, we need to clearly recognize that the Bible does not speak with a unified voice. No doubt you have heard people say you can find support for almost anything in the Bible. There is truth in that because of the wide-ranging views that are expressed. Of course the Bible is all about God. But there is no unity even on that theme. We think of Jews and Christians as monotheists and look for support in places like the Ten Commandments, where we are told to put the one God above all others. Close examination reveals that those commandments don't really point to true monotheism because they acknowledge the existence of other Gods. Jews were commanded to ignore all rival Gods and cling to just one. Real monotheists believe there is no other God than the one and only God. So even on that point the Bible does not speak with a unified voice.

Disturbing as it may be to many people, it is obvious that the Bible expresses a variety of views on many important spiritual issues. Therefore, whenever someone quotes scripture and claims the stamp of God because it is in the Bible, another person often finds a rival quotation with a different answer from the first. Which one carries the authority of God? Having a tug of war with rival proof texts doesn't lead to productive conversations.

A second point is that people often claim the Bible says something as a claim for a moral or spiritual principle that must be obeyed. If it is in the Bible and the Bible has authority that means we must obey what the Bible says. Listen to those who point to Old Testament texts against homosexuality as proof that Christians must never recognize and accommodate that lifestyle. Deuteronomy says it, so it must be obeyed.

Over the years, I can't count the number of times I have heard people claim the world is going badly astray because we ignore the moral commandments of the Bible more and more. But these same people do not follow the dietary laws that many Jews still feel are biblical commands and they don't sanctify the seventh day as the Bible expects. Nor do they follow the rules of the early Christian community as stated in Acts, when everyone shared possessions in common. In fact the book of Acts makes the point emphatically when a couple who holds out on the community are killed by God as punishment (Acts 5:1–6).

For some strange reason, many people who are convinced we must return to the morality of the Bible don't see the contradiction when they pick and choose the moral principles they like rather than follow all of the Bible. Invariably they will engage in an argument that says essentially that the Bible really says what they want it to say and in other cases that it doesn't really mean to say what they don't want it to say.

A third point is that people who say "the Bible says" are claiming that whatever is in the Bible represents eternal and infallible truth. This is contradicted by the two hallmarks of modern thought: science and history.

Science involves the disciplined search for provable truth. In school we all learn of triumphs of scientific knowledge that appear to be discoveries of eternal truth—Newton's laws and Euclid's geometry are historic examples. But we also learn how Einstein used non-Euclidian geometry in developing new principles that went beyond Newton. So science has learned that even the most sacred discoveries can be only early glimpses of still bigger truths to come.

The other achievement of modern times is historical awareness. Science tells us that our universe began with a gigantic explosion from which everything originated and which set everything in motion. We are still in motion today. Not only is our planet traveling around its sun, but our solar system and everything else in the universe is flying apart from everything else at an accelerating speed. That explosion created something called time that was encoded into the very fabric of the universe so that achieving consciousness, as humans have, leads to the realization that everything is always changing.

Human beings are unlike any other living creature in having a culture. Human beings are changing and evolving like every other thing in the universe but at a much slower rate than cultures change. As we study the lives of earlier peoples, we have to learn about cultures that are very different from our own, in which people express the same emotions and experiences we have in different ways. In different cultures, people find it easier to believe different things.

The books in the Bible represent the experiences of people in earlier cultures. They have a universality about them because they were human like we are. But the difference in cultures means that what made sense to them may not even be credible for us. The experiences of peoples and their cultures cannot be carriers of eternal truth. At best our cultural experiences of God are like the story of the blind people feeling different parts of an elephant and deciding what an elephant is like based on their experience of just one body part. We can relate to the beliefs of earlier cultures but invariably we find they lack elements of what we feel are essential to better understanding for today.

At one time it made sense to Jews and Christians that Joshua did a good thing by slaughtering the people of Jericho and Ai in a righteous holy war. Unfortunately, there are people today who would endorse that same ethic in an updated context—but most of us call that terrorism.

Before the printing press spread books everywhere, writing often took on a sacred character. The phrase "it is written" conveyed a sense of permanency that we no longer recognize in written information. Clearly many of the values and opinions expressed in the Bible are out of step with experiences of later cultures and thus should not be seen as enshrining unchanging and eternal truth.

No doubt many people will complain that I have said the Bible is unreliable since it should not be seen as always representing the authority of God for today and all time. I have known people who insisted on the literal truth of the Bible to the extent that if even one letter were shown to be out of place that would mean that the whole thing must be unreliable. Any reasonable person should be able to see that no document coming from human culture can pass that kind of test for reliability.

The question of the ways in which the Bible is reliable and useful today is important.[7] My view is that, for Jews and Christians, it is an indispensable part of the spiritual discipline involved in seeking a relationship with God. Meditation and prayer are part of the spiritual discipline of most religions. The Bible is certainly a source of prayers. It is also valuable as a basis for study and meditation as it becomes what Marcus Borg calls a conversation partner.[8] Interacting with the experiences recorded in the Bible is valuable for spiritual growth. One of the surprising things about prayers in the Bible, as found in the book of Psalms especially, is how often they complain to God. Interacting with the Bible can also involve complaint and disagreement instead of the traditional idea that it must always be obeyed.

CHAPTER TWO

WAS JESUS REALLY HUMAN?

In my junior and senior years at Mercer University, I wrote periodic editorials and book reviews for the school newspaper. Just before the splash made by the movie *Zorba the Greek*, I came across the novel *The Last Temptation of Christ* and did a review.[9] Both novels were by the Greek writer Nikos Kazantzakis.

I was shocked by the implications of the novel, as many people would also be shocked when it was made into a movie in the 1980s by Martin Scorsese. Mercer was a Baptist school and quite a few of my friends were ministerial students who were not pleased at seeing the school newspaper publicize a book they considered too immoral to read. In fact, Kazantzakis had been anathematized by the Greek Orthodox Church and the book had been placed on the Catholic *Index of Prohibited Books*. When he died in 1957, Kazantzakis was not allowed burial in consecrated ground.

The immorality of the book was its treatment of Jesus as an ordinary human being with strong sexual desires and a preference for having a family over dying on the cross. There are some pretty steamy fantasies involving Mary Magdalene. As he is crucified, Jesus comes down from the cross and escapes death. Living an obscure life, he later encounters a maniacal Paul spreading the gospel of Christ and lets him know the true inside story. Paul refuses to believe him, proclaiming that Christ must have died and went on preaching what he knew to be false.

When you think the book is pointed toward a cynical ending, Jesus suddenly comes to himself and realizes he had hallucinated everything about the descent from the cross. He was still impaled and would complete the sacrificial death.

Religious leaders were shocked in the 1950s when the book was published. Here was a picture of Jesus as an ordinary human being with sensual urges and temptations that should not be attributed to someone who was God as well as human. Kazantzakis paid a price for describing Jesus as entirely human.

In the early church there was a tendency to emphasize the divine over the human in Jesus. Some groups found it impossible to accept the combination of divinity with the inescapable sin of bodily existence. The horrible suffering on the cross was too much humanity for some. The human appearance of Jesus must have been an illusion of some kind so that the divine, which was real, was unsullied by corruption.

In modern times there are others who reject the physical existence of Jesus by saying he was mythical. There are serious scholars who have taken a variety of approaches to denying that the gospels have any reliable history in them. To some extent, the attention received by the New Atheism through bestselling books has fueled Internet sites denying the reality of Jesus. The level of attention being given to arguments not taken seriously by most religious scholars led Bart Ehrman to devote a book to refuting the errors underlying attempts to question the historicity of Jesus.[10]

Ehrman's subsequent book, *How Jesus Became God*, described the transformation of Jesus into divinity in the early church.[11] Within twenty years of the crucifixion, Paul's letters refer almost exclusively to Christ when referring to Jesus. He makes some clearly historical references, such as his description of the last supper and his claim that he was one of many witnesses to see the risen Jesus; but his references are a prime example of the Christ of faith taking priority over the events and sayings in the ministry of Jesus. Some important historical information is found in Paul's writings. The history that seemed most important to Paul was letting others know the gospel was spreading as the ongoing work of Christ the Lord. Theology was the focus of Paul's thought, not history.

The long recognized dilemma of a human or divine Jesus—of a Jesus of history or Christ of faith—is a problem of theology and personal belief, not a historical problem. The two hallmarks of modern thought, science and historical awareness, deal with a time-space universe of constant change in an ongoing cycle of birth, aging, and death. Any participation of divinity in our universe is not currently detectable and thus is outside the scope of scientific or historical study. Cultural beliefs about divinity are historical and are studied as changing phenomena rather than as manifestations of any form of transcendent powers. This is not intended to demean theology as a form of study and body of knowledge. Yet it must be recognized that history and science are always on defense against concerns based on theology that are used to block the pursuit of their forms of knowledge.

The New Testament manifests the gradual impact of theology on how the life of Jesus was presented as gospels developed. First, we must recognize that the gospels emerged from a Jewish culture although there were increasing Hellenistic influences as the word spread beyond the ancestral land of the Jews. This culture recognized only one God. Those who shaped their religion—Moses, Samuel, David, Elijah, and other prophets—were emissaries of God but they were not divine. Monarchs in the Near East were treated as gods, and some influence of that environment can be seen as Jews called their kings Sons of God; but the status of Son of God was an adopted special relationship representing presence of the power of God rather than anything approaching equality with God.

This Jewish context must be kept in mind when reading the four gospels. The synoptic gospels of Mark, Matthew, and Luke proclaim Jesus as the Messiah but, prior to the resurrection, it is a human Jesus they present. Manifesting the power of God by healing, exorcism, and other wondrous works was not equivalent to divinity. These gospels show a Jesus whose concern is to build a movement focused on a coming kingdom of God. Dedication to God without proclaiming his own importance is notable in these gospels.

The beginning of John alludes to the wisdom tradition in Jewish history, which tended to personify Wisdom as a woman who was present with God at creation. John turns that picture into the Logos as the form in which Jesus was with God at the beginning. Jewish thought never made personified Wisdom equivalent to God. Some interpretations have seen John supporting a trinitarian view of Jesus, but that is not the case. This Jesus proclaims his special role with God, unlike the picture in the synoptics; but making Jesus as Logos the true way to God, just as Wisdom had been seen as a way to God, did not reach the equality represented by the trinity.[12]

After the resurrection appearances, we see a movement in the early church toward making Jesus into divinity that was not present during his ministry. How the ideas of Christ developed into the trinity is a phenomenon that is the proper study of history.

The conversations in this collection will treat Jesus as an ordinary historical person. Looking at the gospels from this vantage point will bring out features that have been overlooked as theology ruled out this view of Jesus.

Some people I know will be disturbed that my approach will assume that Jesus could be an ordinary sinner. Let me point out that sin is a theological concept with a varied cultural history.[13] There was a time not long ago when any aspect of sexuality was considered sinful. Many people believed that sex itself was the original sin in the Garden of Eden. When Kazantzakis portrayed Jesus sexually, his contemporaries were shocked and religious officials condemned him. Freud was considered extremely shocking when he openly discussed sexuality with female patients and theorized that infants had sexual motivations. Yet today sex is not universally acknowledged as inherently sinful. Recent decades have seen a great many changes in attitude toward sex and other matters that for centuries were presented as evil. The things that are sinful in one time may be taken as natural and unobjectionable in another time.

The gospels tell us Jesus was an ordinary Jew of his time. Like many others, he was drawn to John the Baptist and was immersed in the Jordan as an act of repentance. All the gospels show him teaching in the temple, which means he followed routine procedures for purification by washing in pools before entering the temple courts. Those were rituals expected of all worshipers who must do them to enter the presence of God. Does conformity to those rituals mean that Jesus was a sinner like everyone else? That is a theological question that might tend to interfere with accepting the plain fact that Jesus participated in traditional rites as an ordinary Jew.

Historians and scientists also make decisions as believers or nonbelievers on religious matters. At the end of his famous lectures on *The Varieties of Religious Experience*, William James put aside his role as scholar to address the question of personal belief. His scientific approach had assumed a distinction between an ordinary, material world and a world of strange experiences that claimed to have a transcendent source. He took what he called a pragmatic stand by saying that a transcendent world was indeed a reality even though it could not be scientifically verified other than as internal experiences. In his final paragraph, he took a remarkable personal stand:

> But the over-belief on which I am ready to make my personal
> venture is that they exist. The whole drift of my education
> goes to persuade me that the world of our present conscious-

ness is only one out of many worlds of consciousness that exist, and that those other worlds must contain experiences which have a meaning for our life also; and that although in the main their experiences and those of this world keep discrete, yet the two become continuous at certain points, and higher energies filter in.[14]

James pointed to a line of defense by which historians and scientists can make personal decisions in favor of Christ experiences and other non-verifiable beliefs.

My concern in the conversations that follow is not with the Christ experience, which would lead us off into the development of early Christianity. I am content to see Jesus as a human being in the gospels as a way of understanding his message about the nature of God. To me the crucial issue for personal belief and for the entire Judeo-Christian tradition is the existence and nature of God, which is the overriding concern of the entire Bible. In my view, Jesus points the way today, as in his own day, to a relationship with God that should be the focus of personal values.

Chapter Three

Why Jesus Was Not a Christian

I began my teaching career in 1968 at a university in the mountains of North Carolina, sharing an office with another new faculty member with a doctorate from Duke. He was a really nice guy and we had some good conversations. But right away I began to shock him by making a point of learning the names of all 175 of my students within the first few weeks and learning something about their backgrounds and interests. That was not really necessary. Then I began expressing concern about the lack of writing and study skills, even going so far as to hand out materials on how to read and study history. My officemate was among the first to tell me that my job was to teach history, not English or general study skills. The word got around the history faculty about this really odd guy who didn't understand what it meant to teach history, just plain history.

After the midterm exam, which included the early history of Christianity, I experienced a revolt by all of my classes. They were outraged, so that the chairman of the department heard and then word spread to others in the liberal arts school. Everyone objected to one of the questions on the exam: "Which of the following was not a Christian: (a) Paul; (b) James; (c) Peter; (d) Jesus." Not a single student chose the correct answer.

They had not been listening to me. The question brought to their awareness how radical this guy from Vanderbilt really was. How could Jesus not be a Christian? That had never penetrated their awareness no matter how much I talked about the Jewishness of Jesus. I discovered it had not penetrated the awareness of many of the officials at the university either.

Why would these students not think of Jesus as a Jew rather than a Christian? Every one of them knew the birth stories in Matthew and Luke and their genealogies tracing Jesus back to King David. Most of them probably knew Luke's story of the young Jesus amazing scholars in the temple, which may be seen as part of a bar mitzvah experience. When would he have stopped being a Jew?

Some of the culprits were the speeches in John, which are so very different from those in the three synoptic gospels. Mark begins with a clear statement of Jesus's preaching: "The time is fulfilled, and the kingdom of God has come near; repent, and believe in the good news." (1:14) That is very different from what Jesus says in John: "I am the light of the world. Whoever follows me will never walk in darkness but will have the light of life." (8:12) These selections point to a big difference between the Jesus who proclaims God and his kingdom in the synoptics and the one who proclaims himself and the ability to speak on behalf of God in John. An extreme statement is found in John 14:6–7: "I am the way, and the truth, and the life. No one comes to the Father except through me. If you know me, you will know my Father."

Another culprit can be found in the trial and execution of Jesus. In John 18, he is arrested by a detachment of soldiers (apparently Roman soldiers) and temple police who take him first to Annas, father-in-law of the high priest, for interrogation. Annas sent him to Caiaphas, the high priest, and we don't know what interrogation took place. With the arrival at Pilate's headquarters, the narrative changes characters. Instead of the Roman soldiers and temple police, there is suddenly a crowd with no identified officials leading them. It is an indistinct "they" who arrive at Pilate's location (18:28) and refuse to go into a Roman building because they would lose ritual purity needed to celebrate Passover, which was upon them. Pilate came out and had a conversation with them. The crowd, now identified as "the Jews," (18:31) responded as if Pilate were talking to a single person. After Pilate interrogated Jesus, he returned to "the Jews" (18:38), who chose Barabbas rather than see Jesus released. Pilate then tortured Jesus and once again returned to the crowd to display him to them. This time John says the chief priests and temple police were in the crowd who clamored for crucifixion (19:6). Once again Pilate talks to Jesus and tries to release him but the "Jews" threaten to report Pilate to higher Roman authorities if he did not crucify Jesus (19:12). Finally Pilate asks "Shall I crucify your king?" It is the chief priests who reply they had no king, only the Roman emperor (19:15).

Matthew's version compounds the case against the Jews. Pilate gathers a crowd to ask them to choose between Barabbas and Jesus. The chief priests and elders, said Matthew, "persuaded the crowds" to call for Jesus's execution (27:20). Pilate demonstrated his innocence by washing his hands. When he told the crowd to do as they pleased, Matthew 27:25 says: "Then the people as a whole answered, 'His blood be on us and on our children.'"

So who crucified Jesus? He was not stoned as was done in most Jewish executions. It was the Romans who executed Jesus using their preferred method. These innocent Romans did that horrible thing only because "the Jews" insisted not once but multiple times. Furthermore, they exonerated the Romans by saying the responsibility should fall on them and their descendants.

But execution would not make Jesus a Christian rather than a Jew. In fact the charge was that he claimed to be king of the Jews.

The four gospels are united in showing mounting opposition to Jesus by Pharisees and other Jewish authorities. Jesus was attacked for not respecting the Sabbath. Not only did he do unusual things like healings and exorcisms, he continued to do them on the Sabbath. Pharisees and others in the upper crust of that society were attacked in many of the parables as well as the sayings of Jesus.

Arguments with religious authorities have been coupled with the way Jesus taught "with authority" as in Matthew's Sermon on the Mount where he mentions some aspect of Jewish law they had been taught and follows with "But I say to you." (5:21–38) He seems to be claiming authority to replace what Jews had always been told with something new.

A trend among early scholars looking for the historical Jesus was to distinguish the vital religion of Jesus from the formal and tedious presentation of the Torah especially by Pharisees of the time. Many centuries of blaming Jews for executing Jesus and rejecting their true leader were compounded by flights of scholarly imagination setting up a straw man of Jewish law that Jesus rejected. If he rejected the law, then how could anyone see Jesus as Jewish?

One of the undeniable achievements of the efforts to recover a more historical view of Jesus has been the growing recognition and affirmation of the fact that Jesus was a pious and even strict Jew throughout his life.[15] In fact Jesus seemed at times to be prejudiced against anyone who was not Jewish. When sending the disciples on a mission, he told them to keep to Jewish areas and not to take their mission to Gentiles or Samaritans.[16] He even showed reluctance to heal Gentiles. In Mark 7:24–30 and Matthew 15:21–28, he refused to heal the daughter of a Syro-Phoenician woman, saying in Matthew that he was sent only to Israel. When the woman persisted, he commented that food should not be taken from children to feed dogs. The woman seems to have shamed Jesus into helping her daughter by saying that even dogs get to eat scraps from the family table.

I can hear my old students asking: "But didn't Jesus start the church and doesn't that make him the first Christian?" Jesus undeniably started a movement. One of his earliest actions was to designate twelve close followers, symbolizing his outreach to the twelve tribes of Israel and an intent to get them ready for something important God was about to do. There were other groups identified in the gospels, such as the Pharisees and those following John the Baptist. Jesus and his followers fit in neatly with the pattern of groups within Judaism of that time. After his death, his followers became centered in Jerusalem, according to Acts. Traditionally this group has been called the early church, but now scholars refer to the Jesus Movement within Judaism. Paul joined the movement within a decade of Jesus's death and helped spread it to Roman cities around the Mediterranean in the 50s CE. Paul had important differences in views from the leaders in Jerusalem, but all of them considered themselves a movement within the religion of Israel and not a separate religion. Stating it that bluntly still shocks many people, but that was the historical situation that Christianity covered up for many centuries.

Referring to members of the Jesus Movement as Christians is what historians call anachronism. It is putting something into a time when that something didn't exist. Often anachronism happens as people project something from the present into the past. Old Testament scholars often point to many aspects in Israel's history that were backward projections from a later time to justify the practice of that later time. European history has many examples of kings projecting fake genealogies and laws into earlier times to manufacture support for their contemporary actions.

Roman destruction of Jerusalem and the temple in 70 CE was a traumatic event for all groups in Judaism. Pharisees were a leading group in moving from a destroyed Jerusalem to Galilee where Rabbinic Judaism would develop. Cut off from its original headquarters in Jerusalem, the Jesus Movement bumped heads with the movement toward Rabbinic Judaism and gradually they separated. Some scholars go so far as to say authors of every book in the New Testament considered themselves Jews. That is going too far, I think.

The Jesus Movement that was on the way to becoming Christianity, seeing what happened in the Jewish Revolts of 66–73 and 132–135, accommodated itself to life in the Roman Empire even as it too suffered persecution. Part of that strategy was the picture in the gospels of Jewish leaders being responsible for the execution that was carried out by Rome. Scholars believe that all of the gospels were written after 70 and have detected ways that early Christian communities adapted events in Jesus's time to the needs of their own political and social requirements. This makes the gospels instruments for spreading the message in an environment that was very different from the days of Jesus in Judea and Galilee. It also makes it difficult to rely on some details in the gospels.

One of the tragic effects of historical distortion of Jesus's relationship to Judaism was the persecution of Jews that culminated in Hitler's methodical insanity. The Roman Catholic Church has gone on record that the Jews were not responsible for killing Jesus, but the deep-seated hostility fostered by centuries of distortion has not yet been eliminated from Western society.

Historical study, along with science and a host of related social sciences, helps us achieve an increasingly more accurate understanding of Second Temple and New Testament times. Popular ideas based on distorted histories of those times have been known to use devotion to images of Christ to support terrible "acts of faith," demonstrating the extent to which religion could justify cruelty and murder.[17]

Conservative Christians are still uncomfortable with historical criticism that questions the literal accuracy of the Bible and even doubts the reliability of many words and actions of Jesus reported in the gospels. Historical scholars are not without their own flaws, often presenting a picture of Jesus and Judaism fitting their own philosophies rather than uncovering accurate historical information. Nevertheless, using the best historical information we can obtain as verification for historical claims must be insisted on as a check on theological and historical flights of imagination and devotion.

Christianity claims to have a historical foundation in the life, death, and resurrection of Jesus. Faith in a Christ image that undermines the key values of the Jewish Jesus seen in the gospels does not have a supporting historical foundation. We can't return to the times of Jesus with a camera to catch his very actions and words, but we are coming ever closer to understanding that time. What we learn must be used to correct traditions from later times that seek to distort basic truths such as the undeniable Jewishness of Jesus.

CHAPTER FOUR

MARK IN A NUTSHELL

Teaching Sunday school classes is something I have enjoyed doing in several churches over the years. When visiting classes, I try to be quiet. Having been a teacher in a variety of settings, I appreciate the preparation that goes into teaching and it always bothers me when someone upstages the teacher. In my professional experience, there were many unpleasant times when I worked with colleagues who made a habit of surprising or embarrassing those they were supposed to be working with. Keeping my comments as nonthreatening as possible is often difficult because I have a reputation for knowing the Bible, which sometimes intimidates people in classes I visit even when I am silent.

When not teaching, I often see approaches that get me to thinking about how to do a better job. One Sunday morning when visiting a different class in my church in which there were several friends who knew my opinions, I witnessed an attempt to teach the third chapter of Mark's gospel. The teacher used a commentary written by a well-known conservative scholar as he went verse by verse through the chapter. After the class one of my friends told me he could see that I was biting my tongue and trying to keep silent even though it was hard.

The class included several professionals who worked with mentally ill people. Some were in medical and legal professions. In their professional lives, they would never accept that discipline or mental problems were the product of demon possession. Yet as they read this chapter in Mark, they were endorsing the idea that Jesus was actually grappling with demons. At one point the teacher called on me for an opinion, so I said that most scholars would say that Jesus didn't really talk to demons. The immediate response from the teacher and several of the professionals who should have known better was that the story had to be true as written because it was in the Bible. Jesus was God, someone said, and could talk to demons if he wanted to.

As I thought over that class experience later, it came to me how many significant messages were missed by the narrow verse-by-verse focus and the literal-minded interpretation. It became clear that Mark's third chapter presents a good bit of his gospel message in a nutshell. From this chapter alone we can see the major themes of Mark standing out clearly if we know how to look for them. Furthermore, the humanity of Jesus is very much on display.

The chapter begins (verses 1–6) with Jesus in a synagogue in an unspecified village toward the northwest end of the Sea of Galilee. Many scholars believe that synagogues at this time were community assemblies in private homes or perhaps at the gates of the city and not community buildings similar to churches and synagogues today; however, this location appears to hold a sizeable number of people, an uncounted "they," who are anticipating that Jesus will do a controversial healing on the Sabbath. Jesus finds a man with a withered hand and does heal him. Without any indication of comments by the "they," Jesus seems to know their thoughts and challenges their ideas of what should be done on the Sabbath so that Pharisees and Herodians (now we gather the "they" included them) began plotting to destroy Jesus.[18]

Next Jesus leaves that unspecified place for the sea (verses 7–12), which is presumed to be the Sea of Galilee and which therefore suggests his previous location was close to it. We learn that he is being followed by a large crowd from all over Palestine and Lebanon who pushed against him, seeking cures for diseases. Because of the crowd, Jesus wanted to get into a boat to escape the crush. At this point, without being told any specific episode, we learn that whenever people in the crowd with "unclean spirits" saw him, they would fall down and shout that he is the Son of God. That reference points to the contemporary belief that mental and physical illnesses resulted from demon possession. Jesus clearly wanted to escape the confessions of the sick as well as the crush and demands of the crowd, for we learn that whenever demons confessed who he was, he "sternly ordered them" to be quiet.

Suddenly Jesus has left the sea and the large crowds (verses 13–19) as we see him going up an undisclosed mountain and inviting some of his followers to accompany him. There he appointed twelve "to be with him, and to be sent out to proclaim the message, and to have authority to cast out demons."

After this, it says Jesus "went home" (verses 20–35), and the crowd was upon him again. At this point Mark makes us aware that Jesus's family heard about these doings and told people that Jesus was out of his mind. Also there were scribes from Jerusalem who were making statements that Jesus used the support of a powerful demon, Beelzebul, to overcome demons—making his healing more like witchcraft. Somehow Jesus is aware of those attitudes and takes on the scribes as he denounces the idea that demons would actually assist in undermining their own power. Then he goes further by making a statement about blasphemy. Jesus said, according to Mark, that all kinds of blasphemies could be forgiven but not the things being said against him because "whoever blasphemes against the Holy Spirit can never have forgiveness, but is guilty of an eternal sin." Suddenly the mother and brothers of Jesus have arrived and he takes on what he knew they were thinking. When he is told his family had arrived, Jesus didn't see them but told the crowd around him they were his family as was anyone who did the will of God. Thus Jesus turned his back on his family and dissociated himself from them because of what they said, which he had just identified as blasphemy against the Holy Spirit.

Having reviewed the flow of the chapter, let us turn now to some patterns that emerge when the narrative is analyzed. The chapter represents several of the main themes and tendencies of Mark throughout his gospel, so that in this chapter we can see Mark's interpretation epitomized. Devotional study verse by verse looks at these patterns but often doesn't see them— it misses the forest by focusing on the leaves on the trees.

The first pattern to notice is that the chapter illustrates Mark's use of thematic unity rather than chronological sequence for much of his gospel. Mark appears to be a biography and many scholars argue that it is representative of the type of biography that was written in Roman times. Once Jesus arrives in Jerusalem, events are described day-by-day and sometimes hour-by-hour. Prior to Jerusalem, Mark uses constructions that are generally chronological but which are really thematic in unity with very unclear time references.

Mark is saying these events were associated with the beginning of Jesus's ministry. How old Jesus was is unclear. The time period for these events is unclear. Days, or weeks, or even months may have passed in chapter 3—we have no definite way of knowing what time span was involved.

Also the geographical references in this chapter are vague. It appears he is staying around the northwest corner of the Sea of Galilee, in the vicinity of Capernaum, which we were told in an earlier chapter was home for Jesus. The lake is nearby, so getting into a boat makes sense. But then suddenly "he went up the mountain" (verse 13). What mountain? Where are these mountains? There are a good many hilly areas around the Sea of Galilee but we are given no clue as to where the so-called mountain was actually located. Then suddenly he is back home.

So there is an impression these events happened around the same time and near the northwest corner of the Sea of Galilee. These events were definitely in the villages in or near Galilee rather than in the major Galilean cities of Sepphoris or Tiberias. The specific places didn't seem to matter until Jesus went to Jerusalem. The themes being illustrated at the beginning of Jesus's ministry and the general setting are more important than specifics about time and place.

You may wonder what difference this makes. Scholars have tried to figure out how long Jesus's ministry lasts in Mark but always without success. Many guess that it lasted about a year. But there are no clear indications of seasons of the year until the journey to Jerusalem. Stories and events are grouped to illustrate the conflicts Jesus encountered and then his teachings. Mark organizes into a general chronological pattern, giving an idea where events fall in the progression of the ministry of Jesus; but his form of organization undermines our attempts to see a clear chronological sequence even though it gives a biographical structure.

The main theme being illustrated in this chapter is how there was opposition to Jesus from the beginning because of the popular following he was gaining. We are given a picture of how things went when Jesus first started. There are two stories of opposition and Jesus has an angry response to both. The first is in the synagogue on a Sabbath when he spots a man with a withered hand. Notice that, in the third chapter, there is no confrontation between Jesus and his critics. Apparently they are silent and disapproving, but Jesus knows their thoughts and attacks their criticisms as he heals the man. Then Mark says they started plotting to kill Jesus, which shows that very early the opposition became deadly.

The second story of opposition involves a literary technique called "framing" that is a distinguishing characteristic of Mark. This technique begins a story, interrupts it with another, then comes back to the conclusion of the first story. The effect is to use the bookends at the beginning and end to emphasize the meaning of the central point of the passage, which are the sayings in the middle.[19]

The story begins with a nonspecific description of his family hearing about him and thinking he had lost his mind. The scribes go even further and accuse him of witchcraft or being in league with the leading demonic figure Beelzabul in what appear to be good works. Those verses make up the first bookend. There is a concluding bookend when Jesus's family arrives and he clearly rejects them in favor of the people who are following and supporting rather than criticizing.

In the middle is the heart of the story, which the bookends are intended to emphasize. It is an angry response to criticism, which defends the sanctity of his relationship to God. He claims to be speaking by the Holy Spirit and goes so far as to say that people who make that criticism will not be forgiven. Part of the message here that is often overlooked is that the saying applies directly to the scribes and family in the bookends.

What we see here is a picture of Jesus under pressure. In defending his relationship to God, we see a very human side of Jesus. This passage will be examined in greater detail in a later conversation as we discuss how Jesus handled stress.

Another important theme in this chapter that is easy to overlook is how Jesus suppressed those who wanted to use messianic terms such as Son of God. Keeping this role quiet explains how Jesus could be the Messiah yet not be recognized by the public or Jewish religious leadership. When talking of the multitude at the seaside, a general observation is made about the press of the crowd and what "unclean spirits" said in apparently crowded situations. There is no specific healing or other incident given to explain why this observation happens here. The point is that Jesus was recognized only by demons and he tried to suppress that information. This theme will also be discussed in more detail in a subsequent conversation.

A final overall pattern in Mark that should be noticed in this chapter is the importance of exorcism and healing in the ministry of Jesus. In this chapter, crowds follow Jesus for his power over the forces they believe cause disease, not because of his teachings. One of the significant differences between Mark and the other canonical gospels is how little attention is given to Jesus as a teacher. Mark presents a Jesus who is more healer and exorcist than teacher. The importance of this function is further emphasized when the disciples are sent out to spread the movement, for they are empowered to make healing and exorcism a key part of their role as extensions of Jesus. The theme of exorcism is a third item that will be discussed in greater detail in another conversation in order to more fully understand the personality of Jesus.

In the third chapter of Mark, we recognize major patterns of the entire book. A final point to notice about this chapter is how it gives insight into the personality of Jesus that is often missed. We see a very human Jesus doing things he knows will be criticized and then becoming angry as the pressure and criticism grow. We see a Jesus guided by a sense of mission from God he doesn't want to announce. He exhibits this mission through actions that challenge religious authorities. When the public responds too enthusiastically, he wants to get away. When those possessed by demons make statements about him, he doesn't like it and quickly silences them. He doesn't say anything to make claims about himself, but his actions display a claim of authority. He expects his disciples to figure out the nature of his special role on their own and becomes frustrated when they don't. If we had not been told by Mark at the beginning of the gospel that Jesus is the Messiah, we too would be confused.

Mark is describing the personality of Jesus with this puzzling behavior. By looking more closely at three of the themes seen in this chapter, we can understand the very human picture of Jesus that Mark is presenting along with the message that he is the Messiah. My friends in the Sunday school class mentioned earlier failed to see any of these themes or the humanity of Jesus because they were too busy looking for eternal words from God.

CHAPTER FIVE

JESUS UNDER STRESS

Most Christians are familiar with the picture of Jesus in agony in the Garden of Gethsemane just before his arrest. That is usually the image we have when thinking of Jesus under stress. But what about the stress he must have felt at the start of his mission? As he set himself apart from John the Baptist and went a separate way, there must have been plenty of apprehension and uncertainty. This is an aspect of the humanity of Jesus that is seldom appreciated—but this can be seen clearly in the angry Jesus in the first three chapters of Mark's gospel.

Jesus is not presented as talking about the role he sees for himself, rather we see it through actions described by Mark. Apparently he senses a special relationship with God's power as seen in his ability to exorcise demons and heal infirmities. On the one hand he seems self-assured as he intentionally takes on religious authorities by healing on the Sabbath and challenging their ideas of what is acceptable; but, on the other hand, he quickly becomes irritated with the crowds following him and with the criticisms that reach his ears. The early chapters of Mark show a Jesus who is often thin-skinned and touchy as he does things he knows are bound to draw criticism. This is a man not yet comfortable with the public role he is playing.

We saw previously how the first three chapters of Mark show a pattern of conflict as Jesus exorcised and healed in controversial settings. Crowds were attracted to Jesus so that he was experiencing the stress of too much adulation at the same time that he heard criticisms that could have been devastating. The crowds also pushed and jostled as he healed. At the same time he was shutting up demons who were saying things he didn't want spread abroad and also reacting to criticism. No wonder he wanted to get away with just an inner circle.

Mark's third chapter shows an increasingly angry Jesus as he silences a demon, criticizes silent religious authorities as he heals on a Sabbath, and then pronounces a curse on scribes and his family because they attacked the source of his power for exorcism. The chapter begins with seething anger and ends like the eruption of a volcano in a dramatic statement about an unforgivable sin.

As a child, I heard a sermon on this passage that haunted me. The minister said a truck driver told him he had cursed God but wished to find forgiveness. The minister said the only response he could give was that the man had committed the unforgivable sin. The story ended with the man dying soon afterward, evidently headed for hell. Compare that pastoral advice to something else said by a chaplain friend to a kid incarcerated in a maximum-security facility. The kid told the chaplain not to waste time on him because he had already "cussed God" and was hopeless; but my friend came back with "God is tough enough to take it." Should we give ultimate significance to this kind of sin, or treat it as no different from other problems?

Those who emphasize the divinity of Jesus want to see this chapter as eternal truth from the mouth of Jesus. The result has been a great deal of unnecessary anguish over angry statements like the one on the "unforgivable sin." If we see a very human Jesus getting adjusted to all that is involved in playing a provocative role, we can understand how anger would be a natural part of that process. As he became adjusted, a more balanced Jesus replaced the early angry Jesus. Should we enshrine as eternal truth statements that Jesus himself might later have shrugged off as "having a bad day?"

The saying about the unforgivable sin has troubled people over the years because it appears to contradict the message of forgiveness Jesus teaches elsewhere. The passage has been the focus of many "hellfire and damnation" sermons that interpret the words of Jesus literally. Because of its apparent contradiction of teachings on love and forgiveness, many commentators have taken an approach similar to Jewish Midrash by looking "between the lines" or by seeking deeper insight that gets past what seems like a clear literal meaning. As a result there have been many explanations saying that Jesus appeared to say x but he really meant y or even the opposite of x.

One example of this approach can be seen in the online site "Gracepoint Devotions: Devotional Quiet Times and Bible Commentary." Here we are told to look for positive and not just negative in the passage: "However, the problem is that Christians frequently seize on the negative aspect of this saying—one is 'guilty of an eternal sin'—and neglect the positive statement—'all the sins and blasphemies of men will be forgiven them.'" Ignoring the plain meaning of the passage, this commentator turns to a passage in the gospel of John:

> Since this passage has caused so many such unnecessary anguish, one wisely stresses that the love, grace, and patience of God are never exhausted by our abundant sinfulness. 'Whoever comes to me I will never drive away' (John 6:37). The gospel proclaims that God forgives what may seem to us to be unforgivable."[20]

This approach is called harmonization because it uses a quotation from a different gospel to offset negative effects of the first statement. Thus we have an argument that tries to turn the meaning of the passage into its opposite. This website goes on to say:

> Their sin is that, in the presence of God's grace in action, they have not only rejected it but ascribed it to the devil. They are set on calling the Spirit's work the activity of Satan. It may be that Jesus means that they have not yet reached this point of no return, and that he is warning them against hardening their current attitude into a permanent stance. There is no forgiveness here because such an attitude is incapable of seeking it.[21]

One has to wonder how the clear pronouncing of a curse can be interpreted in such a way that those who are cursed "have not yet reached this point of no return."

There is another example I would like to mention. Marcus Borg is respected for his use of historical-critical scholarship and for using what he calls a "historical-metaphorical" approach.[22] The effect is to support the devotional approach by looking for meaning "between the lines." Here is how he interpreted these verses in the third chapter of Mark.

> The section concludes with a verse that speaks of the unforgivable sin and names it as blasphemy against the Holy Spirit.

The verse has terrified many Christians, including many in my generation. I can remember scary conversations about what the unforgivable sin is. In Mark's context, its meaning is clear: if you do not perceive the presence of God's Spirit in Jesus, if you think whatever was in him came from somewhere else, your life will not change. This passage is not about getting into heaven. Rather, not discerning the Spirit in Jesus is to stay the way you are and to fail to participate in the dream of God.[23]

On the whole, I admire the work of Borg; however, in this case his metaphorical approach turns the clear irritation and irascibility of Jesus into a calm warning to change your life rather a clear damnation of scribes and his family who were the critics he had in mind. Furthermore, none of the commentators I have seen recognize that the saying is directed at Jesus's family along with other opponents. His family will never be forgiven is a clear meaning that is ignored.

Whatever the historical basis of the saying may have been, it was not applied by the early Christian community as evidenced by the leadership role of James, the brother of Jesus, and by the development of stories of virgin birth, which highlight the virtue of Mary. Considering the picture of an irascible Jesus in this chapter, adherents of the literal approach insist on enshrining as permanent truth statements made in anger that may have reflected a human Jesus in a bad mood or having a bad day. The first three chapters of Mark present Jesus as often angry. Treating every statement of Jesus as eternal truth means taking too seriously words spoken in anger that contemporaries of Jesus did not interpret so inflexibly.

These chapters in Mark show an apparently successful Jesus having to deal with the stress of public attention that came with the mission he had launched. What we see here is not a divine Jesus making pronouncements of eternal truth, but a very human Jesus whose anger indicates his level of discomfort as he was getting started. Most adults can empathize with the stress that comes with even the happiest events. A great new job, a happy new marriage, the birth of a child—all these are good events that require a lot of adjusting. In the process, people feel disoriented and normally express it in anger even at times when people would expect to see expressions of joy.

If you look at it logically, we see a paradoxical Jesus who seeks controversy but responds angrily when, as a result, he is criticized or opposed; who intentionally grabs public attention with dramatic healings but then shows irritation when crowds follow so that he finds ways to run away from them. However, if you think of the stress and adjustments that have to be made in setting out on something new and demanding, it is not surprising that human emotions jump out in ways that defy logic. The emotions that come with stress have a logic of their own.

This chapter of Mark presents a portrait of Jesus any parent can recognize in young people growing into responsible adult roles. It is a credible snapshot of some stressful days adjusting to something dramatically new. As parents we learn to "cut some slack" for the emotional consequences of these times in someone's life. I think the same leniency should be allowed Jesus.

Chapter Six

Healer and Exorcist

A few years ago when I was not married, I met a number of women through an Internet dating site. This was often a pleasant experience because of the information you learned about each other before meeting. The online profile I gave was very candid in many areas, including my religious views, so that I usually met women whose views were not incompatible.

One time, the initial face-to-face encounter was over lunch. I saw right away that the woman's appearance was what I expected. That was refreshing because so many women used photographs that were ten years and thirty pounds out of date. We really hit it off and had great conversation over lunch. Time seemed to fly by. Before the end of the meal, I made a cardinal mistake when, overcome with enthusiasm, I said I just had to see her again. When the time seemed right, I signaled the waitress to bring the bill. As I did that, she took my other hand and said: "Please don't go before we get to my favorite topic, religion."

Over the next few minutes she told me of her experiences with demons. She belonged to a church that regularly exorcised demons as part of worship and she had taken training on how to overpower them. She went on to tell about the slow decline of her mother into senility and the changes of personality that came about. Her mother, she declared, was taken over by the Devil and had begun to say terrible things to the one person who was trying to care for her.

Finally, she noticed my icy silence. I sat there wondering why I ever made the mistake of declaring that I wanted to see her again. As diplomatically as I could, I paid the bill, walked her to the car, and never saw her again. She was surprised at the coldness of my reception even though she had read about my religious preferences.

Since the 1700s, there has been much discussion of the role of miracles in the Bible and especially in the ministry of Jesus. A lot of effort has gone into explaining the so-called miracles in ways that would be credible to people who believe in science with its chain of natural causes for events. Some people discount sections of the Bible they consider miraculous. Thomas Jefferson went to the extent of cutting out parts of the Bible he found incredible, preserving mostly the teachings of Jesus.[24] Many scholars follow the example of Rudolph Bultmann by ignoring parts of the gospels they find less reliable and fall back, like Jefferson, on teachings they can accept.[25]

Christian denominations considered "mainstream," which are more sympathetic to education and science, have been losing ground for many decades. Many of the groups that have grown dramatically are "charismatic" in one way or another, actively endorsing the existence of demons as they encourage "speaking in tongues" and emotional participation in services. The woman I dated belonged to such a group and there are many such groups in my community. Even though I attend a mainstream, denominational church, many people there believe in literal interpretations that insist Jesus actually talked to demons because the gospels say he did.

Historical awareness teaches us that we can't understand Jesus without putting ourselves in his shoes. If we apply contemporary standards to pick what to believe, then we miss how the gospels intend to portray Jesus as seen by his contemporaries. Understanding the cultural views of those times doesn't mean we have to ignore scientific and medical advances to the point of endorsing the views of those times. In that time, demons made sense and the actions of Jesus grabbed attention. Charismatic healings still occur today in ways that challenge modern beliefs.

The first three chapters of Mark show that Jesus made a dramatic impression through exorcism and healing in public. This brought crowds from Galilean villages to see him in action. It also brought political officials (Herodians) and religious authorities (scribes and Pharisees) from the cities in Galilee and Judea. Charismatic healing was not unknown in the Roman world or in Judea and Galilee, but it was still an uncommon experience, leading to fame and small crowds hoping to experience healing.

The early chapters of Mark present a Jesus known for his actions rather than sayings or teachings. These actions conveyed a sense of power and authority that was thought to come from God. Mark doesn't show Jesus making dramatic claims about his relationship with God. The actions spoke loud enough.

One of his early actions was to draw away and designate twelve close followers. The number chosen symbolized his intention to impact all of Israel, a message that was understood by his contemporaries. His commission to those followers also included the power to exorcise and heal because that was an important part of his ministry. In this action he was claiming the ability to share the power he received from God.

Jesus and his contemporaries did not consider exorcisms as miracles. Rather, they were demonstrations of power over spiritual forces that often interfered with normal processes of the visible world. We have to put aside modern views of miracles as violations of a natural order of cause and effect if we are to understand how people saw Jesus. We must also put aside modern medical attitudes that focus on disease processes that can be cured. Jesus healed people rather than curing them by showing power over hidden spiritual forces. Therefore, an important question for contemporaries was where his power came from. Jesus wanted them to see the power of God acting through him and became very upset when critics said it showed alliance with demonic forces.

Understanding the times in which Jesus lived involves recognizing that audiences in the villages of Galilee and nearby Jewish territories believed there was a host of spiritual powers between people and God—"powers and principalities," as they were called in Ephesians 6:12. Those with health problems were often understood as being possessed or under the power of demons who could disrupt lives and events in a variety of ways. Being tortured by these powers was the result of sins committed by individuals or their families. The problem was not how to cure a disease, whether physical or mental, but how to overcome the power of spiritual forces.

The first chapter of Mark tells three stories of healing, the first of which involves a man possessed by an "unclean spirit." A literal interpretation would affirm that Jesus actually encountered a demon, that it spoke to Jesus, and that he exorcised it with a single command. A more modern approach would see the man as suffering from a form of mental illness. We can embrace the modern understanding and still recognize that Jesus and the people in this story believed in demon possession. They believed the demon spoke and then obeyed a command from Jesus. They experienced a demonstration of power over spiritual forces that led to crowds following him around, hoping for similar healing experiences. The healing happened within their cultural context and conformed to their perception of the world. Contemporary holistic approaches recognize the psychological and physical effectiveness of human belief in the power of charismatic healing in similar situations today.

In the first three chapters of Mark, there are five healing episodes as crowds become more and more troublesome for Jesus. This sets up a confrontation in the third chapter with those who attack the perception of power that is attracting the crowds. The scribes from Jerusalem are reported as saying that Jesus was in league with a leading demonic figure, Beelzebul, so that what appeared to be power over demons was really a hidden form of demonic power or witchcraft. Thus they attacked one of the foundations of Jesus's mission as presented by Mark. No wonder Mark presents an angry response to what could have been a devastating criticism.

At the beginning of the third chapter, Mark tells of an episode at a synagogue on the Sabbath. In this case a man with a withered hand—clearly a physical complaint unrelated to demons—is singled out, and Jesus makes a public issue of healing on the Sabbath, knowing that Pharisees were present and would be critical of him. In fact Jesus is angry as he performs the healing.

Holistic approaches to modern medicine do not find it difficult to accept that contemporary faith healing experiences can impact what seem to be physical problems at least temporarily. Problems such as the paralysis in Mark 2:1–12 and the vaginal flow mentioned in Mark 5:25–34, along with the withered hand in chapter three, may well have responded to a charismatic healer even if they were not permanently resolved. The intent of these stories is to show that Jesus also had power over conditions not related to demons; that his power extended to being able to forgive sins behind illness and deformity; and that his power generated hostility and opposition by Pharisees, scribes, and Herodians. In fact, Jesus sometimes made a point of publicly and angrily challenging his opponents, as he did in the synagogue in chapter three.

The beginning of Jesus's ministry, as told in the first three chapters of Mark, is characterized by demonstrations of spiritual power through exorcism and healing. These actions bring quick fame, crowds, and criticism by religious authorities. In the fourth chapter, Mark begins to present Jesus as a teacher as he continues to heal and provoke religious authorities.

No matter how enlightened, modern, or educated we are, Christians must be comfortable with Jesus as a healer and exorcist. It was important to Jesus and those who followed him. It was important to the early church presented in Acts as they continued to manifest the power seen in Jesus.

That doesn't mean endorsing a world view full of demonic spiritual powers. But the fact is we don't understand spiritual forces, although most of us
believe in them and claim to experience them in a wide variety of ways. We
don't believe that sin causes natural disasters or disease. But who can explain
the power of evil that continues to be seen especially in human actions—or
the innocent suffering that permeates our world through economic, political,
or disease processes that are impersonal and impervious to their consequences?

The truth is that life remains mysterious in many ways that touch us
deeply and personally. The power of God is something we cannot explain,
even though Christians, Jews, and many others believe they experience it. Life
itself is an ongoing conversation with God. I find that conversation in its many
forms to be meaningful but I do not expect to receive definitive answers to important questions before this life ends. Still, I really enjoy the conversation.

Chapter Seven

Hidden Messiah

When I was a student at Mercer University in the 1960s, we were required to attend a weekly chapel service that always featured a sermon. We heard some of the prominent ministers in the South. There was a special treat in the fall term because we frequently heard the choir sing pieces from the oratorio *Messiah*. One of our annual traditions was a full performance of Handel's famous oratorio around Christmas, so the choir gave students previews during chapel services. I am sure I am not the only Mercer student who has made Handel's *Messiah* an essential part of Christmas festivities since then.

Messiah is an important concept in Christianity. The equivalent word in Greek is Christ. It is a title but many people think it is actually the last name of Jesus. The word refers to being anointed as prophets and kings were anointed in the Bible. That action designated someone for an important and authoritative role that carried with it a relationship to God. We continue the same tradition today as church officers experience the "laying on of hands" as an inaugural event that bestows the office on them—similar to the swearing in of presidents.

The gospel of Mark opens with these words: "The beginning of the good news of Jesus Christ, the Son of God." (1:1) Readers of the gospel have no doubt how Jesus's actions and teachings should be regarded, but that is not so for those within the story Mark tells. He presents a Jesus who does not want people spreading abroad that he is the Messiah. It seems to be a big secret he is keeping from the public that he also hesitates to share with his closest followers. Why would Jesus want to do that?

One reason many people have not wanted to consider is that Jesus may have been trying to figure out just what role he was supposed to play. Matthew and Luke provide rival birth accounts that tell us Jesus was designated Messiah at his birth. John pushes the special role back to being with God at creation. But Mark has an inaugural event. At the baptism by John, a dove descends and God makes a pronouncement, which has the effect of turning Jesus into the Messiah from that moment. That was the moment of anointing. The early chapters of Mark also show a Jesus not yet sure of himself. So it could have been that Jesus was still trying to figure out what his special role was.

Why would there be confusion, you may wonder. Christian tradition has maintained that Jesus was the true Messiah from the beginning and that crucifixion and resurrection were always what the Messiah was to accomplish. But Jews at the time of Jesus and since then have different views.

To understand the confusion over Messiah in Jesus's time and since, let's begin with a very fundamental distinction. Messiah is not a political, religious, or philosophical concept that can be logically explained in a consistent way. Why not? Because it is essentially a poetic concept full of evanescent symbolism. The idea is found in prophetic oracles that were often poetry and not prose. The idea was not explained, only illustrated with symbolic language. Thus the music of Handel is a very appropriate method of seeing this wide variety of pronouncements over very long periods of time by many different people.[26]

The very word Messiah derives from the act of being anointed, being chosen. Prophets and especially kings were chosen in this way, and with it came a special relationship with God in both cases. That relationship carried an aspect of divinity, but there was no mistaking the fact that these Messiahs were humans acting with the authority and power of God and not God himself. Other terms were also applied. In a great many psalms, the term Son of God is used as a designation for the king, showing the same special authority and power relationship to God but not literal kinship. Other literature known in Jesus's time used the term Son of Man in highly symbolic ways. Jesus himself began using this term. It could refer to an ordinary human being and be the equivalent of "this guy" or it could refer to a special divine role. Jesus seems to have used both of those meanings.[27]

What we have to keep in mind is that with poetic concepts, there is no universal agreement on their meaning. We can't explain them logically and consistently. Trying to do that is like grabbing water in your hands or precisely identifying the color of a chameleon as it shimmers from one hue to another.

In Jesus's time, there was not a widespread expectation of a Messiah as many people have asserted. There were uprisings in Galilee and Judea following the death of Herod the Great, and there were three instances of large public demonstrations in the decades between the death of Jesus and the rebellion against Rome in 66 CE. All of these brought Roman military responses but few appeared to be messianic. John the Baptist and Jesus were exceptions in that they did not bring about large-scale Roman intervention, but both of them were executed when their religious movements became viewed as political threats.[28]

In the opening chapters of Mark, we see a Jesus who is dramatically asserting the power of God through provocative actions but who is careful not to talk about himself in any definitive way. He seems very uncomfortable as he is adjusting to the stress and demands of this role and perhaps is figuring out just what God wants him to do. He definitely knows he does not want people spreading the word loudly that he is the Messiah. Nor does he openly attack Herod Antipas, as John did, because that would lead to a similar fate.

The silence of Jesus keeps the public and his disciples guessing. The public uncertainty leads to more and more observation by officials to see if he would slip up and declare himself in a way that could justify their action. But Jesus became upset that his disciples didn't figure out the nature of his role, even though he would not come right out and tell them.

It is only because of the opening words of Mark that we feel confident we know the role of Jesus. When he breaks silence, he uses the term Son of Man in a way that people are still trying to figure out. How were the disciples to understand such imagery with shifting meanings?

As we look back from our time, we are seeing Jesus in light of the crucifixion and resurrection narratives. We look through the glasses of interpretations in the gospels and later traditions that derive the meaning of Jesus as Messiah based on the entire events of his life.

In reading Mark, we must put aside those glasses and look from the perspective of Jesus and his contemporaries at that time in his ministry. What we see is a remarkably human picture of a Jesus convinced that he has a mission from God yet still working out just what it means. We see him dealing with the pressure of perhaps unexpected quick success, yet being smart enough to know that he should not say too much too soon or authorities will scoop him up. When he does speak of himself, it is not in language that would immediately be recognized as a messianic claim. He refers to himself and his role as that of an ordinary human being when he uses the term Son of Man; but the term also referred to a title used in apocalyptic texts and there are times when Jesus appears to refer to that title. This makes it difficult to determine how that term was understood before the crucifixion, for John Collins points out that: "It is difficult to see, however, how Jesus could have been identified with the Son of Man prior to his crucifixion . . . . That identification would seem to presuppose the resurrection and ascension." [29]

In Mark it is possible we see development in the thinking of Jesus although we don't know what period of time was involved. At some point, he decided to leave Galilee for Jerusalem. His comments make it clear he expects to be executed there by the Romans because he refers to crucifixion. If he had provoked Herod Antipas in Galilee, he would have been beheaded in a remote fortress as happened to John the Baptist. He decided to reach for a bigger stage. His comment was that Jerusalem was the appropriate place for the death of a prophet. That was reaching for center stage.

How Jesus himself saw his role is still under scholarly debate. Jews say he could not have been the Messiah because the messianic age has not arrived. The concept itself is still not clearly understood. We must remember that the Messiah is about poetry and music, full of hope and anticipation, not logic and lucidity.[30]

CHAPTER EIGHT

USE AND MISUSE OF POWER

The synoptic gospels agree that Jesus was baptized by John the Baptist and began his movement by separating himself from John. The gospel of John doesn't show Jesus being baptized but emphasizes the testimony of John the Baptist without showing an actual baptism. Mark says Jesus went into the wilderness for forty days but gives no details. Matthew and Luke provide slightly different versions of three temptations Jesus resisted during the fasting in the wilderness.

There is no reason to see the temptation story as historical. Jesus was alone and none of the gospels said anything to indicate he told the story to his disciples. The scholars of the Jesus Seminar were unanimous in declaring these words and actions as not directly from Jesus but they did recognize the plausibility of someone like Jesus withdrawing for a period of prayer and fasting as preparation for launching a movement.[31] The story itself has the simplicity of a parable without the surprise or provocation usually found in parables. Each temptation represents an abuse Jesus could make of special powers he believed he received from God and he responds to each proposition with answers from Deuteronomy. The details of the story, from the forty days to allusions to manna and a mountain, are reminiscent of Israel's experiences in Sinai. As Marcus Borg is wont to point out, this story has deeper significance than historical factuality.[32]

The Jesus Seminar pointed out that this story is typical of the way Greco-Roman biographies began with the story of a trial that forecast the later developments of the hero's career. The story plays a role in Matthew and Luke that is similar to the stories of conflict and response to pressure seen in the first three chapters of Mark. The direction Jesus will take in his ministry is at stake. In all three gospels, it is portrayed in relationship to demonic powers.

There is no reason to doubt that Jesus believed in demonic powers striving against God and the agents of God like himself. The powers he felt sure came from God enabled him to overcome those hidden spiritual forces. In Mark a big problem arises when critics pass the word that Jesus's powers actually result from alliance with demons rather than opposition to them. In Matthew and Luke, the demonic challenge is far more subtle and insidious. It has to do with the motives of Jesus as he used the powers from God.

The nature of the temptations themselves is very credible, considering the possibilities of religious movements like the one Jesus intended. Doing spectacular things like turning stone into bread and making a big public display in the temple are not very far from things Jesus was reported to have done in Matthew and Luke. The issue of going for political power is one that some scholars still debate and that appears to have been the official reason for his execution by the Romans; yet the gospels are united in insisting that Jesus did not have a normal political and military effort in mind when he spoke of a rival kingdom. But in the temptations, it is not just the doing or not doing of something that is at issue—it is the motive that is highlighted in Jesus's responses.

Tempting as it is to see this story as actual insight into Jesus's own thinking about his mission, we must resist that simple and literal answer. Part of the deep truth in the story is that Jesus almost surely did see himself in a contest with demonic powers. The thinking process reflected in the story may well have been part of Jesus's internal struggles over how and when to use his special powers—and for what reasons.

As previously discussed, Mark shows the humanity of Jesus in his struggling with all that comes with sudden success in launching a movement. Mark shows a period of adjustment. In Luke and Matthew, the suggestion is that Jesus confronted similar questions within himself at the beginning and resolved them. Too often sermons interpret these temptations as the divinity of Jesus passing the test and moving triumphantly onward. That is not how the world operates. Most of us discover that when we are successful in resisting powerful temptations in one form, we later experience the same thing occurring in multiple and often deceptive forms. If we have a weakness, reality finds a way to keep probing. Hardly ever is temptation a "one and done" experience.

If we focus on the humanity of Jesus, these temptations take on even deeper meaning. First of all, anytime he used his powers, the issue of who he was serving, God or evil forces, was always an open question. Gaining confidence in his mission would naturally lead to less frequent introspection as the movement developed, but you can bet the question still came up within him. History is full of stories of political leaders who started out with seemingly good motivations but who, in time, found themselves pursuing self-gratification. Napoleon and George Washington were contemporaries that carried great hopes when they took power. Napoleon followed the usual course of mounting egotism leading to his ruin. Washington is one of the few historical examples of someone who voluntarily relinquished power he could easily have retained and enhanced if he had been so inclined. The kind of self-denial seen in Washington and Jesus is rare and comes about from ongoing battles with temptation.

A second point makes us even more aware of the pitfalls of humanity. In the story, Jesus professed a motivation to put God first, but the gospels show that he did actions similar to things mentioned in the temptations. When he took those actions, how could he be sure his motives were entirely based on devotion to God? How often are our motivations pure and single-mindedly altruistic when we do something people admire and praise? One of the realities of the human situation is that our very best motives are always tinged with selfishness—there is always something in it for us. All of us have our critics, and they are keen to see where the best of our goodness serves our own gratification.

I can hear the protest that these mixed results point to Original Sin and the fall of Adam and Eve. This approach of course exempts Jesus from such accusation. Not so fast. Putting aside theological wishful thinking, we must realize that life and death, along with the possibility of good and evil, pleasure and suffering, all came into existence at the Big Bang as part of the texture of reality. If Jesus really experienced humanity, he knew this reality as well. None of us can ever have completely pure motivations and actions. Part of the deep truth of the temptation story is the likelihood of seeing the ongoing struggle within Jesus to which he had no definitive answer, just as we have no definitive answer. We must all do the best we can, no matter what construction others may put on it or how self-serving it will be, and leave the outcome in God's hands. That is no guarantee of success, for too often overwhelming opinion insists on taking what you feel sure is the wrong interpretation of actions and motivations.

This brings me to a third point that has to do with the consequences of our actions. Please bear with me as I take a short detour to talk about one of my favorite novels, *The Razor's Edge* by W. Somerset Maugham. There is a conversation when the narrator figures out something terrible that the leading female character has done under the guise of doing what was in someone's best interest. The narrator tells Matthew's version of the temptation story and then puts a different ending on it.

> That's the end of the story according to the good simple Matthew. But it wasn't. The devil was sly and he came to Jesus once more and said: If thou wilt accept shame and disgrace, scourging, a crown of thorns and death on the cross, thou shalt save the human race, for greater love hath no man than this, that a man lay down his life for his friends. Jesus fell. The devil laughed until his sides ached, for he knew the evil men would commit in the name of their redeemer.[33]

A little further on, the narrator concludes the conversation with this observation.

> I couldn't but surmise that the devil, looking at the cruel wars that Christianity has occasioned, the persecutions, the tortures Christian has inflicted on Christian, the unkindness, the hypocrisy, the intolerance, must consider the balance sheet with complacency.[34]

There is a double edge to this ending, for it suggests that even self-sacrifice can be seen as giving in to temptation along with holding the person responsible for all of the consequences of what seemed to be done for the best of motives.

This does not represent cynicism, but reality. One of the political critiques developed in the Reagan years of the liberal social programs of the Kennedy-Johnson years was how they undermined the very intentions behind them. The term "the law of unintended consequences" was used often in political discourse and it still turns up in different forms today. The idea is that people do things for one reason but then events end up making worse the very thing that was to be improved.

The concept itself is not partial to any political party or set of actions. It recognizes a fact of life. All of our actions and inactions have consequences beyond what we foresee or intend. Should we be held accountable for those outcomes?

The peril of taking action and risking adverse consequences is yet another aspect of the humanity of Jesus as presented in this story. However pure our motives, our actions will have results we could not possibly have anticipated, some of them good and many of them undesirable. We must risk acting and leave the outcome in God's hands. Sometimes it takes quite a while for events to finally move in the direction that was originally intended.

Looking again at the temptation story in Matthew and Luke, we can see a divine Jesus being tested once and passing. That is easy and not really much of a temptation. Of course the story is not historical. Yet it clearly bears deep metaphorical truth. I think it probably represented something not too far from the internal struggles Jesus had in figuring out just how he represented God over and against demonic powers. It was not a onetime test, but lasted through his life and ministry. This helps us to see even more deeply into the humanity of Jesus, to a greater psychological depth than seen in the conflict stories in Mark. This is a picture of a man who truly bore the depth of our sorrows and struggles with the ambivalent realities of life.

Chapter Nine

Did Jesus Use the Bathroom?

The principal of Fell Avenue Elementary School was a disciplinarian who used a wooden paddle on Fridays to solve behaviors that bothered her. She taught fourth grade in that four-room school building with a cafeteria attached and a large supply closet that was also used for paddling kids as parents stood watching. One paddling seemed to correct most problems, except for one little boy with diabetes. Kids always teased him in the cafeteria about how he could never eat what the rest of us ate, leading to frequent uprisings that meant almost weekly paddling. I remember his very meek mother crying and telling the principal she could not understand why her little one could not stay out of trouble.

This formidable lady noticed me when I was in the third grade. I had a condition that has followed me all my life in that my bladder fills quicker than usual. Over the years several urologists have done tests showing nothing was wrong with my active metabolism. But the principal told the third grade teacher something was not right when I frequently asked to be excused during class. The solution was to make me wait. On the second day of the new rule, I had an "accident" in class that girls teased me about for the next three years.

The principal relented until I was in her class the following year. Angry at my frequent need to interrupt class, she sent a note to my mother to come on Friday to witness my paddling. Mama didn't wait for Friday. The next morning she arrived and insisted on a conference. She wouldn't go into the supply closet but stood just outside the door to the classroom so that every class heard as she told the principal she would never lay a hand on any of her children. Then in words that children shouldn't hear, she berated the principal for wanting to punish someone for a condition that doctors had said was normal. The only solution was to simply let me use the bathroom when necessary.

I had no more problems with the principal, but my frequency caused embarrassment in other ways. In church, our minister preached some very long sermons. Well before the end, I usually had my legs crossed and then started swinging them trying to hold back the flood. It was embarrassing to get up and walk all the way to the door beside the pulpit, in plain sight of everyone, to get to the bathroom. If I could wait out the sermon, then he would want to sing extra verses of the closing hymn until someone came and gave their life to Jesus. Having to walk down the aisle then and make a sudden turn toward the door leading to the bathroom was really embarrassing.

Maybe it was my unusual problem that made me notice things. In the movies, none of the cowboys ever had to go to the bathroom. None of the childhood stories I heard ever mentioned the bathroom and neither did the books I got from the library. In the Bible, Jesus was always walking around in the countryside but never needed to drink water or find a bathroom—or so it seemed.

In daily life, we are always having to work around basic physical needs for water, food, and bathroom, but those aspects of life are often taken for granted without being mentioned in novels, movies, and the Bible. We are in the habit of not looking for those normal elements of life to show up in the Bible. This mental habit can lead us to overlook the fact that many ordinary aspects of life are never mentioned in accounts of Jesus.

Just think of the ordinary things we know about people in real life that we don't know about Jesus. Where did he live? How did he make a living? Did he have a wife and children? Could he read and, if so, what languages did he read? And here is a real puzzle—why didn't he go into the cities of Galilee? Let's take a look at each question.[35]

The gospels mention Nazareth as his home town and he is shown visiting but not living there. The synoptics show him moving about in the area around Capernaum and Mark says that was his home. Jesus wanders widely around the Sea of Galilee so that he appears not to have a fixed home. There is one reference to him saying that foxes have holes but he was homeless (Matthew 8:20). Many scholars think he made a point of not having a home as part of his wandering ministry. Perhaps the home referred to in Mark was Peter's house in Capernaum that he used as a base. Various references in the gospels can lead to all kinds of speculation, but the fact is we are not told clearly where Jesus slept at night. He went into deserted places to pray, we know, but he doesn't seem to have slept there or to have had difficulty finding a place to sleep or get in out of the weather.

How did he live? He hung out with fishermen who seem to have been able to keep up their business although we are not told much about how they did that. Jesus was said to be something that was traditionally translated as carpenter. That term could have meant that he was an unskilled handyman or plain construction worker or, on the other end of the scale, a skilled artisan employed in the design and construction of complicated things. During his lifetime, Herod Antipas did a lot of building in Sepphoris, just a few miles from Nazareth, and later built a capital at Tiberias on the lake not far from Capernaum. Jesus could have been employed at either or both locations. The gospels don't report him visiting either of those cities.

Many scholars want to label Jesus a peasant, which would make him a lower-class person unlikely to have been educated or be a skilled laborer. Amy-Jill Levine has made the point that Luke 8:1–3 mentions a female member of his company whose husband was steward at the court of Herod Antipas. That made her part of the retainer class, which was a lower-level member of the elite in that society that centered on the courts of rulers and the temple. That suggests Jesus must have been more of an artisan, for they related to the upper classes and were on the margins of the retainer class so that they knew how to get along with that level of society. In other words, Jesus was not a country bumpkin. He knew how to deal with city folk. This would also be supported by stories of his meals with Pharisees, indicating he was not ignorant of etiquette for relating to upper strata of society.[36] That sounds about right to me, but we don't know for sure.[37]

This leads to the question of reading skill. Most scholars are convinced Jesus was illiterate. The gospel of Luke reports him reading from Isaiah in a synagogue (4:16–20). Was this episode invented? There are some scholars who would quickly line up behind the idea such an episode did not occur. But there is an interesting debate going on right now about literacy in societies prior to the widespread use of the printing press centuries later. Archaeologists are looking for early synagogues around the time of Jesus and for signs that Torah scrolls were used in them. Results are not yet clear. Richard Horsley is among those who argue that what we have translated as "read" meant "recite." Before easy availability of the printed word, all societies were based on oral communication and even the scribes, those whose profession it was to read and write, learned and worked mostly by memorization and recitation from memory. Biblical scrolls, according to Horsley, were mostly stored in the temple for safekeeping or memorialization as in a museum rather than for reading. People heard scriptures recited and in an oral culture it was not unusual for people to know biblical traditions, if not the very words of the scrolls, by heart. That is one reason the wording of the documents changed over time.[38]

William Herzog and Richard Horsley are among those who see Jesus as versed more in the "little tradition" of Judaism rather than the official tradition associated with Torah reading and temple cult. This is to say that Jesus knew oral traditions of Galilee, which focused on the Mosaic covenant teachings and stories of popular prophets, like Elijah and Elisha, identified with northern areas. Herzog concludes that familiarity with this aspect of the tradition resulted in Jesus's ability to read and interpret Torah. "It is very likely that he learned to read and argue Torah in the local synagogue gathering . . . . When Jesus appeared on the public stage, he was already able to debate Torah, the most basic skill needed to become a public figure."[39] Whether Jesus was able to read is not clear, but his knowledge of scriptural traditions and interpretations is undeniable.

The Jewish Scriptures are preserved in Hebrew, but the ordinary language of Jesus's time was Aramaic. Did Jesus read or recite in Hebrew? Again, there is no clear answer but the focus on oral culture would not necessarily rule out Jesus using Hebrew. How about Greek? Greek was the normal language in the cities in Galilee and in Hellenistic cities in Judea. Jesus may well have picked up some knowledge of Greek but we can't be sure—and I don't think it would be very important if he did speak some Greek. We can feel confident that the ordinary language of Jesus was Aramaic and that Jesus lacked the training to read or write. Literacy in his time depended on oral transmission more than on writing, so being what we call illiterate would not have kept Jesus from knowing a lot of the Bible by heart.[40]

How about a family? Most people in Jesus's time would be married and have children. It stands to reason that most of the disciples had wives and children even though they are not mentioned. We know Peter was married because of the story about healing his mother-in-law (Matthew 8:14). Remember that Jesus is reported as saying followers must leave wives, children, and family to come after him (Matthew 10:37 and Luke 14:26). As for Jesus himself, there is silence. He certainly had a lot of female camp followers.[41]

Responsible historical criticism involves being skeptical of the gospels, but, in my opinion, does not involve wild speculation. A romance with Mary Magdalene is the stuff of legends and sensational novels. When someone like Bishop John Shelby Spong jumps on board that train of speculation, it lowers respect for other good work he did.[42] Of course the gospels provide no evidence of such a marriage. I suspect the strongest indirect evidence that Jesus was not married and had no children is the fact that his brother James shared leadership with Peter of the early Jesus movement in Jerusalem after the crucifixion. When James was executed in 62 CE, it appears leadership in Jerusalem fell to a nephew of Jesus. If there had been a son, you can bet he would have been mentioned among the leadership. Jesus's family came to play a role in Christian tradition. If there had been any indication of a wife and children, you can be sure they would have played some role in the Jesus Movement.

Questions about family, education, occupation, and residence are all normal things you expect to know about someone that are unclear about Jesus. Anyone writing a biography would certainly cover those areas. Even biographical writings in the Roman period would have covered them. The gospels are similar to the biographical writings of the Romans but they leave out a lot of information by focusing on the mission and message of Jesus, the good news they are proclaiming.

There is one other biographical area that has more clarity. Mark, Matthew, and Luke show Jesus working predominately in the villages of Lower Galilee, in the area around Capernaum, and going to Jerusalem with a sense of death awaiting. Why didn't he go into the cities of Galilee? There is a very active debate as to how Hellenistic those cities were and whether that was a reason for Jesus to avoid them. It seems clear that the village areas were centers of more traditional Jewish practices. Operating in that locale showed greater comfort with Mosaic and prophetic traditions of Judaism than with environments where Hellenistic and Roman features were more common. This only confirms the Jewishness of Jesus. This was an area where he would expect to have less interaction with non-Jewish populations in a mission directed primarily to Jews.

John shows a different picture. He shows Jesus active in all parts of what had been the kingdom of Herod the Great. Jesus is often in Jerusalem and interacts comfortably with people like Nicodemus who belong to the ruling class that has a working accommodation with their Roman overlords. Even John shows Jesus avoiding the cities of Herod Antipas.

Asking about Jesus's bathroom habits is an attention-getting way of making us aware that we lack a lot of everyday information about him that we expect to know about people. Those who want to speak confidently about Jesus's personal life are building on speculation most of the time. The gospels give us plenty of insight into Jesus while leaving gaps that tantalize. I would like to know more than they tell, but I am extremely grateful for what they do tell us.

CHAPTER TEN

HARMONIZING AND QUESTING

Variety is not always the spice of life. Sometimes people become very uneasy when there are too many choices.

I am comfortable going to the same restaurants over and over, usually eating the same dishes time after time. When I find something I like, I tend to stay with it—a tendency some have described as getting into a rut. I just am not interested in exploring the many choices on the menu when I find something that satisfies enough to keep eating it. A longtime friend of mine gets nervous whenever we go into a restaurant that is unfamiliar. Time and again I have seen him look over an extensive menu without taking the time to look closely at anything. He often seems jumpy until he can ask the waitress "What's good here?" She usually mentions two or maybe three items. This settles him down as he picks the one that sounds best. Too many choices can be intimidating.

Imagine the situation in the early development of Christianity. Books were not a very common item because reading and writing was limited to a small, educated elite. Most information and communication was passed orally so that people listened more attentively and remembered more of what they heard than is common today. Yet there was an extensive literature that was circulating. Many of the books claimed to tell of the life of Jesus and still others claimed to be written by various members of the original disciples. Some of those books are known today only because of references to them in some of the writings of the early church leaders and because archaeological discoveries in the twentieth century uncovered some of them.

Church leaders wanted to set standards by rejecting much of the contemporary literature. A man named Marcion, son of a bishop, became a target of church leaders and was denounced as a heretic in the 140s CE. He disapproved of what we know as the Old Testament and he didn't like many of the circulating books that we now recognize in the New Testament, so he put together his own approved collection. This appears to have been the start of efforts to develop an authorized collection from among all the books of the time. Marcion started what became a trend. It was Athanasius, bishop of Alexandria, whose Easter letter in 367 CE was the first to list twenty-seven approved books that were on the way to becoming the New Testament.

The collection that came to be approved by the early church included four gospels. The variety found in those gospels troubled people in earlier times and it continues to trouble people today. Anyone who reads the canonical gospels can see that each has a distinctive personality, presenting different versions of Jesus's life and even varying interpretations of the same events.

One response to this discomfort has been to try harmonizing the gospel accounts. Efforts were made to combine the four accounts into one comprehensive story. This idea is not far-fetched. Scholars are convinced that Genesis is the harmonization of three different traditions. That is why the first three chapters have back-to-back creation stories, each deriving from a different tradition. They were blended together so that it was taken as one consecutive story for a very long time.

There was one successful harmonization of the gospels by a man named Tatian who became a Christian around 150 CE but was later declared a heretic. He arranged the gospels into a harmonized version titled the *Diatesseron*, which spread widely in Syria and was used, in spite of efforts to stamp it out, until around 400 CE. Uncomfortable as some church leaders were with the variety in the four gospels, the decision that prevailed was to maintain the integrity of the differing accounts.

A variation of harmonization is in common use today. One of the areas of agreement in the gospels is that John the Baptist played an important role as Jesus began his ministry. Sermons and Sunday school lessons often refer to the varying accounts of Jesus's baptism but choose details from one account or another as part of giving "the whole picture." The idea is that the gospel versions complement each other so that one can put together a preferred mosaic from the stories rather than acknowledge that they contradict each other in detail and in interpretation. I have seen this approach used by literal interpreters who insist that the Bible tells the whole story when you know how to put different pieces together to arrive at the "true picture" of events. This seemingly innocent method undermines the integrity of each gospel story.

Probably the most flagrant example of harmonization today is "the Christmas story", which every child learns through pageants, nativity scenes, and television as well as in church materials. The story combines rival birth accounts in Matthew and Luke into a journey to Bethlehem where shepherds greet the child in a stable and to which wise men come so that Herod is stirred up. Joseph is then warned to escape to Egypt.

I love the Christmas season and especially the wonderful music. The fact that churches endorse harmonization that encourages biblical illiteracy is very discouraging. It seems appropriate that rival birth mythologies are repeated at the same time as everyone tells children about Santa Claus flying around the world and dropping down chimneys in spite of central air systems. Letting children enjoy their imaginative worlds is not a problem for me—but adults who fail to see the distortion that is accepted as legitimate understanding of the Bible is something that churches should not encourage.[43]

It is biblical scholars who point to the many differences and contradictions in the gospels. Uncomfortable with just four accounts of Jesus's life, scholars keep searching for more sources hoping to gain valuable information. Archaeology produced a text of the Gospel of Thomas, which lists sayings of Jesus without indicating a context. Some scholars have argued that Thomas should be added to the canon and the Jesus Seminar included it when they published translations of the gospels they relied on.[44] Archaeology has also turned up fragments of what appear to be gospels or collections of sayings. The hope is to find more evidence from which to build a more historical view of Jesus than can be found in the four canonical gospels.

As historical methods began to be applied to biblical study in the seventeenth and eighteenth centuries, scholars began to look for a more accurate historical picture of Jesus than could be found in the gospels. Each of the accepted gospels presents a distinctive religious interpretation of Jesus as they tell of his life and ministry. Scholars have tried to sift through theological views to get closer to what a camera might have picked up if Jesus had been filmed. Cameras take pictures from only one angle at a time, but they don't add their own bias. You can combine multiple films of the same event and get a fuller picture as the bias of the single angle is reduced and a more complete account of an event is put together. But Jesus lived before cameras and any source in writing has multiple viewpoints that make it hard to know for sure if any accurate information about the historical Jesus is included at all.

What these scholars did was the reverse of harmonization in two ways. First, they delved within the gospels looking for their sources and began breaking them into component parts. Luke and John make statements acknowledging they drew on multiple sources for what they wrote. Sure enough, the seams joining various sources were uncovered.

The biggest discoveries of these efforts were the importance of Mark and a sayings source that had not been mentioned in the writings of any of the early church leaders. It became accepted that Mark was actually the first gospel composed and that Luke and Matthew followed Mark's structure even to the extent of copying him word for word in many places. But Matthew and Luke also had many sayings in common that were not in Mark, so these were designated as coming from a previously unknown source who was called Q for the German word for source used by the German scholars making the discovery. The sources for Jesus had suddenly multiplied from within the New Testament itself. Now there was (1) Mark, (2 and 3) the parts of Luke and Matthew that were adopted from Mark but given separate interpretation by each of them, (4) additional material that only Matthew used, (5) additional material that only Luke used, (6) the sayings that Matthew and Luke used that came from an unknown source called Q, and (7) John who seems to have used an unknown source who listed the signs performed by Jesus.

Scholarship focused on Jesus also reversed harmonization in a second way as scholar after scholar tossed out John and gave preference to Mark as the basis for the most reliable picture of Jesus. Early in the twentieth century, Albert Schweitzer described German research on Jesus in a book whose name made the kind of impact that was made by the Watergate scandal. After Watergate, every scandal investigation was described so that "–gate" appeared at the end. The English translation of Schweitzer's book, *The Quest of the Historical Jesus*, set everyone to talking about the quest.[45] Schweitzer's book killed the quest, it seemed; but then a second quest appeared, and a few years later a third quest was claimed. The list of quests could go on, but I agree with James Charlesworth of Princeton that enough is enough. Each of the so-called quests had as an objective to find versions of the real historical Jesus. Schweitzer and others have said that is not possible. Charlesworth agrees that it is impossible to recover the actual historical Jesus, but through ongoing research we continue to learn more and more that sharpens and improves our understanding of him. Charlesworth prefers to refer to "Jesus research" and so do I.[46]

The early questers thought they found a more reliable Jesus by narrowing their focus to Mark. This was the earliest and most primitive of the gospels. In this case being primitive was good. Mark's Greek was not polished like the other gospels and seemed more direct and honest. Albert Schweitzer took the trend to its fullest extent before he burst the quester's bubble at the end of his book. He thought it possible that Mark presented a Jesus whose parables and sayings about the kingdom coming with the harvest actually referred to the very next harvest. That means that the ministry of Jesus was even shorter than had been imagined. Trying to force events to a head, Jesus went to Jerusalem convinced his actions would bring about the immediate arrival of the kingdom he anticipated. But Schweitzer left him hanging on the cross in what seemed to be defeat.

Schweitzer's final blow was to announce the impossibility of finding the historical Jesus. He had shown that each scholar had found a Jesus shaped by their personal philosophies. Schweitzer did not think it possible to get behind biblical sources to see what a camera would have seen if one had been turned on Jesus. In the 1930s, Rudolf Bultmann, the most prominent biblical scholar of his day, seconded Schweitzer's view that recovering a historical view of Jesus was impossible as he limited himself to talking about the teachings of Jesus.[47] In this approach, Bultmann narrowed the material on Jesus mostly to the teachings found in Q, throwing out John and reducing the variety of biblical material even further.

Conservative Christians are not likely to say many good things about the Jesus Seminar at the end of the twentieth century, but at least they were expanding rather than contracting the material on Jesus. Every biblical scholar lets you know which sayings of Jesus they find credible, expressing thereby a multiplicity of views that individuals can hardly keep up with. The Jesus Seminar went public in trying to determine a consensus among a group of scholars representing a spectrum within Jesus scholarship. They published what they thought could be relied on as the words and actions of Jesus as seen in more sources than just the four canonical gospels. Their work also confirmed the tendency to exclude most of John from consideration.[48]

The singularity of John was recognized from the earliest days of the church. The monologues of Jesus proclaiming himself as well as God were very different from the pithy short statements and parables in other gospels where Jesus proclaimed the kingdom of God and not himself. Church fathers held to John, calling it a "spiritual gospel," meaning that it interpreted the meaning of Christ better than other gospels, which may have been more like the Jesus of history. John has always been a favorite among those who value the "Christ experience."

The term source has been an essential part of discussions about the historical Jesus—and indeed in the application of historical criticism to all parts of the Bible. Hidden in that word is a set of assumptions that have come with use of the printed word since the impact of the printing press on the eve of the Reformation. The gospels are assumed to have individual authors who pulled together written materials and some oral traditions to express either their own point of view and purpose or the point of view of their believing community. Authorship, use of written sources, editing and compiling sources—these all came with the spread of printing and literacy on a much wider scale around the time of the Reformation so that it is increasingly realized they do not apply so well to the oral culture of Second Temple Judaism and the early New Testament.

Werner Kelber was among those who began to focus on the faulty assumptions of historical criticism when applied to realities of oral cultures that prevailed before widespread use of printing and literacy. In those times, literacy was most often seen in terms of recitation from memory of important texts and other significant stories by people who did not read or write. The increasing discussion of the Old and New Testaments as products of oral memories performed before communities is beginning to reshape many ideas about the Bible and about the stories of Jesus.[49]

Today the verdict of the historical scholars on John is looking very premature. Archaeology has uncovered features in Jerusalem mentioned in John, indicating that in many details John was more accurate than the synoptic gospels.[50] His chronology of Jesus makes specific reference to festivals in the temple, which allow us to figure a ministry of about three years for Jesus. James Dunn has suggested that John came later than the synoptics, knew their accounts, and may have had additional sources of oral tradition around Jerusalem that were used to fill in gaps in the earlier and more Galilee-focused accounts.[51] It is beginning to look as if John is more reliable than other gospels in some historical features even if the speeches of Jesus do not seem credible.

So the verdict of the church fathers who kept four separate and contradicting gospels is looking better all the time. Efforts to harmonize them into a single story have not worked. Efforts to narrow down to a reliable kernel of truth have not worked. We are left with a variety that challenges us. In other conversations, I will make it clear that I believe there have been real achievements in seeing Jesus with more historical accuracy than in previous times. As research continues, that accuracy may keep improving. I am confident that real progress in understanding Jesus will not mean throwing out any of the four canonical gospels. Each one has its treasures to be uncovered and appreciated.

CHAPTER ELEVEN

FAITH, KNOWLEDGE, AND ILLUSION

Most of my life has been spent attending Presbyterian churches that have as part of the service the recitation of a creed, most often the Apostle's Creed. In the Baptist churches of my childhood, we did not believe in creeds, but we were taught to believe firmly in the plan of salvation that involved giving one's life to Jesus as part of a conversion experience. When speaking of faith, what was usually meant was faith in Jesus as savior and holding certain important beliefs that made you a Christian.

The standard was found in Hebrews 11:1. The King James Version reads: "Now faith is the substance of things hoped for, the evidence of things not seen." If people began to have doubts about the credibility of parts of the Bible, that was a crisis of faith. The solution was to turn back to faith and rely on it as knowledge when deceptive human thinking was leading you astray. Saint Augustine was a strong supporter of this approach, as seen in a sermon on the parable of the Prodigal Son who had to turn to the food pigs ate when he was low. Augustine saw an allegory in which the food represented "secular doctrines, which crackle, but don't satisfy, fit for pigs, not human beings; that is for demons to take pleasure in, not for the faithful to be justified by."[52]

These days Hebrews 11:1 is presented differently. The scholars behind the New Revised Standard Version translate it this way: "Now faith is the assurance of things hoped for, the conviction of things not seen." The commentary in the *HarperCollins Study Bible* points out that: "*Conviction* is not simply a subjective attitude; unseen realities are tested and 'proved' by experience."[53]

The commentary in *The Jewish Annotated New Testament* says: "*Faith* carries overtones of endurance, trust, and insight into spiritual reality."[54] Both groups of scholars are saying that scripture does not represent faith as a credible substitute for normal evidence.

Faith as belief depends on historical verification using evidence. It does no good to believe that the first eleven chapters of Genesis are the literal story of the beginning of the universe when science demonstrates otherwise. Insisting on holding to an unsubstantiated belief of this sort is an illusion rather than an acceptable form of knowledge.

Those who are concerned about holding fast to beliefs are often resistant to questioning them because they see that as intended to destroy their faith. If the security of your belief is in the literal accuracy of the many wondrous events reported in the Old and New Testaments, then you are like the man Jesus said built his house on sand (Matthew 7:26). That foundation cannot stand the test of science, historical studies, or plain common sense. Beliefs can rarely be the rock foundation one desires for building a durable faith.

There is one way in which faith becomes a form of knowledge—it is the intuitive knowledge involved in relationships. The term we use most often for this is trust. Why do we trust some people and not others? Somehow we have a sense of confidence, we "just know" they are reliable. An obvious problem is that this form of knowledge is wrong as often as it is right. "Confidence men" are those who specialize in gaining people's trust in order to steal from those they consider "suckers." People in intimate relationships often feel betrayed by a loved one they trusted. Parents are always having to deal with children who say they can be trusted but who don't act in ways to encourage trust.

Here is the really odd thing about faith as trust. When there is clear verification of betrayal, people can still hold on and insist they know who someone truly is and refuse to give up on them. They can forgive and try to set the person straight. The world is full of people who claim to have found their true selves because of parents, teachers, friends, spouses who refused to give up on them no matter what horrible things they did. All too often, efforts to maintain faith result in failure, but the person of faith still felt obliged to keep trying in order to save the relationship.

The Bible represents a long series of episodes in which prophets say the people have been disloyal to God so that they are punished, followed by other prophecies of continuing relationship that will not give up on a people. It also has prayers of desperation by those who suffer and feel deserted by God but still will not give up the trust that is essential to their lives.

Sigmund Freud called religion an illusion and more recently Richard Dawkins called it a delusion.[55] Both see religion as the projection of a parental figure onto the universe because of human neurosis and wishful thinking. They may be right. There is no way as yet to scientifically validate arguments for or against the existence of God.

My belief is that religion is programmed into the human brain. Michael Schermer has talked about patternicity as the key to explaining religion.[56] Humans, like many other animals, have been able to survive because of their ability to recognize patterns in the environment fast enough to avoid predators and other dangers. I experience a variation of this every time I drive my car. My children were taught to drive defensively by anticipating movements of the vehicles around them. A faint hint of movement or other slight show of intention often gives enough time to slow down just enough to avoid a collision because of someone's carelessness. Sometimes just seeing the possibility of other actions leads to saving action or to action that would have saved but was unneeded because the other person did not do what was anticipated. My children have told me that anticipation has often kept them out of trouble and that has been my own experience as well.

Schermer edits the magazine *Skeptic*, which specializes in exposing hoaxes that are meant to take advantage of human patternicity and the way it can lead to accepting silly and dangerous confidence games. There is no doubt that this inner something behind religion has been and will continue to be deceived. Verification can often bring out abuses by those who build on gullibility with fake substitutes for knowledge.

One of the fundamental patterns essential to human existence is the relationship of parent and child, which is at the base of the ability to form relationships. It is natural to want to project a cosmic parent and to have a relationship with whatever is behind all the mysterious forces operating in this universe. So all forms of religion can indeed be seen as projection of human desire. But the human brain also picks up mathematical patterns in the environment. Are these discovered or merely projected from within our minds? Oddly enough, these have been verified through our space explorations, using mathematics to leave this planet and accurately reach locations at vast distances in space. We have not yet found a way to verify our projections of God, but that does not automatically make them an illusion.

Individual health and survival depend on the ability to form human relationships. There are many stories of experiments to discover the "natural language" spoken by children by intentionally not speaking to infants. The Franciscan monk Salimbene di Adam (1221–ca. 1290) recorded an experiment by Holy Roman Emperor Frederick II in which foster mothers and nurses would care for infants but not speak to them. The intention was to see if infants began to speak Hebrew, Greek, Latin, Arabic or some other language naturally. The infants died because more human contact than holding and nursing was needed. Salimbene recorded "the children could not live without clappings of the hands, and gestures, and gladness of countenance, and blandishments."[57] The psychologist Harry Harlow became known in the 1950s for research with monkeys and then humans on attachment to the mother. He concluded that in humans nursing and physical contact were essential for developing the ability to bond and relate socially.[58] Babies need to be held and spoken to as part of learning communications and relationships, which are essential for life support. In her book on Harlow, Deborah Blum describes the death toll in asylums and orphanages along with the medical advice to limit touching of infants that was documented from the eighteenth century until the studies of Harlow showed the importance of human touch and affection.[59]

My personal belief is that humans desire relationship with God as part of seeking meaning in life. That is a pattern generated by our brains. It is not a matter of belief that can be verified or exposed as a fraud with current knowledge. It involves trust in a higher interpersonal relationship. As in every case of trust, extreme risk cannot be avoided. There is the risk that God in fact does not exist. There is the risk that our concept of God and our expectations are completely wrong so that we cannot avoid feeling betrayed and deserted. There is also the risk that we humans will be unfaithful, as we keep proving in so many ways.

The testimony of the Bible is that God hangs on to commitments to people through our betrayal and through what seems to us as God's forgetfulness, desertion, or wrath. Faith in specific beliefs as if they must be factual or infallible is a guarantee of disillusionment. That is inappropriate use of faith. But faith as trust in relationships, even though always risky and frequently disappointed, offers hope that leads us forward. Many of us can testify to how people significant to us died without seeing the fruit of their trust that helped save us in the course of our lives. Trust in others is one of the saving forces God has put in this world. Faith in a relationship with God that is not tied to creeds can give meaning to life and hope for the triumph of purposes we may not understand or live to see realized.

CHAPTER TWELVE

THE GIFT OF DISCIPLESHIP

Childhood memories can motivate us in later life—and that is especially true for religious memories that are negative. Many people, like Marcus Borg, have written about overcoming childhood impressions of hellfire and damnation sermons that terrified them.[60] My own experience was similar. Childhood memories are not always accurate or fair. Children tend to see the world in simplistic, cartoonish outlines that have to be overcome as they mature into fuller understanding of things they heard as children.

One of my deep impressions from childhood was that discipleship was something that meant pain and suffering. Whenever I heard a sermon on discipleship, the title would usually be something like "the cost of discipleship" and with that went the passage from Matthew 16:24 in which Jesus told disciples they must take up their cross and follow him. Discipleship meant giving things up, suffering, and death when people really followed Jesus. Motivation for all this suffering was the assurance of rewards in the next life. My childhood impressions caught a central message that the reward for real Christians came in the next life through personal salvation that would get us past the terrifying judgment that awaits all of us.

College is a time when a person comes to terms with a more complicated perception of life than was learned in religious teachings in childhood. It was then I discovered that teachings of Jesus in Matthew, Mark, and Luke talked about the presence of God and the blessings given in the present world more than the world after death. God is working on making things better in the present time and not just in an afterlife. This was the message that appealed to the followers of Jesus—this was an often unappreciated "hook" in his sales pitch.

I would like to argue in favor of a changed perception of discipleship, away from the emphasis on cost, suffering, and denial. Discipleship today, as it was in Jesus's time, is a marvelous gift—a gift from God that came through Jesus. Being around Jesus was an experience that drew people. I'm not talking about the crowds who came because they heard of healings. I'm talking about the large circle of men and women who constantly wanted to be with him. Being with Jesus itself was a gift, something those people clearly enjoyed. One of the attractions was the way they felt God in the presence as well as the teachings of Jesus. The gospels of Matthew, Mark, and Luke make it clear that the central message of Jesus was about the nature of God, what God was doing, and what God was about to do. In the presence of Jesus, people felt close to God and wanted to be like Jesus in that relationship of confidence and dedication.

Consequently, Jesus gave his followers a wonderful gift—a gift that could be claimed by disciples then and today. The gift of discipleship I speak of is something we take for granted today, something we call the Lord's Prayer.

In Luke, the Lord's Prayer is a response to the disciple's request to learn how to pray. But there was more to the request. Apparently John the Baptist had given instruction on prayer or a model prayer, and they asked Jesus to do the same (11:1). Because of that context, we usually hear sermons about "how to pray" that include the Lord's Prayer along with injunctions from the Sermon on the Mount in Matthew (6:5–14). But I have yet to hear a sermon that shows real appreciation for the way Jesus gave the disciples far more than they requested, something they really wanted that would have seemed too much to ask. That something was the real gift that came with the prayer.

The prayer itself is powerful in its condensation and simplicity. In very few words it contains an explosive message. Usually we explain the clauses of the prayer and, like so much of the content of the Bible in general, we try to explain it rationally as the presentation of concepts. That leads to theological and philosophical understanding. But we must remember the Bible mixes poetry and symbolism in ways that make rational analysis tricky and even inadequate. A few words draw on associations with images and symbols with deep poetic and emotional power that goes beyond mere rational understanding. This is especially true of Matthew's longer version of the prayer (6:9–13) but is also present in Luke's terse version (11:2–4).

The opening words are a puzzle and a paradox. "Father, hallowed be your name." Calling God father was certainly not new in Jewish prayers. The gospels, all of which were written in Greek, drew on traditions of what Jesus said in his native language of Aramaic. In the account of Jesus praying in Gethsemane, Mark quotes the Aramaic word "Abba" as the way Jesus addressed God (14:36). In Galatians 4:6 and Romans 8:15, Paul also quoted the Aramaic word, so that many people think that must have been the common practice of Jesus when praying. This term implied a closeness and intimacy without violating the usual formality that comes with thinking of the holiness and separateness of God. So here Jesus addressed God in an intimate way but then immediately recognized the distance between humanity and holiness. The phrase about hallowing the name was a reminder of how the sanctity of God was recognized during the lifetime of Jesus as the very name of God was considered too holy to say out loud. The Hebrew in which the Old Testament is written often uses the name for God, YHWH, but it had become a practice that it was never spoken except by the High Priest on Yom Kippur. Whenever reading a scripture passage containing YHWH, as in the opening of Psalm 23 with "YHWH is my shepherd," they would substitute a word that we translate as Lord. Thus English translations of the Bible have perpetuated that tradition so that many readers are unaware that all the places using the term Lord really contained the very name of God. Thus we see that Jesus opened the prayer with a paradox—God is close and intimate like a father, but also distant, separate, and holy.

In the simple words of the opening line of the prayer, we see Jesus reflecting a close relationship with God. The followers had seen and were attracted by what seemed to be a special relationship. What is often missed is that, in the simplicity of a prayer, Jesus is bestowing the same kind of relationship on his followers. Those who truly follow Jesus can lay claim to a relationship with God of deep intimacy and closeness that does not violate the undeniable separation between the divine and human. It is a relationship of confidence in God and in the final victory of his purposes, as is reflected in the clauses that complete the prayer. Of course a sense of closeness and intimacy with God was not new in Judaism, but in Jesus the followers saw a special awareness of God's presence, which the gift of this prayer made available to them.

The synoptic gospels portray Jesus as proclaiming the sovereignty of God rather than himself as the heart of his message. Yet the claim of a special relationship had a prophetic character that could be seen as threatening to religious authorities of the time. William Herzog refers to Jesus's role as a broker of God's power. Through Jesus, and not exclusively through the temple and its leading authorities, the power of God could be experienced. Furthermore, in this prayer Jesus is asserting his ability to share this special power and relationship with God. One does not need to see Jesus as divine in order to participate in a special relationship with God through Jesus.[61]

The next part of the prayer shifts into poetic construction. "Your kingdom come, your will be done, on earth as it is in heaven." A characteristic feature of Jewish poetry and prayer that comes through in translation is the use of parallel statements, which usually give fuller expression to the same basic thought.[62] Next in importance after recognizing the centrality of God is the commitment to bringing about God's kingdom on earth. What is God's kingdom? It is the realization of the complete rule of God just as that rule is found in the world beyond. This clause makes clear how important the kingdom is to Jesus and his disciples, and that the focus is on the kingdom in this world as part of realizing God's true purpose.

In two very brief, pithy statements, Jesus has summed up the heart of his teaching, and done so in the form of a statement of commitment and loyalty to God. In order to understand the teaching of Jesus, one must first see that the role of a sovereign God is central, and that from this follows a mission to realize God's will and rule on earth. So what will life be like when the kingdom is realized? The next clauses provide clues.

"Give us this day our daily bread. And forgive us our debts, as we also have forgiven our debtors. And do not bring us to the time of trial, but rescue us from the evil one." Here again we are in the world of poetry and symbols, as indicated by the double phrasing for debts and for the powers of evil. Most people quickly recognize bread as a universal symbol of the basic needs for sustaining life, for which we depend on God. When God's kingdom is fully realized, people will have their basic needs met. They will live in a world of forgiveness and forgiving, and a world in which we are delivered from the power of evil. Most people in most human societies that have ever existed would embrace that reality as a dramatic improvement on the world as they experienced it. Disciples are pledging themselves to work toward this kind of world, relying on God's help.

There is an ambiguity in these clauses that describe life in the kingdom, for they apply to this world and to the next. Daily bread refers to very real needs in this life, especially with so many people suffering from hunger. But it also refers to eating at the messianic table, a feast of the world to come, and also draws on connections to manna in the wilderness as God provides for human needs.[63] Forgiving debts refers to sins, but also to the very real problem of debt among the peasantry and their desire to have relief from indebtedness that often deprived them of ancestral lands. The time of trial could also refer to impersonal forces and to demonic powers.

These clauses imply political and social criticism of social and political conditions of Jesus's time. One of the facts of life in that society was that people lacked the basic needs for life so that many starved. A great many who were not yet starving were in what might be called debt slavery so that they were on the verge of losing their land and the economic basis for life for their entire family. This does not mean that the society in which Jesus lived was more oppressive or unjust than others, yet these were ordinary concerns of the village communities to which Jesus went. The gospels do not show Jesus as a political or social revolutionary out to overthrow the current regime, but they do present criticisms of unjust behavior and prediction of a more just rule that God is bringing about.

This turns into a political and social program for today that involves working against forces of injustice and economic exploitation in our own time. Jesus lived before the stock market and Wall Street financial communities, which often promote extraordinary wealth for fewer and fewer people, especially as they earn multimillion dollar bonuses as rewards for imperiling the entire financial system and undermining pension funds, 401Ks, and mortgages for millions of victims. Today's financial system is more complicated and worldwide, but the essentials of Jesus's message apply to modern forms of injustice as well as they did to the harsh realities of his own time.

More than just social and political criticism, Jesus's words clearly show belief in powers of evil that God is overcoming. A great many of the "mighty works" of Jesus that caught public attention involved healing by exorcism. Jesus saw his actions as representing the power of God binding and overpowering evil forces in the world. Today we do not accept the belief in demons as behind mental and physical illnesses; nevertheless, we are still at a loss to understand or explain what seems to be evil at work in the world through impersonal forces as well as through human actions with harmful consequences. The Lord's Prayer does not attempt to explain evil; it just calls on disciples to trust God as they face the powers of evil.

In conclusion, how is this prayer a gift of discipleship? First, Jesus is sharing with his disciples the kind of personal relationship he had with God. He is telling them to claim that relationship in confidence. Second, the prayer is a summary of the leading points of Jesus's message and ministry so that the disciples are committing themselves to the same mission espoused by Jesus. In doing so, they are following Jesus in serving God, not Jesus.

In the centuries during which Christianity formulated what would be considered orthodox belief, and again in the Protestant Reformation, creeds were developed as part of having congregations state beliefs that marked their form of Christianity. In every case, they were beliefs about God, Jesus, and the church. What has been overlooked is that Jesus gave a wonderful gift to all followers that was stronger than any creed. The Lord's Prayer, addressed to God, is a statement of commitment to God as found in the message and ministry of Jesus. It is not belief about—it represents life commitment. As Marcus Borg concluded, being Christian is about fidelity to a relationship with God that is focused on seeking justice and compassion.[64] This kind of dedication to God is what it means to follow Jesus—and this should be the paramount determination today of what it means to be a Christian.

CHAPTER THIRTEEN

GOD AND CONSEQUENCES

Many who are raised in the church spend their early adult years maturing out of the misperceptions of childhood. Some people have pictured the human species as needing to mature out of religious misperceptions of the childhood of our species. One example of that is the tendency to explain the results of natural processes as divine anger and judgment. The Old Testament is full of attempts to explain political and natural calamities in terms of God's punishment for human wrongdoing. Some people have even argued it is necessary to leave God behind in order to see our world in more realistic and scientific ways. Some have pointed to daily events in the world, such as the death of a child every few minutes due to starvation or treatable disease, as proof of forces of evil and suffering in life that make a good God something they can't believe in.[65]

All my life I heard about a God of mercy and love. But the paramount image of God that haunted my childhood was the God of judgment—the God of consequences. If you don't accept Jesus and find personal salvation, you will go to hell for eternity. If you commit the "unforgivable sin" of cursing God, you will probably die soon and of course go to hell. What happens when Jesus returns? That did not bring a picture of joy, but one of impending final judgment with lots of people being condemned to hell.

My Jewish friends insist that the notion of an Old Testament God of wrath and judgment is not a balanced picture, for they see a God of forgiveness and love as more central. Yet there is a persistent theme that personal and national calamities are the result of sin, individual in many cases and national in scope when it involves the king or royal policies. The death and destruction of the Assyrian conquest of Israel and the Babylonian destruction of Judah lead to God's mercy and restoration of Judah after fifty years of exile. Why did it take fifty years for God to have mercy on Judah? The message of the Old Testament is that the ways of God are often beyond comprehension. Forgiveness and mercy are eventually shown because of overpowering love, but it may take a good bit of suffering and many decades before the people of God see the results of mercy.

The same can be said of personal calamities today. "Why did this happen to me?" is often heard in the Bible and from those suffering in our own time. Disease, loss of a loved one, loss of a job, or divorce are personal trials that are common events we experience so that it feels like we are being punished even when we are confident we are blameless. It is also a common experience for people today to feel that God caused or allowed bad things to happen. Sometimes it takes people several years or even decades to overcome the negative feelings related to personal trials. When people successfully get past the resentment and other negative side effects of those experiences, they often look back and sense a benevolent guiding hand they were not aware of during the worst of times that ended up making them a better person. This view of hardship goes beyond punishment as the explanation for what feel like divinely inspired negative events and points to even greater mystery surrounding the nature and love of God.

Today we no longer accept mostly theological interpretations of current events. We understand that deeper economic, social, and political currents are at work so that success or failure of a nation's policies is not purely a matter of whether the right religious policy is followed. No longer are disease or disability perceived as punishment for sins of the individual or by someone in the family. Yet many people who recognize the need for more textured understanding of the contemporary world still want to accept the simplistic interpretations of similar events in the Old Testament as divine truth straight from God.

It certainly is not true that the New Testament presents a picture of a loving and merciful God that replaced the vengeful God of the Old Testament. The sermons on judgment and punishment in hell that haunted my childhood were based on New Testament imagery. But it is true that the message of Jesus highlighted the love and mercy of God in ways that captivated audiences then and now. This is the image of God that is overshadowed by the emphasis on judgment that is too often heard in evangelism.

Nearly everyone is familiar with the parable of the Prodigal Son and of the loving God it portrays. Something that I think has been missed is how the story portrays God's relationship to sin and punishment. This is a view of God as not taking personal offense at what is clearly considered sinful. There are bad consequences, but they are the consequences of the actions themselves. What we see is that God is ever loving and available, but we must deal with the consequences of our actions, which are themselves in the nature of life and not direct results of punishments or rewards from God.

In the parable, there are two sons who stand to inherit a good bit of property from an obviously well-to-do father. One of the sons does something that breaks the bounds of respect—asking for his share of property before his father's death. This was an insult that could have caused permanent exclusion from the family as a moral response. A few years ago Neil Diamond and Laurence Olivier did an updated version of the movie *The Jazz Singer* in which the Cantor father discovered what he thought was his son committing adultery. His reaction was to tear his clothing as he sobbed uncontrollably and then to say he no longer had a son. That is still considered correct morality by many Jewish families—and by many other families of all religious persuasions.[66]

Amy-Jill Levine points out that a story that begins with a father and two sons would have reminded contemporary audiences of other stories about sons in the Bible. People would have thought of Cain and Abel, where a favored son is murdered by the neglected one; of Abraham favoring his youngest son Isaac and sending away the older son by a slave because of the jealousy of Sarah; of Jacob cheating his older brother of his rights with the help of his mother; and of the favored younger son Joseph being sold into slavery by older brothers. A story of two brothers would have led people to expect rivalry and even favoritism for a younger, spoiled brother.[67]

In Jesus's story, the father gives the son what he wants and lets him do what he is going to do. Of course no one is surprised when this headstrong young man wastes the accomplishments of his father's lifetime in a very short time and finds himself in desperate straits. Far too many families in our time see this story repeated as people of all ages are caught up in one addiction or another. All forms of practical thinking go out the window as the person goes down into the throes of addictive obsession. Jesus's story becomes the paradigm for what many families hope for—a gutter type of experience, a hitting of rock bottom that leads someone to "come to themselves."

In the story, the son does indeed find himself in a desperate situation with nowhere to turn so that he decides that, no matter how badly his father and family treat him, it has to be an improvement over what he now has to live with. Levine suggests the prodigal doesn't repent. Rather he thinks that maybe daddy will pull him from danger once again. As he is approaching home, he rehearses a speech that may have been more manipulative than repentant. The eager father runs out to greet him so that the story is usually interpreted as illustrating the overwhelming love of God. The son can hardly get out the apologetic words he has rehearsed because his father is so busy greeting and making arrangements to feed and clothe him since he obviously needs immediate care. This is not the God who takes fifty years to forgive and finally restore a people. In fact there is no hint of judgment in this father figure at all. Love and forgiveness stand out. He even admonishes the jealousy and righteous outrage of the son who didn't insult him or squander the family fortune. One message appears to be that God's love overrules the self-righteousness of normal morality.

The picture of all-embracing love has been tempered by Amy-Jill Levine's suggestion the prodigal was a spoiled child who counted on a father who would still spoil him on his return. That means the prodigal didn't risk as much as is usually thought to be the case. The righteous brother, then, was complaining about the continued success of a spoiled brother in manipulating the father—something we would most likely agree with just as contemporary Jews would have recognized the justice of the complaints of the older brother. Levine also compares this parable with the one about an owner seeking a lost sheep so that the brother represents the ninety-nine who did not stray and were relatively less appreciated. This combination points to the parable as a story of counting, of the importance of making sure all are included so that the older son is not left out.[68]

What appears to be God's favoritism for some over others is a theme the Bible recognizes and legitimates, for it is Isaac and Jacob whose line is associated with the covenant of God with Abraham. It is also Jacob's descendants who become a chosen people through the Exodus and giving of the Law at Sinai. This parable shows a father concentrating on a favored son to the extent of forgetting to include the older one in the celebration—unlike the ordinary interpretation that he refused to go to the party. Levine thinks the parable is about a Lost Son with the barb of the story being that the righteous son was lost by the father. He was not lost because of his actions but because the father left him out due to his enthusiasm for the returning son. Yet the father, though allowing himself to be manipulated by a spoiled son, still does not reject the more disciplined and respectful son as the reconciliation efforts of the father demonstrate room in God's love for both sons.

Let's not get carried away with the often repeated idea that Jesus replaced a God of judgment with a God of radical forgiveness and love for the undeserving. There are other parables of Jesus that involve judgment and punishment. In Matthew there is the haunting image of a judgment in which God divides everyone into groups of sheep or goats, with goats symbolizing condemnation. There is also judgment in the story of the Prodigal Son even though this parable is not a novella that fills in all the details of what happens at the end of the story. The judgment is that God doesn't undo all the consequences of our actions.

Look at what happens to the Prodigal Son. He is greeted as a son and recognized as a member of the family. Thus a celebration is thrown for him and he is clothed and fed at his father's expense. But there is no indication the father will try to replace the wealth he has squandered. The father still has plenty it seems, but what is left appears to belong rightly to the elder brother. We don't know how the son will live in the father's house. He says he is ready to be no better than a servant and we expect he will be treated better than that. Perhaps he counts on continued successful manipulation to help him regain wealth he squandered. But there is no promise of restoration to the situation before his sinful actions. The story doesn't go into the consequences after the welcome, so we are left guessing. What I think is that, as in other cases in the Bible, actions have their consequences and God's love does not promise to undo consequences. That is a form of judgment we all must live with on a daily basis.

People who fall into addictions can be restored to love of their families and to self-respect, but they are forever haunted by the toll of their actions on themselves and others. All of us can look back on missed opportunities or terrible things we did or said that we regret.

When I was in college, one of my mother's sisters sent me a cake and some cookies in the mail. For a few days I was a popular guy among my friends as they were treated to some very good food. As the first person in my family to go to college, I had no financial support from my parents and none of my extended family understood why I set out on a different path from what they had known. This was the only show of support and affection I received from my aunts and uncles while I was in college. Being a thoughtless kid, I never thanked my aunt. It haunts me today when I think of how much her gift meant to me and how I never expressed appreciation. But the opportunity for speaking up passed long ago. The consequence—the haunting regret—remains.

There is judgment that is not undone in the story of the Prodigal Son. God loves and forgives without promising a fairy-tale ending in which all the bad is undone. Someone tacked an ending onto Job trying to make the sad story right by saying that God gave him more wealth and replaced the children he had lost. Ask any parent who has lost a child. You may have another but no matter how you love the "replacement" child, you never get over the loss of a child. There is no undoing of that experience as if it had not happened.

How should we live in the face of always having to accept natural consequences as a form of judgment that comes to everyone? That is part of the good news of the Prodigal Son story. We have an offer of forgiveness and restoration. It is not fairy-tale forgiveness that undoes the past. It is a realistic forgiveness that allows us to live with the past and orient ourselves to the future. It is the acceptance of love that offers hope for the future because we are not forever anchored to the past even though we can't get away from some natural limitations that result. If you don't finish high school or college, you must live with those consequences until you do something about it. If you have committed murder, you must live with that experience but it can motivate you to a better life from here forward. Forgiveness makes it possible to live positively for the future even though we can't undo the past.

CHAPTER FOURTEEN

WAS JESUS THE SAMARITAN?

Two of the greatest treasures in literary history are the parables of the Prodigal Son and the Good Samaritan. These stories are rich in meaning that continues to challenge hearers of every age as they did those who first heard them. Since Jesus often criticized the religious leadership of the time, both parables have been interpreted as attacks on respectable religion in Jesus's time as falling short of true religion.

In the Prodigal Son, the older brother is often seen as proper religious and moral behavior that was rejected as inadequate. Augustine's interpretation went to the extreme of seeing the older brother as the representative of Jews who rejected the kind of love Jesus offered.[69] Unfortunately, this approach supported persecution of Jews over centuries as well as distorting Judaism and the way the parable would have been heard in Jesus's time.

The audience in Jesus's time would have been more sympathetic to the older brother, as would most of us today who try to be more responsible than the spoiled younger son. Jesus seemed to show that celebration over the return of the younger brother should have trumped righteous indignation, even if the cost of the celebration was coming out of the share of the father's goods that rightly belonged to the older brother. Amy-Jill Levine has called into question even that criticism of the older brother as she suggests that the father may represent celebration gone overboard as he is complicit in continuing manipulation by a spoiled wastrel.[70]

A similar anti-Jewish interpretation has been applied to the Good Samaritan. An anonymous somebody was robbed on the dangerous road from Jericho to Jerusalem, which was not unusual in that time. As he lay bleeding, two religious figures (a priest and a Levite) go to the other side as they pass. It was the Samaritan, a fellow Israelite whose attitude toward Jerusalem was a major barrier to good relations between cousin peoples, who stopped to help. Thus two representatives of "good religion" or righteousness in Jesus's time are seen as failing to respond to someone in need. Interpreting the story as primarily an attack on the priest and Levite has easily turned into an attack on Jewish beliefs about purity and righteous behavior.

Amy-Jill Levine has made us aware that part of the impact the parables of the Prodigal Son and Good Samaritan is the way they gave a surprising twist to accepted story formulas. Stand-up comedians use familiar rhythms and formulas to get responses to their jokes. For many years on the Tonight Show, Johnny Carson did routines that would end a sentence with a phrase emphasizing how bad something was. Ed McMahon, and often the audience, would then chime in, "How bad was it?" What followed would be a series of funny lines that began with "It was so bad that . . . ." Without being a joke, the story of a father and two sons would automatically recall many cases of younger sons getting the better of older sons, as with Jacob over Essau.[71] Levine pointed out that a story with three travelers, two of which were a priest and a Levite, automatically led to an assumption there would be a third traveler who was an ordinary Israelite.[72] That the third character was a Samaritan promised a surprising outcome.

Encountering a traveler needing assistance was a common experience in Jesus's time as it is in our own. That people would pass without offering assistance surely would not be surprising, but the priest and Levite were expected to help a fellow Jew. Part of the shock of the story was that representatives of dedication to the Torah would violate basic expectations of helping those in need. Having a Samaritan as the third character shocked as well, but not as shocking as if the third character had been a Gentile.[73] Samaritans were also Israelites who observed the Torah, although its wording varied in some particulars.[74] Samaritans and Jews were hostile to one another since the building of the second temple following the return from exile, so this Samaritan overcame traditional rivalry to act as a neighbor and carry out the Torah requirements.

You might wonder what defense the priest and Levite could have offered. Those who jump to the conclusion that they were following requirements of the rules of purity are taking those expectations too far, as Levine explains.[75] Yet, it seems to me their best defense might have been that they had to preserve ritual purity in order to carry out temple responsibilities. In that case, helping the injured man could have meant disqualification from those duties for a while. The income and welfare of their families might have been at stake. But Jesus appears to have taken away this defense because he has them heading away from Jerusalem where ritual purity would have been needed. Nevertheless, for the sake of discussion, let's give them the benefit of what seems like the strongest justification for their actions. Let's assume religious duties required of a priest or Levite would have been claimed and presented as choosing service to God over helping an injured nobody by the side of the road.

It is important to notice the context of the story. Someone asked Jesus about the Torah, but the question could be phrased in more current terms as "What is true religion?" The reply approved by Jesus was that loving God foremost and then your neighbor was true religion. The religious figures, following the line of defense I indicated, could have said their behavior showed love of God taking priority by keeping the purity rules needed for temple service. The next question was about the neighbor, the second part of the response. The story was given as a reply; then came a question. Who in the story was a neighbor to the injured man? It was, of course, the Samaritan. Then Jesus said to go and behave like the Samaritan. This implies that loving one's neighbor represented a higher standard, truer religion, than any justification offered by the priest and Levite.

Amy-Jill Levine pointed out that even if temple service were involved, all Jews were expected to come to the aid of someone in need, but especially to someone of their own community, a fellow Jew. Being a neighbor to someone meant recognizing the necessity of treating others as one's neighbor. The religious officials violated that standard. It was someone outside the normal Jewish community, a fellow Israelite but not someone who would be expected to be kind to a Jew, who did all that was needed to rescue a fellow human being. Love of God through love of neighbor can come from those despised by the community as well as from those who are respected.

In my view, a similar point is made in Matthew 25:31–46 when the Son of Man divides the sheep from the goats at the final judgment. The criterion used is how people treated those in need—those who were hungry, thirsty, naked, sick, or in prison. In other words, the situation in the Good Samaritan parable of acting as neighbor to someone in need is a primary consideration satisfying divine expectations on the Day of Judgment. Drawing this similarity between the two stories has the effect of applying the standard at judgment to the parable of the Good Samaritan: "Truly I tell you, just as you did it to one of the least of these who are members of my family, you did it to me." (25:40)

Another passage from Matthew 7:16 also emphasizes the same point: "You will know them by their fruits." In this statement Jesus warned against false prophets by advising to look to their actions more than their words. What are desired actions? The parable of the Good Samaritan and the story of the sheep and goats illustrate the kinds of actions Jesus approved.

The message of this parable has been adapted to fit the religious ideals of different times. When I was at Mercer University in the 1960s, the Civil Rights movement was challenging the racism found in segregation. Mercer admitted its first black student, a young man from Ghana who wanted to come to Mercer because of the Baptist missionaries who had shaped his life. The Baptists in Georgia opposed accepting this student. When he arrived on campus, the pastor of the church on campus told the student he was not welcome to visit. Members of that denomination had funded African missionaries for over a century but this product of the mission field was not allowed to enter their sanctuary.[76]

I wrote a piece for the university newspaper using the parable of the Good Samaritan to show Jesus denouncing those who treated black people as unclean and beneath their religious standards. The piece caught the attention of Lester Maddox, a rising political figure making a reputation in defending segregation, who denounced me in the Atlanta Constitution. He thought I was abusing the Bible in presenting such an absurd interpretation. Maddox would later become Governor of Georgia and then Lieutenant Governor under Governor Jimmy Carter. My interpretation back then might not survive careful analysis, but looking at how we treat people who are considered outcasts is within the spirit of the story.

My editorial was not entirely original because it was probably influenced by sermons given at Mercer by Clarence Jordan, one of the founders of Koinonia Farm near Americus in central Georgia. Jordan often preached at Mercer translating directly from a Greek text of the New Testament into Southern vernacular. His translations were later published as the *Cotton Patch Gospel*. In his version of the Good Samaritan story, the priest and Levite became a "white preacher" and a "white Gospel song leader" who "stepped on the gas and went scooting by" when they saw an unconscious man on the side of the road. It was a black man who played the role of the Samaritan by putting the injured man into his car and taking him to the hospital.[77]

The most popular way of interpreting the Bible in the Middle Ages was through allegory. Luther and Calvin countered this approach with their emphasis on what they thought was the plain, down-to-earth meaning of the Bible that could be understood by common people. Catholic leadership tried to hold on to allegory as a higher form of interpretation that called for an educated perspective beyond the capabilities of common people.

A key example of this approach was seen in Origin's interpretation of the story of the Good Samaritan. Each character in the story represented an element of deeper truth that could be seen through faith. The Samaritan was Jesus defying the religious standards of the day to tend to the representative for all sinners, whose medical treatment represented the healing impact of the gospel and who was turned over to the church for safekeeping. So Jesus was really prophesying about the coming role of the church carrying out the saving mission of the Son of God.[78]

Although this mode of interpretation is not in vogue, a scholar at Brigham Young University has defended it. He explains artistic representations in stained glass windows of several medieval cathedrals pointing to the use of the Good Samaritan parable as part of showing common people the "plan of salvation." Part of his argument is that allegorical interpretation is sanctioned in church history and in Mormon interpretation.[79] This way of thinking turns the Samaritan into Jesus.

There is another interpretation I see that has direct application to our own time. I spent many years working with top management of government agencies and nonprofit organizations, applying the best of current managerial thinking. Methods have come out of corporate America that were intended to maximize profit as one form of corporate success, but those methods worked in other settings as well. I helped people develop their mission and work on getting the organization (whether a church, a charity, or a public agency) to become mission-focused. This always meant that with success came undesired side effects, trade-offs we called them. Individuals in the organization could find their roles diminished or their jobs eliminated. It was not possible to improve without negative impacts on someone.

This aspect of American capitalism was much discussed because of the candidacy of Mitt Romney in the presidential contest in 2012. He and his partners were successful in taking over failing companies, cutting costs by eliminating jobs, and using technology to pile more responsibility and sometimes lower pay on those who did keep their jobs. This strategy would often save the company, leading to big profits and bonuses for the capitalists who put in the changes. That is a form of capitalism that has been praised too much in our country.

What about those who lost their jobs or the economic and personal impact on those who kept their jobs with less pay and much more stress at work? That is what we meant by trade-offs. It could also be called collateral damage. When you go to war, there is unintended loss of property and innocent life that is bound to happen. The response of business leaders might be the words of the famous classic of American culture, *The Godfather*: it's not personal; it's business. However, whenever that phrase was used in *The Godfather*, murder and other forms of violence were being justified.[80] Business decisions aren't usually directly violent, but those who experience collateral damage would certainly say that, to them, business decisions, however impersonal or objective, become very personal.[81]

Following the logic of my hypothetical defense of the religious figures in the parable, we could see them as examples of good business practice. Their role was to officiate in the temple and other religious sites. Passing up the injured person was not personal; it was business. They were focused on their mission. Someone else in society has to take responsibility for such problems.

In *A Christmas Carol*, the same argument is presented by Ebenezer Scrooge when two men want to collect for charity at Christmas. "'It's not my business,' Scrooge returned. 'It's enough for a man to understand his own business, and not to interfere with other people. Mine occupies me constantly.'"[82]

Scrooge's view was countered by the ghost of his partner Jacob Marley, who described the impact of regret for missing opportunities to help those in need.

> 'But you were always a good man of business, Jacob,' faltered Scrooge, who now began to apply this to himself. 'Business!' cried the Ghost, wringing his hands again. 'Mankind was my business. The common welfare was my business; charity, mercy, forbearance, and benevolence were all my business. The dealings of my trade were but a drop of water in the comprehensive ocean of my business.'[83]

Please don't think I am saying current business practice is always unethical, immoral, or unacceptable to God. The message of Jesus was that love of neighbor was a higher standard than whatever reason ordinarily good or religious people might have for passing by someone in need. The parable of the Good Samaritan and the story of the sheep and goats are placed within a Jewish context, for it is a member of the Jewish community that one is to treat as a neighbor. That doesn't mean that Jesus and others within Judaism would not expand the same concept to those outside their community. The development of Christianity has emphasized the importance of extending the application of the principle to all of mankind, as illustrated so well in Marley's words. The message of Jesus for today is not that business success is unethical or immoral, but many forms of business success create more and more of "the least of these who are members of my family" for whom all followers of Jesus and the God of Jesus have obligations. We would be advised to see God in the faces of those in need and model our behavior on that of the Samaritan in the story.

Chapter Fifteen

Who is this Guy?

Sometimes a movie has a way of catching people's imagination and giving special meaning to what had been an ordinary expression. When that happens, people have lots of fun saying the phrase to friends at an unexpected time so that everyone laughs.

That happened with the western *Butch Cassidy and the Sundance Kid*. The movie begins with train robberies that make you expect it to be a comedy. Just when the pickings seemed really easy, the bandits were surprised to see a special train with a posse following the train they had just robbed. A chase began as the comedic heroes used stunts that had always worked. After some of these failed, the funny bandits became more serious. The chase takes far longer than the audience expects. It seems to go on forever as the dogged pursuers get closer and closer. The two heroes keep looking back and trying to figure out "Who are those guys?" As the chase goes on, the situation becomes ever more serious as our heroes look at each other and desperately repeat, "Who are those guys!"[84]

The gospel of Mark creates a similar atmosphere, but without the comedy. As Jesus goes about healing, exorcising, and making authoritative pronouncements, the crowds gather and pursue. Some of the possessed yell out things Jesus is quick to silence. You can almost feel the people looking at each other and asking, "Who is this guy?" They are not asking for his name. They are wondering if he is some prophetic figure of legend come back for their time.

Jesus had to be aware of the buzzing of the crowd, but he never gives a hint of his thoughts other than forbidding people to make statements about him. He spoke primarily with actions. He said a bit more to his disciples, but he spoke in riddles. He expressed frustration at their slowness in figuring out just who he was—but he would not come out and tell them.

Mark 8:27–30 brings the speculation to a climax when Jesus takes his disciples north of the Sea of Galilee to the vicinity of Caesarea Philippi near Mount Hermon. According to Mark, Jesus asked a question as they were walking along. "Who do people say that I am?" Thus we see he was aware of the speculation. The quick replies were that he was a prophetic figure returned from the dead. Then came another question. "But who do you say I am?" Peter blurted out, "You are the Messiah." But what did Jesus think? He only said to them what he had said to the crowds, as he ordered them not to repeat that statement to anyone.

Did he accept Peter's declaration as true? Mark says he began talking about the death of the Son of Man so that Peter became upset, apparently thinking this contradicted his picture of what happens to a Messiah. Jesus rebuked him by equating him with evil. This can be interpreted as a direct denial of the messianic title that Peter has recently announced. Furthermore, Mark says that six days later, Jesus took Peter and a small group of disciples up a mountain where they saws a dazzling vision of Jesus talking with Moses and Elijah (9:2–8). This experience seems to confirm the earlier guess of the common people about associating Jesus with prophets rather than with David or other royal figures associated with the role of Messiah, for all the figures at the transfiguration were prophets.

Mark says Jesus began talking about a suffering Son of Man and his own coming death. But who was this Son of Man? The term is capitalized in our Bibles, yet it was an ordinary term in Jesus's time meaning "this guy" or "a human being." At times Jesus seemed to use it as a third-person reference to himself and at others as a messianic title, but he shifted meaning so that it is not always clear which use he intended.[85]

Behind the question "Who is this guy?" lies another important question. Who did Jesus think he was? Mark tells us at the beginning of the gospel that Jesus was the Messiah. But when you expect Jesus to say right out that he was the Messiah, he continued to speak in symbols with multiple meanings. This is not the case in John where Jesus declares his divine status over and over. That gives us two portraits in the Bible that contradict one another.

After the conversation near Mount Hermon, Mark begins to show Jesus making statements about himself and coming events. Two debates center on these remarks in Mark, Matthew, and Luke. The first is whether Jesus really said them. Many of them predict his coming death and have an apocalyptic view that some scholars think reflect opinions that developed after the crucifixion and the destruction of Jerusalem in 70 CE. The second debate is about the so-called apocalyptic nature of Jesus's comments. Did Jesus see himself as an apocalyptic figure of some kind? If he did, did that necessarily mean that he expected the world of ordinary experience to come to an end through an otherworldly Last Judgment? Most scholars since the 1800s have agreed that Jesus's outlook was apocalyptic; but in recent years, some have discounted those sayings and pictured Jesus as a sage who also taught and healed.[86]

I'll let others hash out just what Jesus did or did not really say. There is no series of rules that can determine any of those views accurate beyond reasonable doubts in sifting reliable evidence from the unreliable.[87] I am more interested in trying to figure out what Jesus might have thought about himself and the nature of his mission—that is tied up in the question of who he was. All we can do is make an educated guess based on what we can learn about those times from the gospels and other sources, but this question is much more interesting in my opinion.

Albert Schweitzer took an extremely apocalyptic view. He thought Jesus expected the kingdom of God to come very soon, in the next few months. Jesus thought his actions would play a decisive role in bringing about the kingdom. This view sees Jesus anticipating what would later be expected at the Second Coming—an end of ordinary time marked by general resurrection of the dead and a Last Judgment.

If we don't throw out most of the apocalyptic passages, then clearly Jesus did have apocalyptic expectations. That doesn't necessarily solve our problem. How do we know exactly what apocalyptic meant? Richard Horsley is among the scholars who have backed away from that term, preferring to speak of renewal movements.[88] It is clear that literature traditionally labeled apocalyptic, like Daniel and the books of Enoch, are expecting transformation that is divine in origin. N.T. Wright is among those who point to transformation as clearly within the ordinary time-space framework rather than pointing to an end of the world.[89] Are they expecting the end of time and the beginning of heaven or are they expecting something like a juiced-up version of David's kingdom setting the clock and the rules back to a time when things were closer to what they should be? This approach turns traditional apocalyptic focused on the end of time and the world into religiously-oriented social and political transformation of the present world guided by God to achieve God's rule.[90] After all, the term Messiah or anointed one was commonly applied to prophets and kings of Israel and Judah. That was also true of the term Son of God. Some apocalyptic expectations pointed to a king descended from David, some to a high priest, and some to a combination of both figures.

Why is this issue so vague? One reason is that we don't know enough about the times in which the literature was written and the setting of the writers in that time. As our knowledge grows, we feel it is becoming more accurate but not nearly as accurate as anyone would like.

The second reason is one people often overlook. We are dealing with poetry not prose. There is no rational explanation of what a Messiah is or rational debate among religious leaders about the meaning of the term. There are writings built on stories and oracles full of symbolism. Different stories in the same book use different symbols. We are trying to learn more about what that symbolism meant to the groups producing the literature and how they expected it to be interpreted. But the symbols themselves are not consistent. As James Charlesworth points out: "We must not claim as clear what is intentionally imprecise."[91]

Many different terms and symbols are used.[92] Jesus uses the term Son of Man in multiple ways. References are made to passages in Isaiah featuring a Suffering Servant who had been interpreted to refer to Israel and not to a Messiah. Jesus rides into Jerusalem on a donkey projecting an image that had been related to Messiah as king. Are all of these pointing to the same thing or presenting a counterview of common expectations? Is it possible there are hints that Jesus's ideas changed over those last months? The answers are not clear.

The same lack of clarity applies to how "kingdom of God" was used. It seemed to apply to what is true now and to what is coming but not yet a reality. It seems to apply to the ordinary world, but possibly to a world to come when ordinary time ends. Interpreting poetic symbolism rationally is difficult and seldom leads to clarity, much less certainty.

Not many people are aware that Albert Schweitzer wrote *The Psychological Study of Jesus* as the doctoral dissertation for his medical degree in 1913. The degree was needed so he could carry out his plans for mission work in Africa. The book concluded that, from a contemporary medical point of view, Jesus was not sane.[93]

Whoever Jesus actually thought he was, you have to admit his behavior was not ordinary. There were three religious demonstrations in the decades following Jesus's ministry in which charismatic leaders appealed to symbols from the days of Moses and Joshua. Each of them ended with Roman soldiers killing people and breaking up the crowd of commoners. John the Baptist and then Jesus appealed to these same villagers who saw them as prophetic figures. With the discovery of the Dead Sea Scrolls, we know of a community on the edge of the Dead Sea formed by a charismatic priestly leader who proclaimed impending divine action to cleanse the temple of pollution from illegitimate high priests. It seems to me the frequent appearance of religiously motivated movements speaks to the society of the time more than to the sanity of the charismatic leaders.

In our own day, there are people whose lives are characterized by intense fervor for political, social, or religious causes. In college I met a man named Will Campbell who was fired with a passion to oppose segregation and the evils of racism associated with it. He also became a fierce opponent of the death penalty. In graduate school I had the privilege of eating with a group at lunch that he often joined because his headquarters was a few blocks from the campus. People who knew him recognized that he was unusual for the intensity of his religious vision and dedication to a cause. Unusual, yes; but no one ever called him crazy even though he was a contemporary manifestation of the prophets of Israel.[94]

I think the gospels are accurate in showing the contemporary speculation as to who Jesus was. The kind of intensity and dedication seen in Jesus aroused expectations of something important. His opponents wanted to undermine expectations that he operated with divine approval. People in that time wondered who Jesus was. His name recognition over the last two thousand years is quite an answer to that question, yet scholars still debate the nature of his role and the meaning of his criticisms of current times. Every period of history will find itself being looked on as dated by those who come after. Certainty on these questions about Jesus will continue to elude us in the future as in the past.

CHAPTER SIXTEEN

BAPTISM AND TEMPLE

I grew up attending Southern Baptist churches in Savannah, Georgia. At the age of nine, I was baptized. Later, when my grandmother died, I went through a period of emotional instability that was partly expressed in an urgent wish to feel saved. It came to me that I had not really been saved earlier when I joined the church because I didn't fully understand the "plan of salvation" and must not have really been saved. I walked down the aisle during the invitational hymn one Sunday and told the minister I was truly saved now and wanted to be rebaptized. He refused. "Once baptized, always baptized." he said, mirroring the Baptist belief "once saved, always saved." That didn't feel like the right answer to me. I read Paul's description of baptism in Romans 6:1–11 so that I was sure baptism by immersion was part of the process of salvation and had to be done just right. After the minister's refusal, I often walked down the aisle during the invitational hymn to rededicate my life to Christ to make up for not having a legitimate baptism.

As an adult, I became a Presbyterian and had my very young children baptized by sprinkling. My father-in-law was a vice president at Mercer University and a Baptist minister. He often reminded me with great pride that one of his ancestors was a Baptist minister who was whipped on the Boston Commons for preaching against infant baptism. Nevertheless, he gladly stood with our family for the sprinkling of both grandchildren. I had known and admired him at Mercer for almost three years before meeting his daughter. Our children admired him and always wanted to go to his Baptist church during frequent weekend stays with their grandparents. Each of them, at the age of nine, wanted to be baptized by their grandpa. I was glad to come and watch as they were properly dunked by their grandfather, whose presence gave the baptism added meaning for them.

Three gospels tell us that Jesus began his public role with baptism in the Jordan River. The significance of that event in Jesus's mind is not clear because each gospel writer gives a different explanation of its meaning, pointing to apologetic concerns of the growing church rather than what might have been intended by Jesus.

John lived in the wilderness along the Jordan River. It was a real wilderness with animals we might associate with the jungles of Africa. Immersing Jews in running water was not new. John dressed as stories said Elijah had dressed, his diet was unusual, and he proclaimed that God was about to do something that would involve judgment. Immersion in the Jordan symbolized getting ready for God's kingdom. But it also reminded people of the reputed conquest of the land that began as Joshua crossed the Jordan into Canaan. God was about to take back the land and people in dramatic fashion.

Why do I say baptism was not a new phenomenon for Jews? Procedures for ritual purification often involved bathing in immersion pools called *miqveh* (plural *miqva'ot*), which used "living water," the term for running water. One of the items archaeologists look for to indicate Jewish presence in an area is the *miqveh*. For example, there has been a debate over how Jewish Galilee was. It had been outside the influence of Judah for a long time and was retaken during the Hasmonean dynasty that preceded Roman control of Palestine. Archaeology is suggesting that Galilean Jews moved there from Judah under the Hasmoneans and established typical Jewish village life. That the people were traditional Jews is thought to be indicated by the absence of pig bones, the absence of coins with pictures of the emperor, the presence of stone containers (like the ones described in John 2:1–11 that held the wine at the wedding in Cana), and the presence of *miqva'ot* in homes and other locations. Stone containers were expensive but met purity expectations better than cheaper pottery. All of these indicators were aspects of Jewish purity beliefs.[95]

Miqva'ot were at each of the entrances of the temple so that anyone, male or female, who entered immersed and changed clothes to meet the purity requirements of temple worship. John's gospel specifically mentions pools of Bethzatha (Bethesda) and Siloam, which were north and south of the temple. These have been found and there were also other *miqva'ot* for temple entry.[96]

Since all the gospels show Jesus teaching in the temple, he too would have gone through immersion before entering.

Immersion by John the Baptist was based on usual immersion practices but clearly seemed intended as a onetime experience carrying more significance than the usual *miqveh* bath. It did not necessarily eliminate future *miqveh* baths. It was a prophetic act that implied the redemptive action of God without needing the blessing of the temple and its ruling powers. Anything that could be seen as what William Herzog referred to as brokering the power of God independent of the temple was often seen as a threat by the temple state elite.

Here is a puzzle. We are not told whether Jesus habitually used the *miqveh* just as we are not told many features of his ordinary daily life. It is clear that he did not baptize as John did. He gathered disciples and gave them the ability to exorcise and heal. When he sent them out, they were not told to baptize as they preached and healed (Mark 6:7; Matthew 10:1; Luke 9:1). Yet soon after the resurrection we see baptism as a standard practice in the growing Jesus movement. In Romans, Paul equated the immersion of baptism with reenactment of the death and resurrection of Jesus. Clearly the influence of John's special baptism continued in the Jesus movement.

Modern scholars have questions about baptism that were not directly addressed in the gospels. Was it intended as criticism of the role of the temple? Before dealing with this issue, let's take a short detour to understand the role of the temple in society at that time.

There is a temptation to imagine the temple as comparable to modern churches, which are primarily centers of worship. Social functions at churches are extensions of worship and mission activities in the community. Temples had far more significance in the ancient Near East. Most large states were actually temple states. The kingdom of Israel was unusual in that a central temple was not part of extending the imperial influence of the king. Temples were used for collecting taxes, keeping the king's financial and official records, and serving as a central financial institution for the monarchy. Centralizing worship in a temple was a religious reform with strong political implications.

Judah evidently began forming a temple state from the time of David through his use of the Ark of the Covenant. There were high priests, but it was the king who decided the disposition of the Ark of the Covenant, when and where to build a temple, and how to centralize worship in the temple. David, Solomon, Hezekiah, and Josiah made key religious decisions, not their high priests.

The Babylonian exile destroyed the old temple state, but the drive to re-build the temple made possible the reemergence of the temple state. Leadership fell to high priests until the Hasmoneans combined the roles of king and high priest to the horror of Pharisees. Under Herod the Great, high priests were separate from the king who appointed them but who did not reassert the powers of the Davidic monarchy for religious leadership. The extensive re-building of the temple was a dramatic demonstration of the power and influence of Herod the Great as well as an enormous expense that brought economic stress along with extensive employment throughout Herod's kingdom. Normal dues for temple support were paid along with taxes to meet the expectations for Roman tribute and the extraordinary expense of work on the temple and other monumental buildings undertaken by Herod. After the death of Herod, his kingdom was divided among three sons. Judea soon was returned to Roman direct authority, but temple leadership, especially through the role of the high priest, was used by the Romans to carry out local policies. The job of high priest often changed hands as families jockeyed for political influence backed by Roman power, but the ministry of Jesus took place under the rule of Caiaphas (18–37 CE), which accompanied the twelve years of Pilate as Roman representative (approximately 25–37 CE). Galilee and Paraea were under Herod Antipas and thus were not subject to the local government functions of the temple, but their populations continued to pay temple dues and honor religious leadership of the temple authorities.[97]

A key point to understand from this background information is that criticism of social policies implied an attack on secular and religious elites that controlled both temple and state. Jesus's comments were dangerous politically and religiously.[98] John's baptism also had implied criticism and dissatisfaction with standards associated with the temple and the ruling powers supporting it. The practices that Jesus attacked were not essential to the temple itself but related to the wealth and greed of the elite that led to injustice for lower-class Jews. However, his public healing and exorcism could be seen as claiming functions belonging to the temple.

The public activity of Jesus, as well as that of John the Baptist, can be seen as a critique of the temple state and also of the priests, scribes, Pharisees, and Sadducees who benefitted from it at the expense of common people. But criticism of the temple state did not necessarily mean opposition to the temple itself. Whether Pharisees and scribes were always associated with the temple elites is under debate. Richard Horsley and William Herzog maintain they would not have been located outside of Jerusalem unless they were sent as messengers to check out Jesus. Amy-Jill Levine, on the other hand, argues that Pharisees were based in towns and villages rather than in the temple.[99] Galilee at this time was not directly under the authority of the temple because the Herodian Antipas was the political leader. He had building programs that produced a refurbished capital in Sepphoris near Nazareth and then a new capital in Tiberias on the Sea of Galilee, south of Capernaum. But Antipas did not attempt to rival the religious authority of the temple in his provinces by constructing anything that might have drawn people away from the temple. Temple taxes were not necessarily mandatory, but loyal Jews in Galilee felt obligated to continue paying temple dues along with the Roman tribute and special taxes collected by their Herodian government. Herzog maintains that a great many Galileans were unable to afford the temple tax and thus were subject to scornful treatment by representatives of the temple, such as Pharisees and scribes. Even so, Galileans, including Jesus, continued to revere the temple and honor the Torah even though they did not follow the policies of temple leadership, which were often self-serving. Jesus himself frequented the temple, as did the disciples after his execution, so that criticism of those in power did not mean rejection of the temple.

How did Jesus criticize the powers behind the temple? His teaching and preaching gave priority to the poor, who were often victims of the economically dominant groups associated with the temple as well as with secular government. Not all Pharisees or scribes were wealthy although they were among the retainers of the elite. Jesus debated Pharisees and scribes, sometimes making very critical statements about them, but he was consistently harsh in statements about those who were wealthy without distinguishing whether they were scribes, priests, Pharisees, or whatever. One of the issues sometimes raised by religious critics was the question of Jesus's authority for the things he did and said. Clearly he did not have the qualifications expected of scribes and others. He was also on shaky ground because healing and exorcising was a function of the temple—and especially the power to forgive, which was implied, then directly claimed by Jesus. The actions could be viewed as claims to be a broker of the power of God, a role normally claimed exclusively by the temple and its priests.[100]

Add to that the direct criticism of the temple establishment when Jesus went to Jerusalem in conjunction with Passover. The Parable of the Wicked Tenants (Mark 12:1–12; Matthew 21:33–46; Luke 20:9–19) seems to have been understood as an attack on temple leadership. The symbol of the vineyard had been understood to represent Israel since the oracle in Isaiah 5:1–7, so that the tenants who beat and then killed representatives of the owner were recognized as the priests and other leadership in charge of the temple. In that parable, Jesus also gave a twist to usual prophetic tendencies, for Isaiah was speaking against an unproductive vineyard (the people of Israel) that would be punished, whereas Jesus appeared to say it was those in charge of the vineyard who should be brought to justice.[101] Jesus was also described as attacking some of the financial transactions in the temple precincts in what was termed a cleansing (Mark 11:15–19; Matthew 21:12–27; Luke 19:45–20:8; and John 2:13–16), but just what he was objecting to was not made clear in the gospels. He also made statements about the destruction of the temple that would be used in the interrogations after his arrest (Mark 13:1–37; Matthew 24:1–44; and Luke 21:5–33).

So did Jesus turn his back on the temple? Was baptism and devotion to Jesus a replacement of temple observance? Some scholars have argued that Jesus's ministry represented a rejection of the temple and its rulers. This would go along with a picture of Jesus as outside the Judaism of his day. This would also go along with seeing the temple system as oppressive.

The prevailing view, which I think is correct, sees Jesus as essentially a traditional Jew of his time who venerated the Torah and followed a great many purity requirements as part of daily life. He did not extend the purity requirements associated with the temple into daily life as extensively as the Pharisees did and he even reached out to those such as tax collectors, whose way of life excluded them from normal acceptance in the community. All of the gospels show Jesus worshiping and teaching in the temple, which means he went through *miqveh* cleansing like any ordinary Jew. He probably followed a kosher diet and took frequent *miqveh* baths, as did most ordinary Jews of his time. Amy-Jill Levine pointed out that "Jesus dresses like a Jew" by wearing fringes or *tzitzit*, mentioned in Numbers 15:37–40, to remind Jews to carry out all of the 613 commandments of the Torah. It was his fringes that were touched by the woman with a hemorrhage, according to Matthew 9:20.[102]

Jesus started his ministry with baptism in the Jordan. This associated him with expectations of a rapidly approaching divine intervention of some kind that would bring judgment and restoration of correct values. Criticism of the temple leadership and its alliance with Rome seemed to be implied, which meant criticism of the political, social, and religious behaviors of the elite who ruled through the temple and benefitted from it by exploiting those outside their relatively small group. Jesus associated himself with this criticism and gave it his own flavor as he exorcised, healed, and taught. He also did not limit the power of God to the temple as he honored the prophetic status of John the Baptist and claimed to extend the power of God through his own actions.

Jesus's criticism of the elite of his day steps on the toes of political, social, economic, and religious leadership of our own time as it has in every time. There are those in our society who celebrate their success as proof of God's favor even though they see that many people are excluded from their small circle and suffer from the tactics that promote their growing prosperity. There are churches whose ministers draw large crowds and who specialize in raising funds from people who are struggling financially while they live in mansions, drive expensive automobiles, and wear fashions few people can afford. Their lifestyles are what many churchgoers hope for rather than a life of sacrifice and even poverty in service to God. In fact, poverty is often seen as evidence of laziness and failure to honor God, as was the view of religious authorities in Jesus's time.

A great many people in our nation of churchgoers have been baptized. How many people realize that following in the footsteps of Jesus would mean that baptism could imply criticism of ordinary social and economic values of our own society as it did in Jesus's time? Thinking about the implications of the gospels keeps every age on its toes.

CHAPTER SEVENTEEN

WHAT TO GIVE CAESAR

As a young Baptist, I learned the proud heritage of my denomination in advocating the separation of church and state in American political life. Roger Williams, the first Baptist in America, protested the interference of Puritan leadership into private lives and also the combination of religious and political offices in the same persons. He withdrew from Massachusetts and insisted on religious toleration in the colony of Rhode Island.

My Baptist mentors were suspicious of the political motives of Catholics running for public office, especially in the case of John F. Kennedy in 1960. Baptists were extremely anti-Catholic for a number of reasons, but we were also sure the Pope would inevitably dominate the policies of a Catholic president.

Scripture, of course, supported keeping religion and politics separate. We knew that when the Pharisees wanted to trap Jesus into saying something inflammatory against Rome, he escaped with a snappy comeback: "Give unto Caesar the things that are Caesar's and to God the things that are God's" (Mark 12:17; Matthew 22:21; Luke 20:25). There it was: scriptural proof of the correctness of separating politics and religion.

From time to time, there have been scholars who argued that Jesus was a political revolutionary preaching radical values. Most scholars and most Christians have refused to accept that interpretation because Jesus did not openly proclaim political objectives such as were associated with some expectations of a Messiah. What has been less appreciated has been the kind of political and economic criticism contemporaries heard in Jesus's remarks.

It is generally accepted that the main theme of Jesus in the synoptics is the imminent coming of the kingdom of God. The way I was taught to interpret his meaning as a fundamentalist was to see references to his Resurrection and eventual Second Coming. For the most part, scholars have talked about whether Jesus was presenting an apocalyptic expectation of an immediate world-ending (eschatological) event with himself playing a key role as either Son of Man or Messiah, or whether he was a sage in the Wisdom tradition talking in general about God's justice as an ideal. A key difference between these groups of scholars is whether Jesus actually said the things that sound like he expected a cataclysmic divine intervention. Also there is growing agreement that apocalyptic expectations did not mean the end of the world as they spoke of world transformation. In either case, it is agreed these days that the message of Jesus had a clear political, social, and economic message for his time.

In a previous conversation, I pointed to the role of temple states in the ancient Near East. In the time of Herod the Great, all of the territories that reputedly once came under David were united again in a monarchy that was a stand-in for Roman imperial government. Herod relied on temple leadership for governing his provinces in accordance with ancient Jewish beliefs and practices and for support in collecting the funds he and the Romans required. The massive rebuilding of the Jerusalem temple took over sixty years and a lot of money. He also built cities and numerous monumental structures, which ran up the cost to taxpayers. Temple leaders were critical of Herod in many ways and sometimes stood up for traditions they supported, but they also profited while the masses of Jews outside the temple elite benefitted far less than the leadership.

Some of the best documentary sources for this period were written by Flavius Josephus, a Pharisee of a priestly family who was a general in Galilee during the revolt of 66 CE. Through his accounts, we learn of a series of popular movements targeting the policies of Herod, Rome, and the temple state leadership that supported them. When Herod the Great died in 4 BCE, there were revolts in Galilee under Judas, son of a well-known bandit named Hezekiah, and in Judah by someone from Herod's court named Simon and a shepherd named Anthronges along with his brothers. Josephus presents all of these as pretenders to kingship. Anthronges was more successful than Simon as he fought in the hills around Jerusalem for three years before being subdued. The Galilean uprising lasted only a few months and was notable for massive slaughter in the area of Nazareth about five miles from the city of Sepphoris. This would have been about the time Jesus was an infant or young child. No doubt he grew up hearing firsthand accounts of the cost of open rebellion that brought Roman intervention.[103]

The movements around John the Baptist and Jesus appear to have been the first since the death of Herod the Great, neither of which encouraged rebellion, although both represented political and religious criticism of the current establishment. The political criticism of both led to their execution without causing an uprising, but they were soon followed by others with a prophetic or messianic purpose expressed in public demonstrations. One thing all of these had in common was an appeal mainly to commoners in the villages. Jesus brought on execution by making an appearance in Jerusalem at the time of Passover, which in part celebrated national claims to independence, thus posing a threat of public uprising that did not materialize. The three who came after him did organize public demonstrations involving large numbers of people. An unknown Samaritan leader convinced followers around 36 CE to follow him up Mount Gerizim to a spot where he was convinced Moses had buried vessels from the wilderness tabernacle. The large crowd was met with brutal force that led to the end of Pilate's career. Then around 45 CE a man named Theudas gathered a crowd to re-enact Joshua's crossing of the Jordan in a prophetic act to reclaim God's possession of the land. Roman forces attacked by surprise, caught Theudas, and beheaded him. After another ten years, there came an unknown prophet from Egypt who led a group up the Mount of Olives, preparing to march on Jerusalem. He declared that the walls of Jerusalem would fall before them as had the walls of Jericho before Joshua. As before, the Romans attacked the crowd, but this time the unknown prophet escaped into future anonymity. It was ten years after this event that a revolt and civil war broke out in Jerusalem that spread to Galilee.[104]

Each of these efforts were different so that they did not act out what Richard Horsley has called an accepted messianic script. Christian tradition has presented the notion that there were common and well-recognized expectations of a coming Messiah that Jesus varied in a special way. The variety of religious and political movements mentioned by Josephus demonstrated lack of recognition of a clearly conceived role for a Messiah. All of these movements appealed to Moses by pointing to the Exodus, the covenant made at Sinai, and the gift of the land through Joshua's conquest. These were key items in a tradition that was essentially oral rather than based on reading books of scripture.

Keep in mind this was a preliterate society with a small percentage of people trained to read—and most of those who were literate belonged to elites, serving rulers and the temple, and lived in cities rather than villages. The uprisings prior to the revolt of 66 were comprised of mostly common people who lived in villages and venerated ancient traditions reflected in oral traditions related to scripture.[105]

For most of his ministry, Jesus looked to the villages of Galilee for his audience. As his fame spread, villagers from nearby regions came as well. Representatives of the court of Antipas (Herodians) along with Pharisees and scribes (some of them from Jerusalem) began coming to check him out. They saw Jesus performing wonders and heard him talking about the imminent kingdom of God. They did not hear a message calling for revolt. If that had occurred, you can be sure Antipas would have acted before Jesus ever went to Jerusalem to cause trouble. What they heard was a message of hope for changes to improve their lives that involved a subtle yet clear message of opposition to key policies associated with the leadership of Antipas, Romans, and temple leadership.

A common form used by ancient prophets of Israel was a series of woes and blessings. The same format is seen in Luke's version of what Matthew presents as Beatitudes in the Sermon on the Mount (5:1–12). Luke's version is more direct (6:20–26). The poor will be honored in the kingdom; the hungry will be filled; and those who weep will laugh. In short, there will be a complete reversal in God's kingdom of current circumstances for those in his intended audience. Then follows the opposite side of the coin. Woes are pronounced on those who are rich, filled with food, laughing, and have respectable reputations. Those present knew he was talking about their religious leaders who also were the stooges for Rome.

Matthew is less direct as he presents the blessings without the negative implications for those not blessed. Mark is even more indirect. He doesn't have Jesus speaking directly to the downtrodden common people because: "With many such parables he spoke the word to them, as they were able to hear it; he did not speak to them except in parables, but explained everything in private to his disciples." (4:33–34) This statement follows two parables of growth. The first pointed out that when a seed is planted, it grows to full maturity even though we do not know how. But when it is grown, we know it is time for harvest. The second parable compared the kingdom of God to a small mustard seed that grows into a large shrub. Both stories appear to speak of the inevitability of the coming kingdom as it grows by its own inner but foreordained logic.

As mentioned in another conversation, the Lord's Prayer represents a summary of the essential teachings of Jesus. Disciples were told to pray for the coming of the kingdom, which would mean realizing the will of God—the realization of the actual kingship of God himself on earth. They asked for bread on a daily basis, which apparently was often lacking in the present reality. They are told to ask for forgiveness of debts as they forgive debts for others. Richard Horsley interprets that phrase as a direct appeal to something very dear to ordinary peasants in villages, the cancellation of the debts that are threatening to deprive them of ancestral land as rich absentee landlords in cities, especially Jerusalem, take ownership.[106] Finally, they were to pray for deliverance from the power of evil, which was a reference to the demonic forces Jesus saw himself opposed to as he represented the healing powers of God.

Until Jesus went to Jerusalem and made his criticism of temple authorities more direct, he avoided confronting them directly enough to bring arrest or military action. He made sure to avoid the fate of John the Baptist who was beheaded by Antipas in a distant fortress. He seemed to prefer a more dramatic confrontation at center stage for all Jews—Jerusalem and the temple. That would bring more public humiliation by Roman crucifixion.

But what about the apparent support for paying taxes by saying to give Caesar the things belonging to him? When Jesus's response is put in the context of his support for the complete sovereignty of God, who is really in charge now but whose rule will soon become increasingly apparent, it takes on new meaning. Jesus is presenting a political and economic message based on traditions related to the Mosaic covenant, which recognizes God's kingship over Israel. Here is how Richard Horsley interprets Jesus:

> [I]n response to the question about paying the tribute to Caesar—a question that Jesus realizes is an attempt to entrap him, since the direct answer 'no, don't pay it,' would have been incitement to insurrection—he offers an indirect answer instead. But everyone listening to his clever response would have known that, according to Israel's Covenant with God, 'the things that are Caesar's are precisely nothing, since the things that are God's are everything' (Mark 12:13–17 and par).[107]

My Baptist mentors would be very upset with scholarly findings emphasizing a political, social, and economic message of Jesus rather than one that was primarily religious. This is where we must be careful about projecting current values back to earlier times—the historical sin of anachronism. Keep in mind the novelty of the idea of separating church and state when it was proposed in debates over the United States Constitution.

Although no longer a Baptist, I still support the American constitutional value of separating church and state, but that is not to say that religious messages do not have social, political, and economic impacts. The hosts of ministers who joined students and others in civil rights demonstrations of the 1960s saw themselves as carrying out a religious mission that also was achieving principles enshrined in the Constitution. Affirming the idea that government should be neutral toward religion so that many religions are tolerated and recognized is completely out of step with the requirement of the first four of the Ten Commandments. We live in a different time. Christians in today's society can be devoted to the rule of a sovereign God without demanding conformity of everyone in a country to the beliefs of one or even a few among the variety of religious groups, which increasingly reflects the religious views of many parts of the world.

Chapter Eighteen

Prosperity and Capitalism

At college I realized that the churches I had known were extremely fundamentalist in their approach to the Bible and salvation. They were very evangelical, reaching out with intensity to save sinners from hell fire and eternal damnation by showing them the only way to salvation. As I experienced other churches, I found some that reacted to the kind of preaching I had known by advocating a more positive approach based on popular psychology and business values. For these churches, the hero was Robert Shuler, whose style differed radically from Billy Graham but who enjoyed great success as pastor of what came to be known as a mega church.

In recent decades, there have emerged numerous mega churches with ministers known for personal charisma. They preach a gospel of prosperity and success that they say is based on teachings of Jesus. These ministers speak like fundamentalists about sin but their personal lives model success as their clothing, cars, and homes manifest the results of great financial success. Their achievement is held up as a model to anyone who has faith. After all, Jesus said to ask to receive, to seek in order to find, and that faith can move mountains. The key to prosperity is to follow Jesus's plan based on faith. Some are known for saying to "name it and claim it" if you want prosperity. In other words, visualize what you want and if you have faith it will happen.

These ministers also have websites with devotions you can access for free, but each one is a prelude to a more detailed study that is in a book or DVD that can be bought on the site. In fact, if you look closely, everything these ministers talk about in the pulpit or on their websites turns into marketing pitches for how to find out even more for extra cost. A great many Americans are sales people who know the principles of marketing and closing sales, but even these professionals get caught up in a religiously based sales pitch that keeps money rolling in to underwrite a very expensive lifestyle.

During my professional career, I saw the impact of such ministries on two women in my office. One of them was caring for a husband who left a very high-paying job for another but in the vulnerable time without health coverage had a stroke that disabled him. She went to work to support him and their daughter on an income far lower than they had known previously. She always told people that faith was all that kept her going. Part of that faith was centered on Jim and Tammy Faye Bakker and their religious community in South Carolina. Barely able to feed and clothe her family, she sent a tithe of her income to the Bakkers, feeling that would bring divine blessing that would keep her afloat through very tough times.

A second woman in the same office was so inspired by the Bakkers that she quit her job and moved to South Carolina to join their community. Six months later, she was back with stories about meeting all the central characters television viewers had come to know and love. In person, they turned out not to be so wonderful. Even with her story of disillusionment, our first lady continued to believe in the Bakkers and kept sending money even after a scandal broke out after the return of our second lady.

Loyalty to American values has also been a topic of sermons, including praising the virtues of the Free Enterprise System. Among the themes to be heard is how America is the greatest place in the world and our economic system is a key to happiness. One time I heard a sermon based on the parable of the landowner who paid the same wage to workers sent into a field at different times of the day (Matthew 20:1–16). When pay was handed out, the first workers grumbled that those who worked only an hour were paid the same amount as those who worked all day. The sermon compared this experience to those who are saved at the last minute and get the full benefits of eternal heaven the same as those who spent a lifetime being saved. This is a popular interpretation that can be found on Internet sites such as Jack Kelley's Gracethrufaith.com evangelical site.[108]

But the minister also went on to use the parable as Jesus's endorsement of the justice of the property owner setting the wage standard rather than being subject to the gripes of workers. Rather than emphasizing the generosity of God to some without being unfair to the first group of workers, this minister argued Jesus supported the right of property owners to do what they want to do with their property. Thus he supported a key principle of *laissez faire* capitalism. Adam Smith, whose *Wealth of Nations* in 1776 first described the workings of market-based capitalism, would have been very pleased at the endorsement of unrestricted private property rights because he saw that as essential to emerging capitalism. From its beginning, capitalistic enterprises have thrived on laws that give priority to the rights of the people putting up the money for a business over the employees of the business or the buyers of products that are made. The interpretation in this sermon amounted to an endorsement of the new *laissez faire* policies associated with Reaganomics so that the minister was endorsing the anti-union and deregulatory emphasis associated with Reagan Republicans.

This view finds partial support among some scholars who interpret Jesus's parables and controversies based on the dynamics of an honor culture. William Herzog drew on such scholarship in presenting the parable as completely arbitrary behavior by the landowner, which insulted the status and honor of all the workers. By this interpretation, Jesus was denouncing what appeared as overgenerosity to some as fundamentally insulting behavior to all the workers because Torah standards of fairness were not applied to any of them.[109]

The popularity of prosperity and capitalism as themes drawn from Jesus makes quite a contrast with the Social Gospel movement of the 1920s based on Jesus's outreach to the poor. Those views are also out of step with the prevailing scholarly view that Jesus was a critic of the social and economic as well as religious elite of his day because of their exploitation of the large underclass living in the villages who were the focus of his ministry.

There is no credible indication that Jesus was a social revolutionary, but the kingdom of God he described represented an overwhelming change of the standards followed by the ruling elites. Political and religious leaders lived in cities and were subsidized by the labor of common people who lived and worked in villages. Jesus went to the villages and to the common people who did not enjoy the prosperity of the religious elite.

Jesus denounced the rich in sayings, for example by announcing that it will be easier for a camel to go through the eye of a needle than for a rich man to enter heaven (Matthew 19:23–24), or that in the kingdom the first will be last and the last will be first (Matthew 19:30 and 20:16; Mark 10:31; Luke 13:30). He associated with religious and social outcasts. He told parables aimed directly against the practices of rich landlords who unjustly took land from commoners and temple officials who would even take the very small amount a widow needed to live on.

One parable that is often misunderstood is the story of the rich man and Lazarus (Luke 16:19–31). The rich man lives without taking notice of the sufferings of the beggar Lazarus and after death finds Lazarus is "in the bosom of Abraham" while he is in a less desirable situation. Most often sermons focus on the heaven and hell aspect of the story. Emphasis is placed on listening to the gospel while there is time and based on it to treat people justly. But this view misses an important dimension of the story.[110]

The rich man is part of the elite who take pride in being children of Abraham. In other words, they see the promises of old as meant for themselves and don't see that someone like Lazarus is also an Israelite covered by those same promises. The rich man is stunned to see the lowly nobody being treated as somebody after death. But he still doesn't "get it." All the requests he makes involve using Lazarus as a servant, either to ease his personal discomfort or to go warn his family. Even in the afterlife, he wants lower-class people to be treated as not worth consideration. The final statement about his family having the prophets as a guide is not much hope because this rich man didn't get the point even when he saw the beggar being treated as a human being in the afterlife. If a dead rich man is too dumb to see his error, how can his living relatives have much chance of understanding?

Another way to get the impact of this parable is to imagine the rich man as a southern plantation owner before the civil war who dies and sees one of his slaves being treated as an equal in heaven. Even then he thinks the black man must be one of God's slaves and asks God to send the slave in heaven on missions for a white man in hell. That illustrates the extent of the stupidity of this ancient rich member of the Jewish elite.

Jesus makes the same general point in the parable of the vineyard that he tells in the temple in Jerusalem (Luke 20:9–19). His audience included the priests and scribes who profited from the temple state at the expense of the lower populations. The image of the vineyard had been known as a symbol for Israel since the oracles of Isaiah. In this case, Jesus said the vineyard was run by tenants who refused to give the owner his due. When the owner sends representatives, they are abused or killed. The punch line is that the owner will come himself and exact revenge.[111]

The hearers knew very well Jesus was denouncing the leaders of the temple state. They ruled in their own interests and did not honor their responsibility to God, according to Jesus. Part of the accusation was that they were unjust to those outside the elite rather than applying the kind of justice envisioned in the Torah and by prophets such as Amos and Micah. When God sent prophets, they were ignored or killed because they were considered a threat. In other sayings, Jesus had made it clear he saw Jerusalem as a place where prophets were routinely killed by those in charge (Matthew 23:37; Luke 13:34). He was also describing himself as a prophet with a special role in that parable and predicted his own death as being like those of other prophets.

A closer look at the parable of the landowner who gave the same wage to all the workers shows an economic outlook closer to socialism than to the property emphasis of capitalism. The workers in the market place may have been people in desperate situations who had lost land or were in danger of losing their land and needed extra income, or perhaps just ordinary workers needing extra income for various reasons. There was a widespread problem of indebtedness to absentee landlords who lived in the cities. This generous landlord gave employment to as many workers as he found that day. The first workers saw their promised wage given to the latecomers and expected more for themselves based on common expectations of equity—more work for longer hours should equal more pay. But the landlord spread out the pool for wages over a larger number of people without giving bonuses to some. More people were helped but the harder workers didn't get bigger rewards—which is against a key expectation in capitalism.[112]

This parable represents a critique of the economic and social standards of our time rather than an endorsement. Its spirit was caught by Sister Rose Pacatte in a commentary on the National Catholic Reporter website:

> But let me tell you what I see here in southern California when I drive around for school or to visit the sick or to shop. I drive by the parking lots of Home Depot and other large stores and see men of all ages waiting to be hired. I know most are probably undocumented and many have wives and children here or in another country they support, or try to. Work means life to them, any work and any pay. Can you imagine how they feel as the hours tick by and no one hires them? Or can you imagine their joy when someone does?[113]

Sister Pacatte sees this current situation as comparable to the workers of the market place in the parable and I agree.

We live in a time when technology and competition among international corporations are used as justification for moving jobs overseas or downsizing by eliminating jobs and loading extra responsibilities on those who remain but who are often paid less rather than more and are expected to be happy to have a job. Employee benefits are among the first cost-cutting items on the block when a company's bottom line in is trouble. What makes this unjust, in my view, is that this planned suffering of so many makes possible exorbitant profits and bonuses to a very small group at the top. Executive pay and bonuses have been shown to be increasingly out of line with compensation of others in the company. We live in a time of runaway pay for fewer and fewer at the top as the middle seems to be disappearing or at least to be increasingly pushed lower on the scale.

Since the beginning of Christianity, the sayings and parables of Jesus have often been used to support the prevailing views of elites of the day. Appealing to Jesus to support a gospel of prosperity and capitalism reflects the values of many people in our country today. My view is that Jesus's attacks on the elite of his day apply to the elites of our day or any day. It is not wealth itself that Jesus attacked. Rather, it was the egotism of the rich that blocked justice or generosity to those not in the elite.

The religious and political leaders in Jesus's day lived for themselves and too often ignored God's expectation of mercy, justice, and generosity. That critique stings every generation that puts its own economic well-being ahead of the demands of God's sovereign rule and the needs of "the least of these who are members of my family (Matthew: 25:40)".

Chapter Nineteen

The Real King of Israel

Each of the four gospels leads up to the crucifixion by telling of Pilate and Jesus before a crowd. Details vary, but in each account, Pilate refers to Jesus as King of the Jews and offers to release a prisoner as a way of letting Jesus off the hook. The crowd calls out for crucifixion and Pilate gives in. John's account varies from the others by having the chief priests give the final answer that leads to Pilate's concession. Pilate asks: "Shall I crucify your King?" The chief priests reply: "We have no king but the emperor (19:15)."

Whether this exchange occurred or not, this statement is credible for the chief priests because they were the intermediaries through which the Romans ruled Judah. Romans made a practice of respecting religious and social rules of subject populations by relying on a client government, a government claiming to represent local sensitivities while profiting from being the intermediary for an outside power. The high priest in Jerusalem was the foremost local official who operated on behalf of Rome. Loyalty to Roman leadership was expected as part of their role.

On the other hand, such a statement would be embarrassing to the chief priests because their primary loyalty to God was the basis for expecting the Romans to make concessions for their religious practices. It would also be a symbolic denial of the Mosaic tradition, which claims God is the only real king of the Israelites. Popular belief in the Mosaic tradition was behind the emphasis of John the Baptist and Jesus on a coming kingdom of God, a situation in which the now hidden rule of God would become visible to all.

It became traditional in Christianity to believe there was what James Charlesworth terms a checklist or role description for the Messiah. Supposedly "the Jews" in Jesus's time expected a Messiah who would be from the line of David and would bring salvation and independence for the people of Israel as part of an apocalyptic ending of the age that would herald judgment and general resurrection. Supposedly Jesus was different in that he did not seek political conquest and it was through death and resurrection that he would bring about the time of salvation. Insight that came after the resurrection seemed to explain to early believers that Jesus was rejected because his approach to being Messiah was different from what was expected.

A symposium held at Princeton University in 1987 reached unanimous agreement on views that contradict this traditional picture of Jewish expectations of a Messiah. They found that the term Messiah was hardly ever used in Jewish documents prior to 70 CE and was not clear in meaning when it was used. It could apply to a king, a priest, or a prophet. It appears different groups had different views of the Messiah based on the circumstances of the various groups.[114] James Charlesworth, editor of the results of the symposium, explains that the texts that used the terms Messiah, Christ, or Anointed One "do not reveal a coherent picture." As a result, there is "no evidence for the assertion that the Jews during Jesus's time were looking for the coming of 'the' or 'a' Messiah, and there was no paradigm, or checklist, by which to discern if a man was the Messiah."[115] Concerning the Messiah, Charlesworth warns that: "We must not claim as clear what is intentionally imprecise."[116]

Charlesworth also made statements about the ministry of Jesus that are noteworthy. There is no indication in Jewish literature in or out of the Bible that the Messiah would be a miracle worker or that he would bring salvation through his death. The gospels do not associate Jesus's actions with those of a Davidic figure nor is there evidence that after the resurrection Jesus was associated with Davidic kingship. Furthermore, in the synoptic gospels Jesus makes no claim to the title of Messiah and, when Peter blurts it out in Mark, he appears to brand that claim as from the devil. The synoptics clearly associate Jesus with the prophetic tradition associated with Moses and Elijah rather than with traits related to Davidic kingship.[117]

Historical events in the years before and after Jesus also do not support the idea of a prevailing expectation of a Messiah. Just a century before Jesus, the Maccabean revolt led to establishing the Hasmonean dynasty. None of the sources from that period indicate that any of the Hasmonean family was expected to play the role of Messiah, although they fought a long and eventually successful guerilla war leading to independence and monarchy. In fact, Charlesworh believes that the idea of a messianic deliverer probably developed in reaction against the Hasmonean experience.[118] The messianic notion did not seem to occur to the Hasmoneans, for their main ambition was to take over the high priesthood and the religious leadership it had involved since the rebuilding of the temple. Prior to the Babylonian destruction, the king had been the religious leader whose support was needed for policies favored by the high priest; but after the exile, the high priest was the political and religious leader of Judah until he lost political leadership to the Hasmoneans. Then the Hasmoneans introduced the innovation of combining the roles of king and high priest.

Herod the Great also did not appeal to the role of Messiah as part of the semi-independent kingdom that was experienced under Rome. Herod seized the power to appoint the high priest and frequently changed the incumbent to flex his muscle, yet the rule of the high priest through the temple was respected as the temple establishment became members of the client government collecting Roman tribute as well as temple dues throughout all of ancient Israel.

Upon the death of Herod, revolts broke out in Galilee and Judea. From this period until the revolt against Rome, there appear to have been rival traditions at work, according to Richard Horsley.[119] Each of the revolts on the death of Herod made a claim to kingship and may have followed a Davidic pattern, but each resulted in defeat. The revolt in Galilee was put down quickly with terrible destruction in Sepphoris five miles from Nazareth about the time of Jesus's childhood so that he was bound to have heard stories of the consequences of messianic revolt against Rome, which perhaps explains his reluctance to be identified with a similar movement. The Judean revolt lasted longer but also ended in failure and restoration of temple officials.

In John the Baptist and Jesus we see traditions of popular movements appealing to prophetic traditions of the kingship of God rather than asserting anything that sounded like a military or political threat. After Jesus, there came other popular demonstrations based on prophetic examples. Within a few years of Jesus, there came a Samaritan leader who organized a march up Mount Gerizim to find implements from the Mosaic tabernacle, resulting in slaughter by the Romans, which brought an end to Pilate's tenure. About a decade later came Theudas and yet another decade later came the Egyptian. Both of these appealed to images from Joshua's conquest. Theudas gathered people near Jericho to cross the Jordan as it was supposed to part in order to renew Joshua's taking of the land. Someone referred to as the Egyptian assembled people on the Mount of Olives to march around Jerusalem as Joshua did at Jericho with the expectation it would experience crumbling walls and divine defeat. These were purification efforts based on prophetic traditions rather than messianic uprisings.

The movements of John the Baptist, Jesus, the Samaritan, Theudas, and the Egyptian were based on commoners in villages rather than the elites who lived in cities. Moses, Joshua, and Elijah were the paramount figures in these movements, not a Davidic claimant to kingship. The mindset of these people was illustrated when Jesus asked his disciples who people were saying he was, for the response was that they associated him with John the Baptist and others they recognized as prophets.

When the revolt broke out against Rome in 66, it quickly turned into a civil war among factions within the temple elite and then a wider civil war as popular movements of peasants became involved. The leader of one popular faction, Simon bar Giora, resorted to the messianic tradition by claiming the role of king but was not recognized by other leaders. He was eventually captured and executed by the Romans.

Historical events do not show evidence of expectation by the population of villages or by elites in the cities of a king like David, who would bring independence and a new era of peace and divine rule. Look again at the story in Mark of the conversation with the disciples near Ceasarea Philippi (8:27–33). Peter declared Jesus was the Messiah and traditionally that is interpreted as the correct answer. Yet, as he did on other occasions, Jesus commands Peter not to tell anyone without directly committing himself. Soon thereafter Jesus takes the disciples up a mountain and suddenly they see Jesus transfigured in the company of Moses and Elijah. Traditional interpretations have seen this as affirming the Messiah role, but on the contrary it points to identification of Jesus with the leading prophets of Israel. David was not there or any symbol of messianic leadership. This tends to suggest the people who guessed Jesus was related to the prophets were right as opposed to Peter's declaration.

The picture is further complicated by considering how Jesus used the term Son of Man. The expression was an ordinary way of referring to just any person and Jesus seemed to use it as a way to refer to himself in the third person. This was a humble, unassuming way of referring to himself. Yet the use of the term in Daniel and in the books of Enoch (which are believed to have been composed in Galilee) complicates things as the term was used as a title for a special figure commissioned by God. The role of the Son of Man in this sense was not a messianic role because it did not involve being king but it appeared to be what has been termed an apocalyptic role of power at the end of time, part of the arrival of God's everlasting rule. According to John Collins, the apocalyptic use of Son of Man makes most sense in a post-Resurrection context rather than before it because it implies a special role as part of the end time.[120] Even if Jesus used the Son of Man as a messianic title, it did not imply any king other than God himself.

Traditional beliefs about the Messiah have assumed that David was the model king of Israel so that the Messiah would be descended from his line. But it appears the direct kingship of God going back to the days of Moses was a more powerful model among the common people in Jesus's day and in the mind of Jesus himself.

The synoptic gospels make it clear that the kingdom of God was the central message of Jesus—a theme John Calvin captured in his emphasis on the sovereignty of God. Jesus was proclaiming God as king. This was in line with the ancient tradition of God as the proper king of Israel so that turning to the monarchy was represented in 1 Samuel as an unsatisfactory substitute for God's direct rule.

The temple officials who supposedly insisted on the execution of Jesus, acknowledging only Caesar as their king, appear to be rejecting more than Jesus. They were rejecting the kingship of God and following the path of killing prophets who upheld the sovereignty of God to the extent that the power and privileges of the temple elite seemed threatened. It is ironic that the grounds for Roman execution was said to be that Jesus claimed to be king of the Jews. The justification for that basis for execution has not been explained satisfactorily. Bart Ehrman suggests that what Judas betrayed was a claim Jesus made to his disciples of kingship, thus leading to his execution. On the other hand, Richard Horsley suggests that Pilate may have jumped to the mistaken conclusion that Jesus was another of the popular claimants to kingship like those following the death of Herod the Great.[121] That Jesus criticized temple leaders on the basis of God's kingship seems clear, choosing provocative tactics in Jerusalem without overtly trying to generate revolt.

It is possible that Jesus saw himself as Messiah because the concept of being an anointed leader and the Son of Man may have been so ambiguous and fluid that they may have been intended as messianic hints if not claims by Jesus. Yet the thrust of the message of Jesus was on the primacy of God, which he saw being rejected by the leadership that repeatedly executed prophets in Jerusalem. In Jesus's mind, the real King of Israel was clearly the God he proclaimed.

We live in a time when legitimacy of political and religious leadership is not determined by dynastic descent. Our election processes are more like the old-fashioned, prophetic anointing as leaders are chosen and then inaugurated with solemn oaths that carry legal obligations. Religious leaders usually claim to be called by God, but they have to go through education and certification processes by religious groups and they too experience an anointing that gives them official status.

We also live in a time of sovereign nation states pursuing their own interests internationally and internally. Religious leaders function within organizations that have their own interests and internal political dynamics. In fact, we live in a society dominated by multiple layers of organizations and their interests, all competing to advance their own aims. Some organizations are nonprofit and intend to serve the public good and some are profit-oriented and seek ways to continually maximize their monetary gains.

Our society is far more complicated than the one Jesus knew and our political processes are significantly different. John Calvin wisely saw that the issue for modern times is not the question of who is king, but who is sovereign. What power and values should be of paramount concern in our day? The question of who the real king of Israel was turns into asking who we look to as holding sovereignty over our lives.

There are many competing loyalties and choices in our time—our nation, employer, church, professional groups, and charitable causes are just some of the organizations pulling for loyalty. The answer of Jesus still applies today. God is sovereign over all. We don't elect or inaugurate God; but it is the power of God and divine standards of justice, mercy, and love that should receive our primary loyalty.

Chapter Twenty

Washed in the Blood

I have known a lot of people over the years who are terrified at the sight of blood. All of us have times when we are cut and bleed a little. And of course if you have children you get used to many little cuts. These we take in stride. But I have also witnessed people becoming very upset at mealtime if someone at the table has a sudden nosebleed. That is a much more public event with blood sometimes gushing and people using napkins for pressure so that everyone around sees it becoming bloody. People lose their appetite and some react more viscerally. Public spilling of blood is not something people want to be around.

The general skittishness about blood always puzzled me because I grew up in a church environment in which flowing red blood was persistently referred to as a good thing. As a child it never occurred to me to wonder if all the ministers who talked about the importance of spilled blood were themselves afraid to be around when blood actually was flowing.

I remember often singing a hymn that asked, "Are you washed in the blood of the lamb?"[122] The refrain of this hymn asks: "Are your garments spotless? Are they white as snow?" Another hymn, written by Fanny Crosby, repeated several times: "Though your sins be as scarlet, they shall be as white as snow."[123] That's how I learned that scarlet suggested sin. It sounded like blood had powers usually claimed by Tide and Clorox—but my mother told me lots of Tide and Clorox were needed to get blood out of clothes.

Washing in blood is not a practical notion, but it was in many hymns and sermons in the Baptist churches I attended. In stained glass windows and history books, I saw pictures of a lamb that had been stabbed so that its blood was gushing into a cup. I learned this represented Jesus, the Lamb of God, spilling his blood for us. The cup related to the Mass, which I knew as Communion, in which Christians actually drink the very blood of Jesus.

As I grew older, I heard an explanation of the bloody imagery. It always came with John 3:16. You see God loved the world so much that He sent His only Son to die for our sins. And He had to spill His blood on the cross to make it possible for our sins to be forgiven. Then I learned the big word Atonement as the doctrine explaining why blood from God was necessary before God could be reconciled to humanity.

An important basis for the focus on blood was the treatment of Jesus as he was crucified by the Romans. The four gospels present a consistent picture of brutality that came with the Roman judicial process for commoners who were not Roman citizens. The books of Daniel and Maccabees illustrate reactions to executions of martyrs under Seleucid dominance, but the gospels provide descriptions that are graphically violent and bloody like no others in scripture. Mel Gibson's movie *The Passion of the Christ* caused a stir because of its violence and brutality, which were intended to reflect faithfully the depiction in the gospels.[124] Mel Gibson made an international reputation through a series of violent movies, as have a number of other actors, as movies with mounting sequences of violence have consistently drawn crowds of young people to theaters. Still, a great many people were shocked to see the story of the gospels portrayed so graphically. Imagine a world in which such public displays of violence were almost routine and the humiliation of the victims even more extreme than portrayed in Gibson's movie, for crucifixion victims would have been completely naked when paraded in public and then executed. Their nude bodies would often have been left hanging for some time as a lesson to others who might consider revolt.

The arrest and swift execution of Jesus evidently caught the disciples by surprise, for there was no indication of organized resistance. The gloom and despair of followers is reflected in Luke's story of the travelers to Emmaus (Luke 24:13–35). Two of the followers of Jesus are discussing their disappointment over recent events when they are joined by a third person who begins to give them a different insight into events. As they are about to eat, they discover it was Jesus himself who was pointing the way to a different understanding of the crucifixion. I doubt this story reflects a historical event, yet I believe it indicates the frame of mind of disciples and their efforts to find a new interpretation in scripture as a result of the resurrection. The story reflects the conviction that the new interpretation was inspired by the risen Lord himself.

In 1 Corinthians 15:3–11, Paul described the account that had been passed to him, which he had passed to his readers. He told of resurrection appearances, the last of which was to himself. His account built theology into the story, for he said "Christ died for our sins in accordance with the scriptures" and he also "was raised on the third day in accordance with the scriptures." This account, written about twenty years after the crucifixion, indicates the Jesus movement found theological justification for what happened to Jesus in scripture and that it was a sacrifice necessary because of human sin. From this theological connection emerged beliefs about atonement as essential for understanding the sacrifice made by Jesus.

As an adult, I have learned to be cautious in relying on childhood impressions because children don't perceive things accurately and often fail to understand what they perceive. Many Christians will say it is a distortion to overemphasize the imagery of blood in Christianity. Something else I have learned as an adult is how often we adults accept traditional language without really thinking about what it means. I am convinced that the adults I knew in childhood routinely accepted religious language filled with bloody images that related the crucifixion to the sacrificial system of the Old Testament without giving much thought to the implications of what they were saying. This is true of much of our religious language taken from the Bible. That language is filled with images from times when animal sacrifice was a normal form of worship and when God was assumed to sit on a giant throne surrounded by a magnificent court as was the practice of powerful kings of those times. Since the practice of animal sacrifice is no longer accepted in most cultures as a form of worship, why do we continue to use images that explain our relationship to God in terms of bloody sacrifices? Some people continue to describe God as sitting on a throne. Do we have political leaders today whose power is symbolized by a throne? A more up-to-date religious image would have God behind a desk in a large oval office.

Bloody images and theories of atonement seem to derive support from the sixteenth chapter of Leviticus, which describes rituals in connection with the Day of Atonement, Yom Kippur. A closer look at that chapter shows that the use of blood for atonement, as prescribed in Leviticus, does not support what Christians have imagined for the blood of Jesus.[125]

Aaron, as high priest, is commanded to select a bull and two goats. This is all to be done in connection with the Tabernacle as the Israelites wander on

Sinai. It was a tent that foreshadowed the temple in Jerusalem because it had an area for God only, a "holy of holies," an altar, and an area for the people to gather. Aaron is to sacrifice the bull to make atonement for his sins and the sins of his "house," which is his extended family. After sacrificing the bull, Aaron is to enter the holy of holies with incense from the altar and make sure its cloud covers the mercy seat, or cover of the Ark of the Covenant, or he will die. Apparently this cloud is to keep him from actually seeing God and thus dying because of such direct contact with the holy. Then he is to dip his finger in the blood of the bull and sprinkle it on the mercy seat and in front of the mercy seat seven times. That is all to take care of his own sin so that he does not die upon entering the holy of holies.

Before sacrificing the bull, Aaron was to choose two goats and cast lots to see which one would be sacrificed. After his actions in the holy of holies with the blood of the bull, he is to sacrifice the selected goat. At this point, Leviticus summarizes the purpose for these actions, as follows in the *Jewish Study Bible* translation of verse 16: "Thus he shall purge the Shrine of the uncleanness and transgression of the Israelites, whatever their sins; and he shall do the same for the Tent of Meeting, which abides with them in the midst of their uncleanness." Then he is to go to the altar and with his finger put bull's blood and then goat's blood seven times on each horn of the altar to cleanse the altar from the sins of the people.

All of this cleansing with blood so far has done nothing for the sinfulness of the people. The priest who is to enter the holy of holies, literally into the presence of God, is to be cleansed, then the sanctuary, and then the altar. So atonement thus far is a housecleaning to make the worship site suitable for the holiness of God because the uncleanness of the people accumulates and soils the place where they worship God.

The central problem in this chapter is the separateness and holiness of God, which must be preserved from the uncleanness that human contact can bring. Sin is used in a general and extremely vague sense. Jonathan Klawans points out two kinds of impurity in Jewish worship, ritual and moral impurity. Ritual impurity involves things that are natural and often unavoidable, such as menstruation, sexual intercourse, and contact with dead bodies. Ritual impurity must not come in contact with the holy. "Because ritual impurity is contagious, the danger here is that defilement if left unchecked will accumulate and defile the Tabernacle or Temple, rendering it impure and unfit for divine habitation. It is for this reason that the refusal to purify oneself would constitute a transgression (Num. 19:20). But this does not make being ritually impure sinful in and of itself."[126] He goes on to state emphatically: "It is not sinful to be ritually impure, and ritual impurity does not result directly from sin."[127] Moral impurity, on the other hand, is clearly sinful. "Moral impurity results from committing certain acts so heinous that they are considered defiling."[128] These actions would include idolatry, adultery, and bloodshed, all of which are considered "abominations." Moral impurity, which is definitely sinful, is not contagious by contact as is ritual impurity; is not temporary but potentially permanent; and does not keep one from entering sacred precincts of the Tabernacle or Temple. "While ritual impurity can be ameliorated by rites of purification, that is not the case for moral impurity. Moral purity is achieved by punishment, atonement, or best of all, by refraining from committing morally impure acts."[129]

The purpose of the sacrificial offerings in Leviticus 16 is clearly a house cleaning to rid the sacred of the accumulated contagion of human impurity, which is opposed to the holiness of God. If Aaron and other high priests fail to follow exact procedures, the penalty could be death—not as a punishment but as the natural result of the unholy getting too close to the holy.

The last thing Aaron is to do is take the live goat and lay both hands on it, all the while confessing over it the sins of the entire people. Sins are literally put on this goat. Then the goat is sent into the wilderness. That is what happens to sin itself—it is not washed away from the people, it is transferred and sent away. There is nothing about Yom Kippur that says God can only forgive sins if they are washed away with blood.

Blood also played an important role in the Jewish festival of Passover, which was being celebrated as Jesus was executed. The story of the institution of Passover is told in Exodus 12. Each household is commanded to take an unblemished, one-year-old male lamb (or goat), slaughter, cook, and eat it all that night. Some of the blood is to be put on the "two door posts and the lintel of the house in which they eat it." Each person is to eat it hurriedly and already dressed for a journey. The explanation is that God will pass through Egypt and kill the oldest male child where the houses do not have blood on the doorposts and lintel. Moses summarized the entire procedure with a command to the people:

> Then Moses called all the elders of Israel and said to them,
> "Go, select lambs for your families, and slaughter the
> Passover lamb. Take a bunch of hyssop, dip it in the blood

that is in the basin, and touch the lintel and the two doorposts with the blood in the basin. None of you shall go outside the door of your house until morning. For the Lord will pass through to strike down the Egyptians . . . ." (12:21–23)

Blood therefore is the marker for identifying Israelites to spare from the punishment that is happening to the Egyptian people. Atonement for sin is not involved. Yet in hymns and sermons, I have often heard references to soaking hyssop in blood as part of cleansing human sin.

Blood plays a prominent role in Christian observance of the Last Supper. The earliest historical description of this ritual is in Paul's first letter to the Corinthians approximately twenty years after the execution of Jesus. In I Corinthians 11:17–33, Paul says that people are abusing what should be a ritual. He goes on to explain the purpose of the ritual. His words have become common place in Christian worship, but too often we don't hear their meaning because of their familiarity.

The observance, Paul says, should not lead to drunkenness or overeating. It is a solemn ritual commemorating a meal to which Jesus gave special significance. He says Jesus took a loaf of bread, returned thanks, and then broke the bread for distribution. As he did so, he anticipated his coming death by saying that the bread represented his broken body, a body broken for them. Then a soft command: "Do this in remembrance of me." (11:24) A meal, which we assume was the Passover meal, followed. Paul jumps over the meal by saying that after supper Jesus took a cup of wine and said: "This cup is the new covenant in my blood. Do this, as often as you drink it, in remembrance of me." (11:25) Paul then adds his own interpretation: "For as often as you eat this bread and drink this cup, you proclaim the Lord's death until he comes." (11:25) The commentary in the *HarperCollins Study Bible* notes: "Paul interprets the tradition he has just cited by accentuating Christ's saving death (see 15.3–5) and expected return (see 1.7–8)."[130] This has been taken as standard interpretation, but it should be noted that such interpretation came only after the resurrection. Nothing in the ritual described by Paul involves dying for sins.

Thus Jesus turned the Passover meal into a ritual of remembering the death he anticipated was about to happen. Nothing in this ritual suggests forgiveness of sins. Just as Israel commemorates Passover annually, followers of Jesus are told to associate remembering the new covenant and the death of

Jesus as a ritual of continuing discipleship. Clearly Jesus intends this ritual as a legacy of ongoing discipleship after his death. There is no anticipation of resurrection or of forgiveness of sins.

A notable difference between the Jesus depicted in the synoptic gospels of Mark, Matthew and Luke as opposed to the gospel of John, is that Jesus proclaims God as his central message in the synoptics while he proclaims himself as divine in John. Paul's description of the ritual established at the last supper shows Jesus calling on disciples to remember him, his message, and his death. It is asking them to continue as disciples. This is not inconsistent with the picture in the synoptics of discipleship as following Jesus in making God central. Jesus is still not proclaiming himself, just asking them to continue the movement he started. This makes the last supper an action that anticipates a transition from a movement under his leadership to a movement without his leadership.

Too often worship falls into comfortable patterns built around familiar language that no longer makes sense if we stop to think about it. Worshiping God is important and the Bible plays a significant role in helping us understand the many forms of worship within our Judeo-Christian tradition. We need to have an ongoing conversation with the Bible that sometimes challenges and updates what is said. This includes applying thought to language and symbols, like our use of blood in connection with forgiveness. This process will make us uncomfortable while leading to worship that is truly alive today rather than mouthing old formulas that have become meaningless.

CHAPTER TWENTY-ONE

RELIABILITY OF THE GOSPELS

Knowing when your child is telling the truth when dealing with serious consequences is not easy. Should you stand up for him against authorities who don't believe his version of events?

I faced that situation as I waited to be interviewed by the police chief of the small town in which my ex-wife lived with our children. My eleven-year-old son was being accused of arson at worst and malicious mischief at best. He looked perplexed and didn't understand because he said all he did was wait for friends who didn't come and then he left.

I could tell the police chief expected only denial from my son and angry responses from me. He was judicially neutral as he began to go over the facts. First he heard my son's version; then he listed the witnesses who saw him hanging around the sign at the entrance to the apartments where he lived and saw him running away as fire consumed the sign. My son had mentioned that the lights focused on the sign were still lit even in the brightest part of the afternoon. He had kicked up some of the pine bark mulch around the lights. But he had noticed nothing and just suddenly got tired of waiting and ran off.

Slowly the picture came together in his head. The bark must have caught fire because of the hot lights. He sat back, looked at me, and said, "I guess I must have started a fire. I didn't even notice." I felt relief, and I saw a change in the police chief. He too was relieved. Here was a really innocent boy who was facing up to his responsibility. There were no charges, but he had to pay to replace the sign. I came away proud of the way my son accepted responsibility.

Credibility is a legitimate concern when we make decisions or take actions based on trustworthiness of the information we have been given. Many Christians have traditionally insisted that everything in the Bible is reliable and even beyond questioning. That position is hard to defend because every other aspect of normal life shows that credibility and trustworthiness are hard to find. When we think we have found it, events often show that parts of what we were told may not have been entirely true.

In the case of the gospels, we have already mentioned how they have distinctive personalities and present conflicting details and interpretations of events and sayings. They can't be harmonized to present a consistent set of information. Does this amount to saying the gospels are unreliable?

My answer is a definite no to unreliability and yes to overall credibility even if many details are not accepted. It is not a reliability that results from literal truth or documented historicity. In this conversation I will explain how I defend the gospels in the face of such variation. The next two conversations will follow that position in looking at what is credible for the course of Jesus's ministry and then for his crucifixion, burial, and resurrection.

Scholars typically try to identify which parts of the gospels they accept and which they reject, thus narrowing them to a kernel that gets closer to sayings and events that are more likely to have been historical. This is all part of seeking a historical Jesus—the living, breathing person that might have been captured on camera if such technology existed at that time. The process of rejection uses criteria to identify which sayings and events were added by the early Jesus movement in various stages until the gospels reached final written form. We must understand how the gospels developed in order to make sense of this elimination process.[131]

First, there is no evidence that Jesus or anyone around him kept written records during his lifetime. Disciples and others remembered and began telling people what they remembered. This would be considered the first layer of the tradition—actual memories that originated and truly represented what happened before the death of Jesus. It should be recognized that many people heard and saw Jesus and that he most likely made similar comments or told the same stories in multiple places to audiences that did not always consist of the same people. That leads to the conclusion that there could not have been a standard version of the actions and teachings of the historical Jesus. If there had been a camera present to record the "historical Jesus," odds are that record would vary dramatically from the accounts of those who witnessed the events in person because cameras don't record the interpersonal factors that lead to deep impressions and emotions of many kinds in the memories of people. This leads to what James Dunn has called the "historic Jesus," which is to say the impressions made by Jesus that resulted in multiple oral versions. So it turns out this early layer could not have been a standard or consistent picture of Jesus to begin with.[132]

One of the indicators of the earliest layer was that no one seemed to expect Jesus to be executed or rise from the dead. Those events came as a shock to all those associated with Jesus. As they passed along the oral traditions, the pre-execution memories were naturally blended with resurrection experiences and efforts to understand their meaning. Quite naturally, those interpretations influenced how they began to remember and tell what happened before the execution. This became the second layer of the oral tradition. Once again this was personal experience passed on orally rather than in writing for quite a while so that this layer also manifests great variety as many people had earlier memories affected so that the oral testimony reflected current and past reactions to events.

There is clear evidence that the surviving and growing Jesus movement was centered in Jerusalem rather than Galilee. This headquarters was affected, as were all elements of Jewish social, political, and religious life throughout the Mediterranean, by the Roman conquest and destruction of Galilee and Judea as the result of a revolt from 66–73 CE. Jerusalem and the temple were obliterated in 70 along with leadership of the Jesus movement. Therefore, interpreting and adjusting to the destruction of Jerusalem and the temple led to another layer of tradition as the movement blended their attempts to understand those events in light of what was remembered of sayings and actions of Jesus. The genuine letters of Paul originated in the 50s but the gospels and other books of the New Testament came about after the traumatic destruction of Jerusalem, although some scholars think that parts of the oral tradition began to be recorded before the Roman war.

The point is that ongoing history interacted with memories of those in the community to alter an oral tradition that was not standardized before some of the tradition was recorded into gospels or as it was being recorded into gospels. Getting back to a more accurate view of Jesus as he was actually experienced in his public activity has been approached on the model of the archaeologist who excavates from the outer layers downward to more fundamental layers underneath. More and more it is becoming clear that such excavation operates on the assumption that written documents with single authors or compilers were involved rather than with the more challenging reality of circulating oral traditions that rarely had identifiable authors when recorded.

The Jesus Seminar sought to identify authentic words and actions of Jesus on the assumption of layers of tradition identified with original documents that were edited over decades. They used a well-publicized voting method to achieve consensus among a group of scholars on four levels of reliability. Two of the categories (represented by the colors red and pink) indicated degrees of basic credibility. The third (gray) meant there was no agreement on the items while the fourth category (black) meant those items were inventions by the community and thus completely unreliable as testimony about the historical Jesus.[133] This procedure represents the capstone of the approach that treats sayings and actions of Jesus as deriving from original accounts that can be dug out of surrounding matter added by later generations.

Let's take a look at a case for a different approach to finding credibility in the gospels. We begin by recognizing the impossibility of achieving something called the historical Jesus. No matter how extensive the kernel of truth we find in the gospels, we will not find documentation to satisfy historical standards. We are dealing with the product of human memory and interpretation with every level of the oral and written tradition. In every case, we are dealing with probability and not documentation. Something is more credible as it seems more nearly likely to trace back to the ministry prior to the execution. Supporting testimony for credibility is now being sought in archaeology, anthropology, and social scientific approaches as well as literary and historical analysis of sources—but the fact remains we are always dealing with degrees of probability rather than verifiable knowledge.

This point is often resisted by conservative Christians, but it is finding more expression in study materials for mainline churches, as in the case of a recent book by Ronald J. Allen entitled *The Life of Jesus for Today*. In his preface, Allen acknowledges that

> [W]hen writing about the life of Jesus, we deal less with certainty and more with likelihood and probability . . . . Indeed, I myself wish I could describe Jesus in a way that makes him a mirror of my twenty-first-century values. However, to honor the integrity of Jesus as I think he was in history, I must report what I think was most likely characteristic of him in

his own time. The church then needs to explore ways in which Jesus is authoritative for today.[134]

Rather than look for a historical Jesus, we need to support the movement for Jesus research emphasized by James Charlesworth of Princeton University. The point is to move ever closer to more accurate information about Jesus and his times.[135] What is the goal? It was described by Craig Evans in his recent account of the impact of archaeology on Jesus studies when he talked about the importance of verisimilitude. Evans began by pointing out that archaeology usually provides clarification of the gospels rather than proof because discoveries have a way of bringing to light new ways to understand details in the Bible. Then he explained

> There is also a very important argument in favour of the general reliability of the New Testament Gospels, and that concerns what is called verisimilitude; that is, what the Gospels describe matches the way things were in early first-century Jewish Palestine. The New Testament Gospels and Acts exhibit a great deal of verisimilitude . . . . The verisimilitude of the New Testament Gospels stands in contrast to the lack of verisimilitude in the second-century Gospels and Gospel-like writings, such as the *Gospel of Thomas*, the *Gospel of Peter* and the various Gnostic Gospels.[136]

One way of thinking of verisimilitude is by comparing it to the use of models in scientific efforts such as weather forecasting. Computers try to incorporate as many factors of a weather system or storm as possible. As the model becomes increasingly accurate and inclusive enough, the model allows scientists to mimic what is happening in the actual weather system and then to predict likely future behavior. The model is not the historical event but it becomes more and more useful as it successfully approaches the complexities of the actual weather system. This has resulted in weather forecasts that have become increasingly more reliable.

Modeling approaches can be applied to past cultures. As we learn more about the times in which Jesus lived, it becomes possible to recognize with greater accuracy statements and events in the gospels that credibly reflect those times and therefore can be considered more reliable (although still not completely reliable) even without historical documentation. What is achieved is not historicity but enough credibility—enough verisimilitude to the times—to support reasonable acceptance or rejection of parts of the gospels. This standard will not lead to certainty that Jesus said or did specific things, but it can attest to whether memories of sayings and actions were consistent with what we know of the times and patterns of Jesus that stand out in earlier materials. The more verisimilitude, the greater the likelihood of reliability. Overall verisimilitude indicates general reliability as to what probably happened.

A second application of verisimilitude is to discover more about how oral traditions circulated during and after the time of Jesus and the process by which those traditions became recorded. This involves deeper understanding of the dynamics of the cultures of those times than previously known. Biblical criticism has focused on source criticism, which is to say it has sought original documents and their authors and how those documents were edited, combined, or otherwise arranged into the accounts in the gospels. Form criticism tried to get at how oral traditions were remembered and transmitted but broke the accounts into small elements that were constantly rearranged like bricks that have no independent context of their own until placed in a structure. More recent studies of oral transmission emphasize that whole accounts were kept in memory and transmitted—a process that seems to have also happened in the development of Homer's *Iliad* and *Odyssey*. The traditions were part of performances that would vary in some ways depending on the performer, the group, or the current situation—yet it was expected to maintain an identifiable integrity.[137]

When we come to the composition of the gospels, Mark seems to have been the first to give a distinctive shape to that tradition—a combination of teachings and events along with a more extended and detailed account of the final week in Jerusalem. James Dunn says Mark invented a new genre. His was not "a gospel" but the telling of the "gospel according to Mark", which launched a particular format for recording gospel materials. That format was followed by the compilers of Matthew and Luke, then later by John. When we deal with these four works, we find that each incorporates and interprets oral tradition in ways that show fidelity to a tradition.[138] This fidelity, I am arguing, is a form of verisimilitude. In spite of distinctiveness of each account, they are tied together by clearly recognizable themes and events emerging from a tradition. Later attempts at gospels diverge from the original traditions in ways that clearly distinguish them from the four canonical versions.

Let me also point out that we are talking about the reliability of historical developments not theological interpretations. As we apply the standard of verisimilitude in the next two conversations, we will not be able to avoid some theological issues because they are built into gospel accounts. Affirming the reliability of historical events does not automatically affirm the accuracy of theological interpretations by the generation of Jesus or by subsequent generations as they told, adapted, and recorded oral traditions. For example, historical discussion can look at the event of the resurrection and how it was described but can't substantiate the various interpretations presented in early Christianity. There are people who want to support theological views by trying to prove the historical certainty of the resurrection. Even if demonstration of the resurrection were possible, it would not prove the validity of any theological interpretation.

In a previous conversation we looked at efforts of harmonizers and questers. In this reflection and the next two, I will use verisimilitude as a substitute for harmonization and the search for a historical Jesus in making a case for the basic reliability of four distinctive and frequently conflicting gospels.

CHAPTER TWENTY-TWO

RELIABILITY OF JESUS' BIOGRAPHY

The four canonical gospels follow a biographical structure so that many people tend to assume they are equivalent to biographies of Jesus. All of them are clearly gospels, which means their primary concern is declaring what each considers to be exciting news of Jesus. Just like the variations in headlines and lead stories on all the news channels, each one has its own idea of what was newsy about Jesus. That means each had its "news slant"—its interpretation.

There is much agreement on biographical information in three of the four gospels because two of them, Luke and Matthew, followed the structure of Mark. They even went so far that, in modern terms, they plagiarized and violated copyright by copying wording or changing it only slightly. John follows a different series of events within the same general structure and adds some really interesting characters like Nicodemus, Martha, Mary, and Lazarus.

There is a perennial temptation to beef up the biography of Jesus by harmonizing the structures. Blending the birth narratives of Luke and Matthew, adding the story of boy Jesus in the temple, and then throwing in Nicodemus somewhere early when the others have Jesus exclusively in Galilee fills gaps in the story line nicely. Then, in connection with the final trip to Jerusalem, you throw in a side trip to raise Lazarus. Voila, we have what looks to be a more complete life story.[139]

But harmonization doesn't work. The early church fathers, who decided harmonization would not fly, were not dummies. We have four separate gospels that follow two conflicting biographical sequences. The reason for saying there are two versions is because most scholars throw out the genealogies and birth stories of Matthew and Luke and other childhood accounts that are clearly theological mythology. What remains is Mark's telling of a Galilee ministry that included wandering around all sides of Lake Galilee and culminates in a trip to Jerusalem for Passion Week. John, on the other hand, shows Jesus frequently in Jerusalem and even in Samaria as well as Galilee. Noting the sequence of temple festivals he attends leads to the conclusion his ministry lasted three years.

Another reason harmonization doesn't work is the completely different style of conversation seen in the synoptics and John. The Jesus who tells parables, hits his opponents and disciples with snappy, comeback one-liners, and amazes us with the Sermon on the Mount (or in Luke, the Sermon on the Plain) is in the synoptics. The teaching of Jesus is notable for a claim to authority. Apparently Jesus made a habit of prefacing significant pronouncements with "Amen," a way to tell people to sit up and listen. The prophets had a similar habit by saying "thus says the Lord." No wonder people were amazed at his audacity to suggest authority in his teaching when he clearly had no formal training to give him needed credentials. Also, Jesus was very coy in what he said about himself. Mark has him keeping his self-concept a secret. Matthew and Luke follow that general approach in that Jesus does not make open and obvious claims about himself.

John's presentation of Jesus is remarkably different. His Jesus gives monologues and sometimes dialogues full of theological messages rather than parables and short memorable sayings. Rather than proclaiming the kingdom of God, as in the synoptics, Jesus proclaims himself in relationship with "the Father." This is further emphasized with "I am" statements with implications far stronger than the authority of prophets and official religious leaders suggested by "Amen." Saying "I am" was direct reference to the unspoken name of God himself, YHWH, the great "I AM."

When deciding what statements are more likely to be accurate reflections of Jesus himself, scholars usually throw out almost all of what John reports. The justification is that the theology presented in those statements reflects beliefs of the church that come well after the destruction of Jerusalem in 70 CE. That leaves the sayings in the synoptics as more genuine. But parts of them are usually thrown out as well, such as the apocalyptic sayings made in Jerusalem that many scholars believe were written after the destruction of Jerusalem, which of course was the fulfillment of their prophesy.

A great many scholars have thrown John out altogether when considering historically valid information about Jesus—but that should no longer be the case. As previously discussed, Mark is vague on geographical and time specifics as Jesus wanders around. Matthew and Luke mimic that vagueness until, like Mark, they become very time specific when he arrives in Jerusalem. This is not the case with John. He gives us pretty clear geographical and time information in Galilee, Samaria, and especially around and in Jerusalem itself. John mentions features of the temple such as its pools and several other notable structures associated with the priesthood and Roman officials.

Behold! Archaeology has found and identified many of the features mentioned in John. One of the distinguishing features of Jewish areas is the presence of *miqvu'ot*, the plural of *miqva*, a pool for ritual bathing. These were in private homes and at Qumran. There were *miqvu'ot* at the entrances to the temple so that anyone, male or female, bathed and changed clothes as part of purification upon entry. John spoke of two of those pools.

There are notable ways in which the four gospels agree on key life events. They all have Jesus associating with John the Baptist and being baptized by him. In John he seems to be a disciple who goes out on his own taking some of John's followers as his own disciples. They all show him choosing twelve disciples and teaching them. Details may vary, but Jesus is an exorcist, healer, and worker of wonders that astound. He is also the target for criticism over what he does on the Sabbath and critics discuss killing him in all four accounts. The culmination comes in Jerusalem in connection with Passover. Jesus teaches in the temple that week and says things that disturb temple authorities. The synopitcs have him "cleansing" the temple, which John had him do at the beginning of his ministry. He is betrayed, arrested by temple police, tried by the Romans, brutally beaten, and executed by crucifixion.

How can we possibly see these four accounts as reliable? Obviously their credibility can't be a matter of literal accuracy in every detail.

We do have to make a choice when it comes to the teaching of Jesus. Scholars prefer the synoptic version. Why? Keep in mind that scholars believe Matthew and Luke incorporate a sayings source, the unknown Q, while each has special material of his own. That turns into four witnesses to that style for Jesus. It is not just Mark using that style and then being imitated by Luke and Matthew. Discoveries of fragments of other sources and the *Gospel of Thomas* also seem to support that picture of Jesus. The early church fathers saw the difference and they too preferred the synoptics for history and saw John as "spiritual," that is deep insight into the meaning of historical events. Since John has Jesus presenting theological interpretations of himself, the view of the church fathers was basically accurate.[140]

My contention is that when you consider the items that are common to four gospels, you begin to see verisimilitude. The specifics of John and the vagueness of the synoptics cannot be harmonized into a coordinated account, yet there is verisimilitude in them individually and together. The Jesus movement centered in Jerusalem after the resurrection and there are indications there must have been support in Judea and other Jewish areas outside Galilee. The conflicting views may not be mutually exclusive. They each have the ring of truth about them. We are unable to justify picking one over the other.[141]

Why complain about not being able to actually document which accounts are more accurate? One thing I had to learn over the years is that when I was convinced I was right and my opponents were wrong I had better be prepared for surprises. They usually came as somehow each of us turned out to be partially right even though we both may have been wrong. Discoveries are still being made. Don't be surprised if parts of these gospels we just knew were phony turn out to be accurate after all. At any rate, I am not prepared to give up any of these four precious gems.

CHAPTER TWENTY-THREE

CRUCIFIXION AND RESURRECTION

The four gospels in the New Testament bring their accounts to a climax in Jerusalem at the time of Passover as Jesus is betrayed, arrested, interrogated, brutally scourged, and crucified outside the gates of the city. Then he is buried on Friday. No one visited the grave on the Sabbath. On the morning of the third day, the tomb was found empty. Three of the gospels then relate appearances demonstrating a resurrected Jesus.

Applying historical skepticism to these events is welcomed by Christians as much as having a root canal without anesthesia. The biblical phrase "fear and trembling" comes to mind when applying our parameters to this subject. Nevertheless, this conversation will consider what our principles of historical verification, science, and verisimilitude tell us about these very important events as reported in the Bible.

There are a great many details in the gospel accounts and, not surprisingly, they vary and even contradict. There are five components of the story: betrayal and arrest; trial or interrogation; crucifixion; burial; and resurrection. Let's take them in order.

The gospels agree that Judas betrayed Jesus so that he was arrested during the night with only his disciples as an ineffective force for resisting the temple police and perhaps some Roman soldiers who took Jesus into custody. It has never been clear exactly what Judas betrayed. The story is dramatic as he kisses Jesus to identify him for the police. The most common answer is that Judas betrayed the location Jesus could be found that night. Bart Ehrman in a recent book suspects that Judas let out a secret Jesus had only told his disciples—that he claimed to be the Messiah or coming king. That would explain the placard on the cross naming Jesus king of the Jews as well as the charge of sedition, which would justify crucifixion. Ehrman's explanation is credible but he admits it is only a reasonable hypothesis.[142] On the other hand, this explanation of the crucifixion is not needed if one agrees with N.T. Wright that the gospels are accurate in showing Jesus prompting the charge through symbolic actions in the temple and then confirming it in the interrogations.[143]

There are some who doubt that Judas was a historical character at all, making him a convenient fiction of the early church. That is just one more example of speculation built on the psychology that appeals to supporters of all kinds of conspiracy theories.[144] The original story makes sense in that time and place. There is no good reason, I believe, to doubt it, as Ehrman shows.

Was Jesus tried by the Sanhedrin? A hurried gathering late at night was not the way they were supposed to operate so that many Jewish writers have doubted there was a real trial.[145] Interrogation by officials of the temple and by Roman authorities is very credible, I believe. We must keep in mind that the disciples scattered in terror when Jesus was arrested, so they were not present at the events after the arrest to report the exact sequence or the words that were said. The accounts show Jesus saying little that was direct but enough that could be used for a charge of sedition. On the whole, that picture is credible based on the indirectness shown in the synoptic gospels and on the way power was exercised in that time.

There can be little doubt about the crucifixion itself although the exact way in which Jesus was placed on the cross has been much discussed. John places Mary and a disciple at the scene of the crucifixion, which may have happened. For the most part, it is clear the disciples ran away, so there is no accurate account of what happened that terrible day. The descriptions of scourging and having Jesus carry his cross were typical experiences and probably happened. The events at the cross mirror the description of extreme torture and suffering in Psalm 22 so that many conservative Christians insist on seeing prophecy of the events of the crucifixion. Of course the dividing of clothes and mocking are credible as possible events but cannot be relied on as derived from eyewitness accounts. Some scholars think this is one example of how the early followers of Jesus imported scriptural passages into their accounts as the basis for events and then argued that the events fulfilled the requirements laid out in scripture. That explanation is credible but does not represent documented evidence.

The burial of Jesus has become a really interesting point of debate in recent years. John Dominic Crossan is the best known of those who emphasize that the gospel versions were inconsistent with usual Roman practices. Crucifixion was part of the terrorism used by the Romans to show the consequences of rebellion. Death by crucifixion meant hanging naked in public as you suffocated slowly because the muscles of the diaphragm became too fatigued to allow breathing. Victims were usually left hanging there to be eaten by birds of prey—as was also done in the Southern tradition of lynching black men in order to send a lesson to others who didn't want to be appropriately submissive. When taken down, the bodies were thrown to the dogs or buried in mass graves without the usual dignity Jewish and other cultures would normally show for dead bodies.[146]

The gospels are united in claiming that Jesus was buried in one of the caves near Jerusalem so that followers could come after the Sabbath to perform some of the rites of mourning. The very earliest written account claiming the burial of Jesus was Paul's statement in 1 Corinthians 15:3–8, which was probably written in the mid 50s. Paul insists that what he passed on and what he received are true: that Jesus "died for our sins in accordance with the scriptures," was buried, and rose on the third day "in accordance with the scriptures." This appears to show that very early explanations among the followers of Jesus insisted on burial and rising on the third day. It also shows that scriptural references were used to combine descriptions of events with theological understanding from an early date.

In a recent book, Bart Ehrman has joined those who question whether Jesus was buried, doubting that Romans would have made an exception for him of their usual terroristic use of crucifixion. He points out that the empty tomb was not considered decisive in the earliest versions, as indicated by its omission in Paul's statement and by the hasty ending of Mark with women running from an empty tomb in disbelief. He also concludes that Paul's statement probably reflected an early creedal statement because of its formula-like language. Paul added his own content when he mentioned the appearance to James, others, and Paul himself.[147]

Craig Evans has taken a different approach by relying on archaeology and nonbiblical writings. He maintains that in peacetime Romans were known to show respect for Jewish sensibilities so that burying Jesus was not as improbable as Crossan and Ehrman think. Furthermore, Jewish burial traditions involved showing only minimal regard for executed bodies, which included burial, treatment of the body with spices, and grieving in private rather than in public. He argues that it was also traditional that the authority deciding on execution would be responsible for burial, making it credible that some member of the council would see to the burial in a less respectable site than normal family graves. On the morning after the Sabbath, the women would have known where the tomb was and came to perform their traditional limited grieving rites when they found the body gone.[148]

There can be no doubt that from the beginning the followers of Jesus blended events of the crucifixion and resurrection with theological explanations, because they consistently maintained those events happened in accordance with or as required by scripture as they came to understand it. The question of the burial of Jesus is a matter of probability and can't be proven one way or the other. Evans maintains it is credible and bears the stamp of historical verisimilitude. I think that historical criticism has been shown to err on the side of too much skepticism, so my inclination is to go with the opinion of Evans over Crossan and Ehrman. It seems to me archaeology is showing more reasons to see much of the information in the gospels as reflective of the times of Jesus, so my bias will be to accept items like Roman accommodation to Jewish sensibilities until there is stronger evidence that Jesus was not buried.

The really difficult issue to unravel is the resurrection itself. What happened and how? Unfortunately, we cannot know an answer to that simple question. The best we can do is make guesses, and for the most part, those guesses have been founded on theology rather than history.

Even though the gospels show Jesus talking about his coming resurrection, the followers seemed to have been shocked by the crucifixion and not to have expected a resurrection event. What seems to have definitely happened was that some of the followers experienced what they called appearances of a risen Jesus as Lord. Although there have been many skeptics, the one clear historical foundation for the rise of Christianity seems to be that followers became convinced that Jesus returned from the dead in some fashion, and they continued to experience his presence. Paul mentions an appearance to five hundred people that is mentioned nowhere else in the Bible. There is a wide variety of appearance stories in the gospels, some of them indicating much doubt among some of the followers. Ehrman's hypothesis is that very few people, Peter being one of them, actually experienced the appearances so that many accepted the testimony of those few while lots of others continued to express skepticism.

There can be no doubt that Paul counted himself among those to whom a risen Jesus appeared. [149]

What happened when Jesus appeared to people? Some accounts emphasize a physical body that was definitely not a resuscitated body. People were less familiar with the experience of resuscitated bodies after a near-death experience than we are today, but they knew that Lazarus and Jairus's daughter as well as others who experienced resuscitation in scriptural accounts had later died in the ordinary course of events. They were convinced that what happened with Jesus was different and that it raised him into a spiritual category not experienced before.[150]

In several writings, Bart Ehrman insists the resurrection itself is beyond the scope of historical study because it was a miracle. By definition, miracles violate the natural order, which allows historical explanation.[151] I agree with Ehrman in not trying to use various historical tactics to "explain away" the resurrection as many others have tried to do. However, I don't think that calling it a miracle lets us off the hook because of modern science.

Of course, science is usually the reason given for doubting the resurrection. People do not come back from the dead with greater than normal powers as a normal experience in our universe. But quantum physics shows us that in the world of subatomic particles, there is no predictability or certainty. We can see where particles have been but can't say where they will go or why. Energy seems to go in and out of existence in unpredictable ways. There even seems to be evidence that particles that are separated cause movements of each other without any indication of means of causality that we can detect. Furthermore, we live in a universe that exploded into existence for no reason we can determine. In the first second, it inflated to enormous size at a rate of speed far exceeding the speed of light, which is ordinarily the fastest speed in the universe. Therefore, we must be careful about making assertions based on ordinary scientific expectations when we live in a universe that science shows to violate normal expectations.

My position does not give us a scientific justification for a resurrection event as claimed by the followers of Jesus. What is clear is that they could not understand it in their normal categories of explaining things and neither can we. They could only explain it as a theological event with a historical foundation. Somehow God raised Jesus and then exalted him so that he returned as a living body that was more than physical.

N. T. Wright has given extensive justification for seeing Christian accounts of the resurrection as more concrete and reliable in spite of the apparent differences and contradictions. This leads him to endorse theological explanations of forgiveness of sins as part of the resurrection from the beginning.[152] He might endorse my position that those who had resurrection experiences could not fit them into their ordinary categories for explaining such phenomena just as we can't, but he would phrase it more theologically. For example, he says the resurrected body had a "new physicality" equally at home on earth and in heaven. By that he is referring to a distinction he made between ordinary human space and divine space beyond us and around us rather than a special place. In other words, somehow the resurrected Jesus was part of the time-space universe with its cycle of birth, death, and decay, yet he was also outside it. That indeed is a kind of physicality that goes beyond ordinary categories.[153]

There was an expectation of a general resurrection that could only be expressed in poetic language. Initial explanations of the resurrection saw it as part of that general resurrection. Paul called Jesus the "first fruits" of the dead returning to life. Amy-Jill Levine pointed to the account in Matthew as suggesting that other events around the resurrection show it was a form of the general resurrection.[154] But a cataclysmic end of time did not occur with the resurrection of all those who previously died. Eventually the explanation of the resurrection came to include a postponement of the general resurrection until a Second Coming of Jesus to complete the resurrection experience with a Last Judgment.

We do not need to treat the resurrection as a miracle in order to recognize that historical study can neither confirm nor deny an event that is known primarily as a theological explanation of experiences that were more personal than public. Ehrman calls them visionary experiences and that is the best we can say about them from a historical vantage point. They were things that people believed they saw, whether their experiences corresponded to physical reality or not. They may have been hallucinations but that is speculation and not verifiable knowledge. If a camera had been present when Jesus appeared to Peter, James, Paul, or Mary or anyone else who had a resurrection experience, odds are it would not have recorded exactly what they saw and felt as reality.

The general conclusion I have been pointing to is that biblical accounts of events around the crucifixion and resurrection are generally credible even though highly colored by theological interpretations presented as history. Jesus was probably betrayed by a disciple to temple authorities who interrogated him and sent him to the Romans for execution because of sedition. He was almost certainly tortured and executed in the usual Roman fashion with maximum public humiliation although there probably were not followers who witnessed those events. He may have been buried in less than normal respectable circumstances because of his execution. Discovery of an empty tomb may be a later belief that was not considered essential to the first believers in resurrection or it may have been covered up because of the role of the testimony of women, as suggested by N. T. Wright.[155] What was considered essential was that believers had experiences of a resurrected Jesus who was more than a resuscitated body and who represented an unexpected version of the general resurrection. Their explanations of the resurrection were theological because they had no ordinary way to explain the visionary experiences that were described.

Historical and scientific explanations of ordinary reality have no way of explaining the resurrection other than as very personal experiences of individuals. Yet the theological explanations of the resurrection claim to have a basis in history and to represent a transformation of ordinary experience in a way that can't be detected by current science or history. Paul was sure the resurrection meant victory over death and his message can be heard from pulpits on a regular basis. (1 Corinthians 15:54–56, which draws on Isaiah 25:8 and Hosea 13:14.) N. T. Wright sees the emphasis on the arrival of the kingdom and transformation of the present world as essential from the earliest layers of testimony about the resurrection.[156] Today the experience of the risen Christ is considered essential by many Christians around the world.

It is important to realize that theological interpretations based on faith in personal experiences can't be presented as having the same footing as experiences verified by history or science. The spread of what became Christianity through affirmation of personal experiences of resurrection as a historical experience strongly colored by theological interpretation is undeniable. Here we have a mixture of history and theology that itself becomes significant historically although the actual historicity of the resurrection and its transformation of reality itself is as yet beyond support by science or historical studies.

CHAPTER TWENTY-FOUR

CONSISTENCY, IMAGINATION, AND TRUTH

When I was in college, I read selections from Ralph Waldo Emerson in an American literature textbook, but I don't remember reading his famous essay "Self-Reliance." Everyone who knew me then would have said I didn't need to read Emerson to learn about being an individualist and breaking away from many kinds of conformity. At some point I heard about the famous quotation from Emerson's essay: "A foolish consistency is the hobgoblin of little minds."[157] Emerson linked too much consistency with lack of individuality. On that point I definitely fell short and so did a lot of the better students I knew in college and graduate school because rigid insistence on consistency is very often caused by an emphasis on always being right. When you are right, that means just about everyone else is wrong. This was definitely a fault of mine.

Having to be right brings a rigidity to one's thinking and approach to life. People who think differently, have different moral standards, or more flexible attitudes toward various religious beliefs and the Bible must be set straight because not being right can ruin a life and send one to hell. At least that was the religious version of consistency I learned from church. There are also many other forms of inflexible consistency to be avoided.

Previous conversations in this collection have built on historical criticism, especially based on literature about the historical Jesus. I have emphasized that beliefs about Jesus need to be grounded in historical awareness rather than follow all sorts of theological ideals not based on historical realities. The remaining conversations in this collection will turn away from the historical Jesus to themes in the Old Testament and to some that unite both testaments. History and science will continue to be essential parameters, but other approaches to the Bible also need to be appreciated.

As we turn to the remaining topics, it is important to understand that too much consistency and insistence on always being right must be avoided. Those who resist historical criticism and scientific evidence of evolution are examples of rigid insistence on literal interpretation of the Bible. It would also be too rigid to insist on history and science as the only values to use in studying the Bible. Harmonization and allegory should be avoided; but there are other approaches, many of them building on different aspects of the Christian tradition such as mysticism, which offer very imaginative interpretations that are valid and meaningful. History and science are not the only avenues to truth.

I have made a point of avoiding theology. Seeking a more historical picture of Jesus often leads away from traditional theological perspectives, so it is easy to give the impression that reliance on history or science means opposition to theology. Yet I do not want to suggest that theology is something that is always negative.

A very refreshing perspective on theology is presented by Colin Harris in an article entitled "Our Need to Be Right Undercuts Theological Process."[158] Theology, he reminds us, is the organized study of God, like other uses of "ology" in sciences like biology. The meaning of science in this case is systematic study using disciplined procedures that combine reason, faith, and history—as opposed to theology as specific answers. Harris's point is to pay attention to the discipline and flexibility of the process rather than getting too enamored of specific theological concepts. This approach leads to flexibility and openness to discoveries as opposed to automatic rejection of new ideas. In another context, Harris points to an important connection between theology and history: "without the history, the narrative becomes fiction and fantasy; and without the theology, it becomes dead fact unrelated to the larger scope of life."[159]

Consistency can sometimes be a value that is pushed by history and theology. I think that one of the truly interesting aspects of the Old Testament is how often there appears to be intentional use of inconsistency. Many people who want to discredit the Bible think that having entirely different creation accounts back-to-back in Genesis robs the Bible of credibility. In my opinion, this view commits the historical sin of anachronism because it is imposing modern ideas about consistency on earlier times.

Embracing contradictions is not only seen in Genesis but in numerous other places as those responsible for collecting and editing scripture decided to preserve strands of tradition that presented differing points of view. In Exodus, for example, the story of escaping Egypt by miraculously crossing a body of water that closes to drown the pursuers (14:1–31) is followed by the Song of Moses (15:1–19), which evidently was a ritual retelling the Exodus with differences in some of the details of the historical account preceding the song. The same thing happens in the book of Judges as there is a story of the woman Jael killing an enemy while he slept (4:17–22) that is followed by the Song of Deborah (5:24–27) telling the story as if Jael killed him when he was awake and looking at her. Still one more example would be how the prophet Nathan announced a new covenant to preserve David's dynasty (2 Samuel 7:4–17) as he was refused permission to build a temple. Yet we also read of Nathan denouncing flagrant adultery (2 Samuel 12: 7–15), which David tried to cover up by arranging to have the husband killed in battle.

Critics and those dedicated to literal interpretations are missing the extent to which the scribes responsible for the Old Testament thought consistency was not all that important.

A second point to keep in mind as we turn to the Old Testament is the role imagination plays when interpreting the Bible. Sometimes imagination leads to theology; but there are also uses of imagination that correct old theological understandings.

The early interpretations of the resurrection point to the role of imagination. The earliest written testimony about the resurrection is Paul's statement in 2 Corinthians 15:3–5 that Jesus died for sin and rose from the dead according to scripture. This is historical evidence within twenty years of the crucifixion that members of the early Jesus movement believed Jesus was resurrected. But it also shows the role of imagination in trying to understand what happened. Jesus was identified with Jewish expectations of a Messiah, but those hopes pointed to a victorious king who would restore the independence of Israel based on the rule of God. There had been no anticipation of a dying Messiah or that he played a role in redeeming people from sin. A theological view based on imaginative reinterpretation of the Old Testament had taken place fairly soon after the resurrection.

Luke's story of the travelers to Emmaus gives a hint as to how this early reinterpretation of scripture came about (Luke 24:13–25). In the story two travelers are disillusioned by the unexpected execution of Jesus. A mysterious fellow traveler challenges their depression by "opening the scriptures" to them to show that they really did point to a dying messiah. As they sat down to eat, the travelers suddenly became aware that it was the risen Jesus himself who had shown them true insight into recent events.

I do not think the Emmaus story is an accurate historical account. It is a beautiful story with the clarity and force of a parable. To me it illustrates the mindset of the followers after the execution as they went from a sense of utter defeat to new confidence in resurrection. They were still part of the Jewish community of belief, so understanding what happened with Jesus in terms of scripture was important to them. As they came to new and very imaginative insights, they saw it as following the leadership of Jesus himself in reaching true understanding of scripture as a key to understanding the cross and resurrection.

Aspects of traditional theology have been challenged by Marcus Borg using a combination of historical criticism and metaphorical interpretations.[160] For example, he is less interested in analyzing the many variations in the resurrection accounts in the gospels and more concerned to affirm the symbolic messages he finds behind those stories, messages that he believes bring out real truth more than determining the exact chain of historical events.[161] In his book, *Speaking Christian*, he applies this combination of history and metaphor to reinterpret traditional language and beliefs of Christianity.[162] In doing so, he is arguing against an emphasis on heaven and sin in order to show that Christianity is more interested in effective living in this world. His application of imagination in combination with history has been extremely influential with a growing number of mainstream believers who question many traditional theological beliefs.

Another example of contemporary use of imagination is the Franciscan priest Richard Rohr. He appeals to a large number of people by combining the Christian mystical tradition with psychology that speaks to personal struggles of contemporary life. In the popular *Falling Upward*, he describes the human dilemma in terms of learning how to live in the two halves of life, each of which has particular challenges.[163] His central message is the importance of understanding and achieving success in the second half of life, a time of fulfillment and growing maturity. Rohr is well versed in historical criticism, but that is not his focus in using scripture. The death and resurrection of Jesus are used as a paradigm for understanding the key issues in life. Appealing to the kind of psychology found in Erich Fromm and Scott Peck,[164] Rohr speaks of the discipline of dealing with failure (crucifixion) in order to reach new life (resurrection) within this world rather than in the next world.

A final example of the legitimate use of imagination is *Learning to Walk in the Dark* by Barbara Brown Taylor. The book is an extended metaphor of day versus night that turns around many normal expectations. Solar Christianity, walking in the daylight with the security and certainty it brings of seeing things in the world as they really are, is compared to the kind of Christianity that involves navigating without clearly visible markings. Walking in the dark means facing things that are scary, including a sense of the absence of God, yet learning to be spiritually confident. She points to the many instances in Old and New Testaments when darkness is bad, offering a counter opinion that reevaluates the meaning of darkness.[165]

Finally, Christians invariably read the Old Testament through New Testament eyes, as in the case of finding scriptural justification for a dying Messiah who brings remission of sin. This tendency is inescapable because, as Bernhard Anderson observed, "the Christian community has appropriated the whole body of Jewish scriptures." In this way, the identity of Israel was incorporated into Christian identity.[166]

It will be important to honor the integrity of the Jewish experience in the Old Testament and to be on guard against imposing standards of later times. But it will be impossible to avoid recognizing cultural changes brought by Christianity and later experiences of Western culture. For example, the relationship of parent and child and of wife to husband have shifted away from the demand for subservience and obedience to the male head of the home. My view is that we should not judge outdated standards of male dominance in an earlier time or try to use the Bible to perpetuate clearly outmoded values in our time.

Our aim will be to continue to rely on history and science while balancing them with appropriate use of imagination and theology. Above all, we need to avoid falling into the trap of rigid consistency that leads to judgment rather than appreciation of the full riches of the entire Bible.

Chapter Twenty-Five

Let There Be Light

In childhood I heard of Humpty Dumpty through nursery rhymes and picture books. It was through picture books that I learned Humpty Dumpty was an egg. But why couldn't he be fixed? People and things are broken all the time and they get fixed.

Later in school, I learned about entropy as part of the second law of thermodynamics. It seems the universe is in the process of running down. Things irresistibly go from order to disorder or chaos. That is why young people turn into old people and a broken egg can't be reassembled into a whole egg again.

But then a history professor named David Christian turns everything on its head as he introduces groups to something he calls Big History. His video explanation begins by showing an uncooked scrambled egg in a bowl. Before our eyes, the egg unscrambles itself, gravitates upward into a broken eggshell that closes neatly and seamlessly, returning to its original unbroken condition. He does this through the magic of cameras and their ability to show events in reverse motion. What point is he making?[167]

Evolution of the universe violated the rule of going from order to chaos. Science tells us there was a sudden explosion about 13.8 billion years ago for no reason we have yet determined. This event brought into existence every-thing in our universe all at once and the force of the explosion set everything in motion flying apart from everything else. Within an infinitesimal fraction of a second after the explosion, the universe appears to have inflated for a short period at a rate of speed far surpassing the speed of light, ordinarily the fastest thing in our universe.

This is only the beginning of the story. What came into existence was chaos in motion—ultimate disorder. What happened over the next several billions of years was the evolution of patterns of order so that eventually stars formed and planetary systems developed around them. And these stars developed into endless numbers of galaxies. In short, our universe began as the most gigantic superheated mush imaginable and sorted itself into patterns of order that led to life on our planet and the emergence of the human species to the point of being able to figure out this amazing story.

Unfortunately Americans have tried very hard to resist a great many implications of modern science, although we want to enjoy the technologies it makes possible. Increasingly those technologies are being made elsewhere because we don't want to take the difficult science courses with their weird ways of undermining our traditional value systems. Polls have shown that even people who are well educated in science still express a preference for so-called creationist views of how the universe began.[168] It is not religion itself that is the problem, but efforts to hold onto biblical mythology as science and history. However, this same public is increasingly ignorant of what is really in the Bible, so they have anecdotal awareness of the Genesis story but haven't really studied it closely.

Let's take a look at what Genesis actually says, then at the picture given by science, and finally at a historical narrative incorporating the Big Bang into World History, something known as Big History.

When we think of the Genesis story, the traditional idea is that nothing at all existed until God spoke to bring everything into being. This rests on outdated translations. Here is the updated New Revised Standard Version translation:

> In the beginning when God created the heavens and the earth, the earth was a formless void and darkness covered the face of the deep, while a wind from God swept over the face of the waters. Then God said, "Let there be light"; and there was light. And God saw that the light was good; and God separated the light from the darkness. God called the light Day, and the darkness he called Night. And there was evening and there was morning, the first day. (1:1–5)[169]

The first point to notice is the "when" that should have been in the older versions. The story described God as working with a formless pre-existing something, which is consistent with other Near Eastern mythologies that are kin to early Israelite beliefs. God's first creative act was to speak light into existence, a full three days before creating the sun and moon. Even without those celestial lights, God divided day from night and a first day passed. Notice the phrasing "there was evening and there was morning" signaling that days begin and end with evening as is the habit for Jews and Muslims.

There is poetic beauty and majesty to this description of creation as order is imposed on chaos by God's verbal commands. With each creation, God affirms it as good. The presence and authority of God stand behind the goodness of this creation, giving it meaning as well as existence.

There is an interesting parallel to the Genesis account found in *The First Three Minutes* by the Nobel laureate physicist Steven Weinberg.

> In the beginning there was an explosion. Not an explosion like those familiar on earth, starting from a definite center and spreading out to engulf more and more of the circumambient air, but an explosion which occurred simultaneously everywhere, filling all space from the beginning, with every particle of matter rushing apart from every other particle.[170]

The universe was filled at that time with superheated particles of the kind studied by quantum physics. His account continues.

> Finally, the universe was filled with light. This does not have to be treated separately from the particles—the quantum theory tells us that light consists of particles of zero mass and zero electrical charge known as photons.[171]

Weinberg can describe the physical processes taking place for the first three minutes after the Big Bang because science is able to deduce previous conditions from present ones all the way back that far in time. This is an incredible claim. Weinberg's description is awe-inspiring. What does he think of it? At the end of the book there is an epilogue in which he puts science aside to express a personal opinion.

It is almost irresistible for humans to believe that we have some special relation to the universe, that human life is not just a more-or-less farcical outcome of a chain of accidents reaching back to the first three minutes, but that we were somehow built in from the beginning . . . . It is very hard to realize that this is all just a tiny part of an overwhelmingly hostile universe. It is even harder to realize that this present universe has evolved from an unspeakably unfamiliar early condition, and faces a future extinction of endless cold or intolerable heat. The more the universe seems comprehensible, the more it also seems pointless.[172]

There are odd parallels and oppositions between Weinberg and Genesis. The Big Bang generates chaos at enormous speed and unimaginably hot temperatures, then, over billions of years, evolves toward order. The God of Genesis starts with chaos of earth and water and speaks it into order, beginning with the creation of light as his first effort. Weinberg's account sees nuclear particles as the first creation, among them photons, which fill the universe with light. Indeed, the creation of light preceded the evolution of any suns. Also, it seems the development of stars came billions of years after the explosion led to large distances of darkness in the universe so that the process involved the separating of day and night long after the creation of light itself. It is very interesting to see how a completely poetic vision anticipated some of the unusual aspects of the evolution of the universe.

The most significant difference in these accounts, in my opinion, is the presence of a creative force with personality who intends and does make a universe that is "good." This creative God stands behind the work, thereby giving purpose and meaning to everything. Weinberg presents a description of creation at work in an environment that is overwhelmingly hostile, even as order and life develop. Scientifically the whole process can be explained, but there is no indication that meaning or purpose is present in the universe. Why did Weinberg conclude the whole process is pointless? Because human beings look for purpose and meaning. Weinberg ventured an opinion at the end because his readers would naturally be wondering: "Shouldn't there be a point to all this?"

The Genesis story is mythology, not history or science. It is the good kind of mythology because, in the absence of reliable scientific or historical knowledge, it is a poetic story that expresses a majestic view of creation that is not really far off the mark; and it sees into deeper truth than science by finding meaning, purpose, and the goodness of creation. If we can't use Genesis as a substitute for science or history, what alternatives do we have for seeking meaning in the world that science presents to us?

My answer is that we usually turn to history as well as religion. In fact there are many different ways in which the Old Testament shows the ancient Israelites expressing meaning as a religious community by recounting histories as a form of worship. Human beings have always turned to stories of one kind or another to express meaning and identity as groups or individuals. Mythologies are poetic recreations that sound historical but usually were clearly recognized as not reflecting actual events. Historical accounts in the form of rituals and psalms as well as narrative throughout the Old Testament embodied the belief that God was experienced through the history of the ancient Israelites. An important example would be the Exodus account that was seen as the founding of the people of Israel and continues to be celebrated annually at Passover with family involvement in telling the story.

An interesting twist to usual assumptions about biblical views of creation is the argument that ancient Israelite beliefs about creation, although influenced by the mythological views of the Mesopotamian and Egyptian cultures around them, developed first from belief in the creation of the people of Israel. This view sees the experience of creation of a people and simultaneous salvation of that people through the Exodus events as prior to the development of the idea of universal creation seen in Genesis. Support for this view is in the hymns found in Psalms 100, 111, and 114, which see God first of all as creator and savior of Israel and seem to precede the awareness of God as creator of the world and ruler of history found in other psalms and other biblical passages as well as in Genesis.[173]

As a high school student, I had to learn Georgia history and American history. One justification was to be a better citizen by understanding the traditions of my state and nation. Often a clear objective of the courses was to teach patriotism and support of the United States Constitution in a period after World War II, when our country was in the grip of many fears of pervasive communist conspiracies against our way of life. This was not a religious interpretation, but a sense of identity as a loyal Southerner and patriotic American were considered important values in those days.

One of the products of the Civil Rights Movement of the 1960s was Black History Month. I remember when college professors scoffed at the wasted time digging into a nonexistent field. Behold, a significant heritage was dis-covered along with the shameful methods used to deny the humanity and achievements of African Americans in almost every conceivable way. Not long afterward, other groups began to want their story told—women, Native Amer-icans, the disabled, and recently the gay movement. People find meaning in the history of important groups with which they identify.

In my opinion, one of the most significant developments in professional history in my lifetime was the genuinely international framework for World History first presented by William H. McNeill in *The Rise of the West: A History of the Human Community*. [174] The McNeill paradigm has become the approach used in most college World History texts these days. In the college where I teach, students tell me that World History is what they find most interesting. This is partly true because these students increasingly represent international birth places and can see their native land reflected in a genuinely international perspective. At last count, Georgia Gwinnett College had students from ninety-one countries in the world. Students from almost every continent are routinely in my classes.

The approach to World History is in the process of changing again. The new and rapidly emerging model is called Big History, which was named by David Christian.[175]

Professional history has traditionally distinguished between prehistory, before writing, and real history, since the emergence of written documents. There are many problems with that approach. Writing in early civilizations was the product and most often the propaganda tool of the ruling elite, which was served by a very small literate elite. The concerns of people at large and many of the concerns of society outside the ambitions of the ruling groups were not considered proper material for history. Archaeology and many social sciences have expanded knowledge far beyond the limits of writing, but we lack the individual stories that we like to associate with history. Furthermore, as we saw in Weinberg's book, science has pushed our knowledge of physical processes in the universe 13.8 billion years back to the Big Bang.

Christian came up with the idea of merging scientific knowledge with the McNeill approach to World History in a grand historical narrative that leads to life on our planet and the human species with its many cultures.[176] Science itself doesn't provide a narrative through which people seek meaning, as we saw in Weinberg. But history is storytelling that seeks understanding. It of course will not endorse an openly religious interpretation such as the one in Genesis. Rather, Big History is World History that embraces all cultures and their searching for meaning. It also presents the story of a developing universe and of life on our planet on a bigger canvas leading to meanings at a higher level than seen in ordinary myopic historical, philosophical, and religious approaches. The newer insights are based on combinations of multiple sciences and social sciences that bring out the importance of environmental issues that are not centered on our species as are traditional historical and religious views.

If you haven't heard of Big History yet, get ready. It's coming. Already high school students are responding to online resources through a Big History Project funded by Bill Gates.[177] Dominican University near San Francisco pioneered its use in college education and found students so receptive that it is now a requirement for all freshmen as a foundation for their higher education. Their experience points to the value of this approach for promoting student engagement and for getting faculty across the university involved in unifying science and liberal arts disciplines.[178] This success is possible because Big History puts science into a story of the universe in a way that allows students to learn basics of science without getting lost in all the technicalities of the individual sciences. It encourages students to understand the global dimensions of contemporary issues. It also brings urgent awareness of issues not often seen in usual narrative histories, such as environmental sustainability and the challenge of the pace of change in an increasingly global society.

It should be noted that reliance on evolution as established science can stir up religious concerns among students, especially since there has been a bias against evolution in local educational systems in many places in our country. It should also be noted that questions about religion and the meaning of life are usually generated when students internalize the liberal arts even without emphasis on evolution. Nevertheless, the impact of Big History on religious concerns of students has been recognized as an issue worthy of special handling. Harlan Stelmach of Dominican University pointed to the need to recognize and respect the religious beliefs that students bring with them. Teachers need to address religious issues directly by being open with their own religious suppositions and encouraging students to explore their own values through discussions in which the teacher does not function as the representative of the official answer. He also encourages recognition of strains of scientific research that suggest that religion is "hardwired" into human beings and will not go away.[179]

In my opinion, Big History will soon complement the usual survey approaches to history seen in high schools and universities. It may replace Western Civilization courses but not national histories or World History as it becomes recognized as the best introduction to both science and a universal approach to history that sets the context for a more contemporary understanding of pressing issues that go beyond ordinary daily political experience. As this happens, more conservative and religiously based views, such as those in Islam or among evangelical Christians that cling to Genesis as history, will be challenged to modify old beliefs. And of course educational and political views in our country will be challenged to be sensitive to concerns of the many ethnic and religious views that are increasing in our pluralistic society that is mirroring the ethnic diversity of the entire globe.

Genesis tells a story of a powerful, creating God. Science and history have not detected such a God, but the story they tell does not exclude that possibility or an underlying purpose behind the universe. While history and science displace religion, mythology, poetry, and literature at one level of knowledge, they do not replace the importance to human beings of the kind of knowledge seen in the poetic vision in Genesis or in the search for deeper meaning in the histories of human communities. Many religious views are founded on experiences of revelation that cannot be verified or disproved by science or historical approaches. Advocates of religious views, as well as those who apply science and historical methods, must always recognize they all represent cultural expressions that inevitably become dated and will be replaced by later discoveries and interpretations. Humility and tolerance is required by all points of view in the face of ongoing change and mutation that is part of life in this universe.

I know people who want to insist the Genesis story is true, by which they mean it is literal truth as science and history. That is not the kind of truth to be found in Genesis. The real question is whether Genesis is correct in describing a creative force responsible for our universe, sustaining it, giving it meaning, and assuring that it is good. This is a matter of personal conviction based on a concept of reality that goes beyond the limits of current knowledge. We can be sure there will be more discoveries showing the failings of current understanding and dating all that we now accept. Still, my answer to the question of the essential truth of Genesis, in concert with the entire history of the Judeo-Christian tradition, is a resounding Yes.

Chapter Twenty-Six

The Story of Everyone and No One

The job of a parent is not just to care for a child but to watch and assist as it crosses one threshold after another on the way to maturity. There are few things sadder than a parent who tries to keep a child from growing into independence or a child so dominated by overbearing parents that the assertion of independence leads to emotional incapacity. In the give and take involved in growing toward independence, many children develop scars and internal battles that haunt the remainder of their lives.

The joy of birth leads to heavy parental responsibilities for feeding and caring for the round-the-clock needs of a totally dependent being. There is relief when the first words and steps come, but these are the first signs of budding independence. Judgment does not come with communication and mobility, so parents have to be vigilant and forever giving commands that have to be obeyed to protect the child from harm. As the drive for independence increases, there can often be a struggle for power as children resist the quick obedience that parents think is necessary. Willfulness soon leads to growing signs of rebellion against authority that seems too controlling to them.

As adults, we see things children don't perceive accurately and don't understand when they do perceive them. A fifteen-year-old mother can see the many ways in which her understanding of reality surpasses that of her growing infant. This experience can sometimes lead young people carrying adult responsibilities to understand the sense of responsibility and concern that led to behaviors they had recently found so objectionable in their own parents. With the awareness of maturity comes a sort of God's point of view in trying to care for a creature that doesn't have the benefit of that higher-level point of view.

Built into all of us, even at the height of adult independence and through the greatest extent of old age, is the desire to have the companionship and guidance of a parent who cares for us and always has that higher-level point of view, someone whose judgment we feel is often more reliable than our own even when we resist it. Often the last words of many dying people of all ages are a call for their mother.

I remember the progression of little rebellions among my children. Along with increasing willfulness comes the realization of nakedness as they must be alone to change clothes or use the bathroom. This is a notable sign of increasing sense of individuality that parents are expected to honor.

These universal experiences as we grow through infancy and as we see our infants repeating the same progression is part of the appeal of the Garden of Eden story (Genesis 2:4–3:24). There has always been a tendency to see this as the early history of humanity, full of significance for every human being that followed. That is in fact what this truly represents, but not as the actual history of two specific people who were the very first human creatures. Douglas Knight and Amy-Jill Levine refer to this account as describing a "primordial period, when life as we know it is still in the process of being established," and "is suspended in time or before time."[180] This is indicated by the name of the first human, Adam, a play on words for the earth, so that Amy-Jill Levine in a lecture in her Great Courses series, says that Adam should be translated as "earthling from the dust of the earth."[181]

Many Christians become offended when it is said the Bible contains mythology. There is no reason for taking offense. The Bible is filled with poetry. The first eleven chapters are clearly poetic in nature, from the majestic and beautiful description of chaos being turned into an ordered universe through God's spoken words in the course of seven days to the poetic story of the early days of human creatures in an idyllic garden.

The Garden of Eden story is a deeply significant picture of God as cosmic parent who can walk in the garden enjoying the evening and set childish humans in an environment that has few dangers but clear rules about some things to avoid. There are two trees that are out of bounds, but God does not warn them about the snake with the unusual ability to speak.

The two humans are clearly on a childish level. The environment is friendly and they are cared for. They have little self-awareness. Their bodies function naturally as does that of any other animal and they accept the way things are. Then in a willful act, they taste of one of the forbidden trees and suddenly develop new awareness. They have crossed a threshold. They are aware of nakedness even though nothing about their natural bodies has changed, so they hide from God out of fear and embarrassment. Needless to say, God recognized the change immediately.

This is described as realizing the difference between good and evil. There is a mental change and a transformation of the entire nature of the relationship of humans with God and the natural world. Their willfulness was a form of revolt against the perpetual care of God, so they are expelled from the garden and face the many risks that come with independence. This means that God no longer walks and talks to them as before. The closeness of the parental relationship has departed along with the perpetual childhood before their awakening.

Most Christians grow up hearing this story told with a negative emphasis. This is how sin entered the world through human rebellion. All kinds of theological misdirection has taken place, looking for the aspects of humanity to blame for this downfall. This approach has turned the story into a fairy tale built around villains and the beginning of wickedness.

The continuing appeal of the story is built around its essential truth at a deeper level than mere history. First of all, this is a poetic telling from the human perspective of the transition in evolution from being just another living creature to becoming that unique thing we know as a human being. There is an awareness of being separate. There is awareness of a being and point of view above the level of creatures. With the transition came a greater self-awareness, an assertion of independence, a redefined relationship with God, and also incredible hardships in living out the newfound independence. This story happened for a first time to someone, but it also happened multiple times as a species made a leap of awareness. This story can only be told in poetic symbols that suggest the outline of events but carry the emotional depth and spiritual yearning essential to the experience. It is mythology because it is history that is truer in essence than would be a prose account that described these events scientifically and historically from an external and superficial point of view.

A second reason for the continuing appeal of the story is that we see it repeated as we watch our children grow. This point of view should lead to a more generous interpretation than is often found in theology. The parent who resents the growing independence of the child resorts to domination, trying to keep the young human always dependent. This is the version of the story with a God who resents the independence of the creatures and is always trying to reassert control and domination through punishment and wrath. Thankfully, this is not generally the way the story recurs generation after generation. The parent encourages and even facilitates the budding independence of the young person, bearing with the years of obtuse teenage rebellion, so that parent and child enjoy an enduringly positive, loving, and even nonjudgmental companionship as the child becomes an adult with their own children.

The overall point I am making is that there is historical verisimilitude in this story but not accurate history. It suggests an evolutionary jump. It also tells of the cultural transition from the hunter-gatherer lifestyle of the species that lasted approximately 180,000 years to the agricultural lifestyle, which made civilizations possible.

There is deep truth in seeing the loss of paradise in that transition. Societies have been exploitative from the beginning, with an upper crust of soldiers supporting religious and political leaders who find ways to take the agricultural production of approximately 90 percent of the population to build the cities and monuments and fight the incessant wars of the upper 10 percent. The upper crusts in those early societies seem to always function in the name of various gods. Society brought a transformation from the God of the garden to people being dominated by human substitutes for God through whom they were to know what God wanted, which served the interests of those at the top of society.[182]

There appears to have been continuing development of human awareness over the five thousand years since human civilizations emerged. Today many people see the vast period of hunter-gatherer lifestyle and early civilizations as the childhood of a species that is now mature or just coming into real maturity. Many people think that losing the awareness of God is a mark of that maturity. It is true we live in a society that is increasingly secular although there continue to be strong minority voices.

I agree with the general view that our species is maturing in a great many aspects. We think we live in a prose world of science, history, philosophy, medicine, and psychology. But movies still draw crowds when they appeal to fears of the supernatural in various forms. Many voices are saying that religion is something to be left behind with the terrors of childhood fears of monsters.

No matter how mature people may feel we are becoming, we still find the universe and this small part of it that we inhabit beyond our comprehension. Life is more mystery than knowledge still. There is something built into the human brain, I believe, that leads us to seek meaning in the world around us. That inner something wants more than explanation—it wants relationship, which is best modeled on the relationship of parent and child. We pray, read the Bible, sing hymns, perform rituals, and meditate. These are spiritual disciplines that shape lives and bring a sense of relationship with God. There is no sign of an evolutionary change eliminating this particular something within us.

Vocal atheists say God is mere projection of our desire for a cosmic parent. That could be true. Thus far no method of human knowledge has been able to prove or disprove the existence of God. If God is mere projection, it is because of this something within the human brain that needs the projection. If we did in fact learn that our brains are misdirected in wanting a God that does not exist, that knowledge would undermine a basic desire of the species.

My attitude is that it is not worthwhile to worry about whether there is or is not a God. It is part of humanity to need that relationship, I believe. If that need is based on something that doesn't exist, if people were forced to live without God, then life would be joyless. Enjoyment of life at its best means living in accordance with that something deep within us as human beings. Even if I knew for sure God did not exist, I would continue to live as if God did exist.

So let's not waste our time worrying about something completely out of our control such as the existence or nonexistence of God. Let's focus on what little we can know of that God. The Bible recounts the experience of people seeking relationship, much of it from a less mature period in human development that does not reflect the kind of relationship I want to see emphasized today.

We are changing and it is natural that our relationship to the cosmic parent would change. Parents of humans make adjustments in their parenting patterns as a natural part of life. Don't you think God would know that the relationship with our species has to change as we are allowed to change? Let's work on finding and living to the fullest the positive aspects of that change.

Chapter Twenty-Seven

The Origin of Israel

Have you ever wondered about the difference between an Israelite and a Jew? If I asked students in my World History classes about the difference, there would be a lot of puzzled looks. Some of those raised in Christian religious traditions would likely respond that Israelites were the ancient name of the Jews. Others might say they were the people who had a covenant with God.

Many people are not aware that Samaritans, who still live in the state of Israel and have their own version of the Torah, are Israelites but not Jews.[183] This makes more sense when one realizes that Jews derive from the land of Judah, just a part of ancient Israel, and that rivalry within the tribes of Israel stands out in the historical sections of the Old Testament.

Technically, an Israelite is one who is descended from Israel, the name God gave Jacob in Genesis 35:10. There were twelve males and one female born to Jacob by four wives. The Bible ignores the daughter, so an Israelite is someone born through the sons of Jacob. But birth is not everything because people can be converted to Judaism today by embracing covenantal features of Jewish religion. The notion of a covenant with God is a central feature of Jewish history and of the Old and New Testaments. Christians also embraced covenantal features of Israelite religion and claim they succeeded the Jews as the true Israel, the bearers of the covenant.

When you look at the development of the covenant people in the Old Testament, you see twists and turns, more like an old-fashioned road up a mountain than a straight highway. First there is the call and promise to Abram who is told to leave his father's country and go to a new land where he will become a nation (Genesis 12:1–3). An interesting detail is that the command comes as Abram is traveling with his father, who had already left Ur but had stopped in an area that today is in Turkey (11:31–32). Abram got up and went to Shechem, where God made a promise to give this land to Abram's descendants (12:7). Abram kept wandering and went to Egypt because of a drought. When he returned to Canaan, he separated from his nephew Lot and remained in Canaan. At this point, near Bethel where he had previously constructed an altar, God promised again that he would have numerous descendants who would inhabit that land (13:14–17). As he continued to wander, he began to doubt the promise since his wife continued to be childless. God reassures him in a vision that repeats the promise (15:1–21). Abram then has a son by a slave and worries again about the promise, so God renews the covenant, assuring him the slave will not bear the people that are promised, changing his name to Abraham, and inaugurating circumcision as a sign of the covenant (16:1–15, 17:1–27). Still Sarah has no children, so in Genesis 18, the promise is repeated again as God appeared in the form of three travelers. This is when Sarah laughed and God seemed to take offense, but in chapter 21 we learn that Sarah finally conceived and had Isaac.

The covenant was repeated to Abram/Abraham four times yet no son by Sarah appeared for apparently decades as Sarah passed menopause. Circumcision became a mark of the promise and applied to all males in Abraham's household, even slaves; but the promise only applied to male heirs through Sarah and not to Ishmael, the son of a slave. When Sarah had Isaac, she became jealous of the older child and had Abraham throw mother and child out.

Isaac carried the promise and passed it to part of his male line. He had twin sons and the promise went through the younger son, Jacob, not the older Essau, who was tricked out of his posterity. Essau then is recognized as the ancestor of Edomites who were neighbors and opponents of Israelites in Canaan. Jacob at one point struggles with God all night and is renamed Israel (35:9–15). That is how the descendants of Jacob became the people of Israel, but the covenant was not repeated in the renaming. Even so, the covenant with Abraham becomes interpreted as a covenant with the people of Israel.

Jacob's descendants wound up in Egypt for several hundred years and began to be treated as slaves, doing forced labor on building projects. The people of Israel were delivered from Egyptian bondage by Moses, an Israelite brought up at the court of Pharaoh who spent much of his adult life on the run for murder but who returned and hooked up with a brother and sister he had not grown up with in order to lead the Israelites to the land promised to Abraham. In an event celebrated as the Exodus, Moses leads the people across a body of water that closes and drowns the pursuing army in order to escape to the desert of the Sinai Peninsula. Somewhere in Sinai the people encountered God on a mountain and a new covenant was made. This was a covenant to obey commands, especially ten specific commandments handed verbally from God with Moses as an intermediary.

The covenant with Abraham meant that the land of Canaan was the destiny of Abraham's descendants. The covenant through Moses brought requirements to be kept and punishment was to be expected if the people didn't follow all the commandments to the extent that suited God. The new covenant was far more difficult than the first one but it promised success and prosperity as long as the people honored it. Of course, anytime something went wrong, such as when Joshua lost a battle at Ai, it meant someone among the Israelites had done something to displease God, no matter how small an offense it may have been.

When the twelve tribes of Israelites occupied the land of Canaan, they had no central government. According to the book of Judges, God allowed Canaanite peoples to continue as occupants of Israel because the Israelites broke the covenant (Judges 2:20–23). After the death of Joshua, God was their ruler and raised up judges when the people were challenged by various opponents. Some of the judges seemed to try to establish a monarchy but failed.

In Samuel there are opposing versions of how a monarchy came about, following the habit of inconsistency that has already been noted for the Old Testament. In both stories, Samuel anointed Saul king after trying to resist the people's request. The difference was that in one account God picked Saul and commanded Samuel to go anoint him (1 Samuel 9:15–17) and in a second version God selected Saul through a public process of casting lots (2 Samuel 19:20–21). However it happened, we are told that a big strapping man named Saul was the king and that he was a failure. God then had Samuel anoint a rival who eventually became King David. In spite of the blemishes on David's record, the book of Samuel considers him a model king and announced a new covenant to preserve the dynasty of David into perpetuity. This promise didn't specify any responsibilities in order to continue deserving the privilege, but the books of Kings and Chronicles make it clear that many Davidic kings displeased God, while the changing dynasties of the northern tribes who broke away always did what was wrong in the sight of God.

That makes a total of three covenants. Which one defines what an Israelite was or is? The Davidic dynasty disappeared from history shortly after the return to Jerusalem from Babylon. The belief in a liberating Messiah sometimes, but not always, involved the emergence of a new member of the line of David to achieve independence and justice that once again represented the true leadership of God. The Jews of today are associated with the kingdom of Judah, which represented the tribes of Benjamin and Judah. Descendants of other tribes are associated with the Samaritans, who do not recognize traditions based on Jerusalem or the line of David, all of which were associated with Judah.

So which covenant is most important to the people of the covenant today? The answer is clear—it is the covenant of the Exodus and Sinai. The liberation from Egypt is celebrated annually as Passover and the 613 commands of God found in the Torah and the products of the oral law, the Mishnah and Talmud, all spring from the experience of Israel on Sinai. That is the origin of the true Israel. This heritage is claimed today by Jews and Samaritans.

I have been describing what are presented as historical events in the Torah. Christians as well as Jews and Samaritans acknowledge those events as historical. With the emergence of biblical archaeology in the twentieth century, it was natural that historical evidence of the covenantal events and leading personalities would be sought to verify biblical accounts.

For about forty years, it looked as though archaeology confirmed a patriarchal period resembling the picture in Genesis and Exodus even if documentation of the leading personalities was not found. Evidence of destruction was found at sites mentioned in Joshua as having been victims of the Israelite invasion. Monumental remains also seemed to confirm statements about the building program of Solomon.

Recent decades have produced archaeological results that undermine much of the historical information in the Torah, Joshua, Samuel, and Kings. There is no longer support for a "patriarchal period" and efforts to match the Bible with Egyptian records have failed to confirm Exodus accounts. In a popular book about archaeology and the Old Testament, Israel Finkelstein and Neil Asher Silberman point out that peoples of the Near East were passing in and out of Egypt all the time because Egypt had a predictable water source while surrounding areas frequently experienced droughts. If a people the size of Israel as claimed in Exodus had left Egypt, there would have been a record of it. The destruction of an Egyptian army at the Red Sea would not have meant liberation because Egypt had forts in the Sinai from which troops would have been sent as well. Those forts were important for enforcing Egyptian policies as they dominated Canaan in that period of time.[184]

Furthermore, they point out that exhaustive studies have been made of the Sinai. A group far smaller than the size mentioned in Exodus would have left traces, but no evidence of a wandering large people has been found: "And it has not been for lack of trying."[185]

The American archaeologist William Dever joined Finkelstein and Silberman in recognizing the lack of evidence for the Exodus and also in rejecting the conquest of Canaan described in Joshua. It appears the tribes of Israel emerged mostly from inside Canaan as city states collapsed for internal reasons rather than conquest. The traditional tribal structure of Israel that is supposed to be founded on descent from Jacob appears to have developed as a way of uniting many disparate peoples into some form of common identity based on legend.[186]

Dever suspects there was at least one group that actually emerged from Egypt and carried with it a tradition of miraculous liberation that gradually was adopted by the larger group. That would mean the Exodus stories were not entirely invented but evolved from within the traditions of a small group to become important to the identity of the larger group of Israel.[187]

There are indications in the biblical accounts that point to the diversity of origin suspected by archaeology. The group of people leaving Egypt in the Exodus included a large group of non-Israelites who made common cause with them. The book of Joshua appears to tell of a rapid conquest of the entire land, but there are gaps in the geographical description where it appears non-Israelites continued dominant. The book of Judges makes it clear that Israelites do not control all the territory claimed by Joshua.

On top of that, there seem to be a least two rival traditions that have been blended so that again contradictions pop up in biblical accounts. The rivals are the accounts around the House of Joseph and accounts around Judah. The Joseph accounts make Judah a villain, as Joseph is the big hero. In the tribal structure itself, it appears the House of Joseph is dominant because the sons of Joseph, Manasseh and Ephraim, make up the two largest and most fertile tribal territories and in fact comprise the bulk of the northern part of Israel. Judah is in the barren hill country around Jerusalem and comes to include desert land to the south associated with Benjamin. The covenant with the line of David and a focus on Jerusalem are part of the Judah tradition, which finds fault with the monarchy in the north, which was based on the House of Joseph. So biblical accounts indicate internal rivalry and division that led to the breakup of a united monarchy into two rival kingdoms.

Has archaeology disproved the Exodus and the story of Passover? Those who are fast to answer YES to that question may well be jumping to conclusions prematurely. Archaeology thus far has not found evidence to confirm the biblical story—that is a true statement. The account as presented in the Bible is not a literal account of whatever historical events did occur. But we have the archaic Hebrew of the Song of Miriam (Exodus 15:20–21) and the Song of Moses (Exodus 15:1–18), which indicate a community ritual based on the Exodus experience going back centuries.[188] It was not invented during the monarchy and projected backward. Literary and oral sources during the monarchy show the existence of a Mosaic tradition that was an aspect of common culture, not invented as royal or priestly propaganda. The annual tradition of Passover came from somewhere, although no one can clearly say just how it came to be.

To be an Israelite today means identifying with the covenant and tradition connected with Moses, Passover, and the Exodus. Jews are Israelites who venerate Jerusalem and Davidic traditions while Samaritans associate Moses with Mount Gerizim near their ancient capitals of Shechem and Samaria. Both groups of Israelites have the Torah. Their versions differ in details but clearly emerge from a common tradition.

Christians gave a new twist to the meaning of Israel when they claimed to represent the true Israel through a new covenant made through Christ. They appropriated Israelite scripture but labeled it as the Old Covenant to which was added the New Covenant, which proclaimed the gospel of Jesus and the developments based on his resurrection.

Being a Jew makes one an Israelite, but one does not have to be a Jew to be an Israelite.

CHAPTER TWENTY-EIGHT

WHO IS THE NEIGHBOR?

I have always loved comedy teams. When I was twelve years old, almost every Saturday was spent at the movies with my younger brother and two sisters. We loved cowboy movies and each of us had our favorite hero. But we all were excited whenever there was a Bud Abbott and Lou Costello movie. As I grew up, I liked Rowan and Martin and hardly ever missed Johnny Carson. Johnny, of course, was a solo act, but the chemistry with Ed McMahon, who often played an excellent straight man, was really special.

In a comedy duo, a really good straight man is essential. I think the best straight man ever was Jewish—it was George Burns. Only after the death of his wife Gracie Allen did the world begin to see how good he was by himself. He, of course, gave all the credit for his career to his partner Gracie. How could we have appreciated her nonsense without the easy softballs he lobbed her and those unforgettable facial reactions?

Jesus was not a comedian, but he had some very famous straight men who served him lines that he made memorable with his responses. Of course these straight men were not trying to be funny or even help Jesus because usually they intended to trap or insult him. One notable encounter happened when a conscientious young man asked him about the essence of the Torah. Then he followed up with the wonderful straight line: "And who is my neighbor?" That set Jesus up to tell the parable of the Good Samaritan, as nearly everyone knows. Oh how many sermons have been preached with that title "Who is my neighbor?"

Having lived in Georgia all my life, I know a lot of people who are convinced that many of the problems of the world would be solved if we went back to biblical morality. Placing copies of the Ten Commandments in public settings is a religious calling to a great many people. My daughter lives in a small town not far from Atlanta that has a very small city hall and a police department building. They don't even have a courthouse on a square in the middle of town like other small towns in Georgia. But someone made sure this town stayed moral by placing an expensive-looking miniature stone monument of the Ten Commandments in the small space between the city hall and the police department. These people are adamant about cutting taxes for all kinds of unnecessary programs to help people in need, yet they support the cost of displaying the Ten Commandments.

I often wonder just how many of the people who are so convinced of the moral value of the Ten Commandments have actually read them carefully. I would wager that none of them could answer a simple question that should have been asked. Who is the neighbor mentioned in the commandments? Figuring out the identity of that neighbor takes very close reading. A great many people think they know what the Ten Commandments say, but they don't read them closely enough.

Jews traditionally maintain that the Torah has 613 commandments. There is a story that Rabbi Hillel was asked to summarize the Torah in the time he could stand on just one leg. His response was a version of what we know as the Golden Rule. In Luke 10:26, Jesus had a similar opportunity but threw back the question of the young lawyer about the essence of the Torah so that the man gave his own answer. He replied it was to love God and then love your neighbor. Whether that accurately reflects all 613 of the Torah commands is something for my Jewish friends to debate. What is clear to me is that what the lawyer said and Jesus affirmed was an excellent summary of the Ten Commandments.[189]

The Torah has two accounts of the giving of the commandments to Moses and the people of Israel. Most are aware of the version in Exodus 20:1–21. The second account is in Deuteronomy 5:1–21. The book Deuteronomy actually derives its name from the fact that it is a second telling of the commandments given as Moses recalled them in a series of long statements before he died. The two versions differ in interesting ways.

In Exodus, the context is a bit unclear. Moses brought the people of Israel to the foot of Mount Sinai to meet God. Moses went up and spoke with God who told him to bring Aaron up with him but not to let the priests or the people get too close to the mountain. Then suddenly we are told that God spoke the commandments just after Moses told the people to keep their distance. At the end of the commandments in verse 18, it says the people at the foot of the mountain "witnessed the thunder and lightning, the sound of the trumpet, and the mountain smoking." Their natural reaction was fear as they stood at a distance. Then the people said to Moses, "You speak to us, and we will listen; but do not let God speak to us, or we will die." But God had just spoken. Had he spoken to everyone or just to Moses? Although the situation of the giving is not clear, no one doubts that the commandments derive from God himself.

In Deuteronomy, Moses convened all of Israel and began by reminding them that at Horeb, God "spoke with you face to face at the mountain, out of the fire." There is disagreement between the accounts as to the name of the mountain where the commandments were given and some other details, but in both versions the commandments represent the direct words of God to the entire people. Everyone is held accountable for these rules.

The first four commandments spell out how God is to be respected. Both accounts say "you shall have no other gods before me." This is not a declaration that there is only one God. Rather it is a statement that God does not allow competition with the other gods known to this people. It is a requirement to give up all other gods. The competitors are known through images, but this God will not allow images or recognition of the images of the other gods. This God also does not want his name to be misused when taking an oath—in other words, one should not use God's name in order to lie or deceive. In later years this statement will be interpreted to mean that the very name of God itself was not to be pronounced aloud. Finally, God wants the seventh day honored as a holy day on which no one labors.

These four commandments begin with the words "you shall" or "you shall not." All the people are being addressed, so it appears that the "you" represents all of the people. In describing the details about Sabbath observation, the "you" becomes more specific. "You shall not do any work—you, your son or your daughter, your male or female slave, your livestock, or the alien resident in your towns." The Deuteronomy account varies by listing specific types of livestock.

The fifth commandment is transitional as we move from loving God to loving neighbors. The transition category is your parents, father and mother, who are to be honored. This is the only commandment that lists a consequence—in this case a good one, which is the possibility of a long life.

Commandments six through ten are all prohibitions that are essentially ethical. Murder, adultery, stealing, and lying are common things outlawed in societies. The last commandment is interesting because it goes into detail in naming things that "you" are not to covet. "Neither shall you covet your neighbor's wife. Neither shall you desire your neighbor's house, or field, or male or female slave, or ox, or donkey, or anything that belongs to your neighbor." That is the Deuteronomy version, which separates the wife from a listing of other things. In Exodus a similar phrasing is used, but the wife is not distinguished so clearly. "You shall not covet your neighbor's house; you shall not covet your neighbor's wife, or male or female slave, or ox, or donkey, or anything that belongs to your neighbor."

I come back to our earlier question: Who is the neighbor in the Ten Commandments? The phrasing in both versions makes it clear that the neighbor is someone who owns property or who is over the household, parts of which are not to be coveted—and a wife is part of what belongs to the one in charge. It doesn't take much thought to realize that, in this context, women are excluded from being the neighbor.[190]

Next question: Who is the "you" being addressed in the commandments? It appears to be the entire people of Israel, which would include women and children. Clearly these laws apply to them—but are they really addressed to them? Look at the wording of the fourth commandment about the Sabbath. It lists children and then property that is not permitted to labor. Children were also part of the household as were wives, and the father of the household was the key person being addressed. The fourth commandment does not list wives among property as the tenth commandment does, but it is clear that the primary audience of the commandments are the circumcised men of Israel. It is men who own property, rule over the family, and are the neighbor mentioned in the commandments.[191]

Do you think this is farfetched? Look again at the story in Luke 10. Jesus is asked who "my neighbor" is. His answer is to tell a story in which all the characters are male. I don't take this as an endorsement of the male dominance standard in Judaism at that time because we know that Jesus did challenge the exclusion of women in some ways; but it is a tacit recognition of the standard of that time. The question of including women in the category of neighbor just did not come up. It should also be noted that Jesus did not need to include women in the parable because its implications were already shocking enough. His parable and concluding injunction to behave as the Samaritan meant that the essential question was the kind of behavior expected of a neighbor and not who the neighbor was.

Consider that the temple known to Jesus was divided into courts for specific groups. Nearest the holy of holies was the court for the priests and next came the court for Israelites. Outside that was a court for women. A court for Gentiles surrounded the other courts, marked off by a wall with a warning in Latin and Greek of the point beyond which Gentiles should not go. What was an Israelite? It was a male who was circumcised. For a female to enter the court of the Israelites or beyond was blasphemy. Any non-Jew who went past the wall into the inner courts, which were considered the temple proper, would be put to death. Paul was arrested after a riot caused by accusations that he had taken a Gentile past the wall (Acts 21:27–36). According to Acts 22:25–29, Paul used Roman citizenship to avoid the torture that would have been used on him. Acts goes on to show how he was protected from Jewish execution and sent to Roman officials for interrogation and trial.

Models of the temple based on more recent archaeological work indicate that the court of the Israelites was very small and that the court for women was where a great deal of activity took place. Women usually stayed in certain areas of the court and worship activities took place in other parts. It was known as the court for women because it was as far as women could go in approaching the holiest areas, but it was really where most of the worship activity occurred. Strict segregation by gender was not required in the women's court but it was considered improper for men to loiter around talking to women there as in most other public places. This court is also where imageless coins were contributed in special containers. It was where Jesus would have seen the poor widow making a contribution of the small amount of money she had.[192]

Synagogue worship has traditionally perpetuated this separation of men and women so that it is a big issue for some very conservative Jewish groups. In 2011 the Israeli Prime Minister Benjamin Netanyahu was embarrassed by one of the ultraorthodox groups in his political coalition. This group takes the separation of men and women in worship and in public very seriously so that they feel it their duty to publicly insult females, even an eight-year-old on her way to school who did not meet their very stringent dress code. This group and others consider it irreligious to listen to women or loiter with them in public. A good many Jews in Israel and around the world were offended by the male-centered holiness rules of this group.[193]

It should also be noted that some very conservative Jewish groups continue to honor the prayer attributed to Judah the Prince, the codifier of the Mishnah, by which males begin the day thanking God they are not gentiles, uneducated, or women. There are, of course, explanations that attempt to explain away the negative message about women. This leads naturally to some ambivalence among modern Jews, as indicated by Amy-Jill Levine, whose response to what her young son learned about this prayer was: "I do not find such contemporary explanations convincing. However, I do understand how the tradition attempts to limit the negative implications." One negative implication seems to be that males are the primary bearers of the promise because of circumcision.[194]

Consider again the claims of groups in America today who insist on putting up copies of the Ten Commandments in public locations. Critics have pointed to this as a violation of the separation of church and state required by the United States Constitution. These groups often violate the ninth commandment by denying religious motivations or implications. What other motivation makes sense? Commandments five through ten are covered in thousands of pages of laws and court decisions in our country and all others around the world. What is different are the religious requirements of commandments one through four. These views are endorsed by Jews, Christians, and Muslims. But they are religious views that are not endorsed by many elements within a secular society permitted by the United States Constitution.

An important point to be realized is that these commandments also imply outdated gender roles. Many of the groups wanting to display the commandments want to enforce those outdated standards as well.

Again we face the question of the reliability and authority of the Bible. Thousands of legal codes and rulings endorse the reliability of the ethical commandments but go into more detail for cultures and a wide variety of specific situations. Jews, Christians, and Muslims support the religious views of the four religious commandments for their members. However, it is necessary to recognize that the cultural setting has changed substantially. There no longer are male and female slaves. In our society women and children have legal rights and are not classified as property or under the domination of the male head of household. It is important to recognize that these commandments in their original cultural setting are not eternal and unchanging truth even though we continue to find great value in them.

Values change as cultures mutate over time. I am opposed to rendering moral judgments on the times in which the original intentions of the commandments were followed. It is not fair for one time to impose its standards backward on an earlier period. No doubt our grandchildren's culture will have values that find many of ours offensive. I grew up in a world in which black racism was accepted as the natural condition that should be preserved. I am thankful those values have changed. I believe the generations of my parents and grandparents should have recognized the error of racism sooner than happened. But I am not in favor of projecting judgment back on earlier times, for example, by denouncing Abraham Lincoln as a racist rather than appreciating the wonderful things he accomplished.

The Bible speaks of our obligation to our neighbor. We should recognize that today the neighbor means something different from what it meant during the Second Temple and earlier times in Israel. The standard is valuable as long as we don't take a "strict constructionist" point of view that insists on enshrining the original cultural assumptions that came with those standards.

CHAPTER TWENTY-NINE

DEUTERONOMISTS, KINGS, AND TEMPLE

When I became aware of current events in the 1950s, I learned the meaning of insecurity. Until that point in life, a crisis was when I was sick or injured. For those problems, the recourse was always my mother, the best solution for all problems. But then I learned our country had just won a world war only to find our situation more threatening than ever because Russia intended to take over the world through military conquest or internal subversion. I also learned about the nuclear threat, especially as we received materials in school about what to do at home when air raid sirens went off, signaling the approach of an airplane that might be carrying an atomic bomb.

Sometimes the media paints the 50s as a time of tranquility before the havoc of the 60s. They point to television shows like *Father Knows Best* or *Leave It to Beaver* as symbolic of the cozy family life of the times before so many ordinary features of life began to change. That is not how I remember the 50s. It was a time of fear and uncertainty. Joseph McCarthy was one of the people who exploited the national mood. Even after he was exposed and discredited, national political figures were careful to avoid being linked with free speech that might be portrayed as sympathy for communism. Even the hero of D-Day, the very popular Dwight Eisenhower, chose the anticommunist Richard Nixon as Vice President to protect himself from right-wing slander when he ran for president.

The insecurity of the 40s and 50s was a new thing for our country. Protected by oceans, we had distanced ourselves from conflicts in Europe. Suddenly we found ourselves in a world of increasing air power in which oceans no longer provided security.

Most countries in the world have not been insulated from constant wars on their borders that inevitably bring fear and insecurity. That was especially true of ancient Israel. The people of Israel were located between powerful imperial centers in Mesopotamia and Egypt that pioneered the development of early civilization in the western part of Eurasia. The land bridge of Palestine, Phoenicia, and Syria that connected those empires was often the site of wars as domination of the area frequently shifted from one empire to the other over a number of centuries.

The story of these years, recorded in the books of Joshua, Judges, Samuel, and Kings, is referred to as the Deuteronomistic history because those books are believed to be the product of a group of scribes and priests responsible for the book of Deuteronomy. These books describe the occupation of Canaan, periodic resistance to various threats, the emergence of monarchy to deal with the increasing threat of the Philistines, and then the progress of rival monarchies until the destruction of both by empires from Mesopotamia. The interpretive point of view is almost exclusively religious because political and military success are presented as depending on whether the people followed the commands of God. Standards of justice and morality based on the Mosaic covenant are part of those religious views. As the story moves along, it also becomes clear that God's commandments involved preserving the Davidic monarchy, Jerusalem, and especially the temple in Jerusalem.

Growing up in the 1950s, I learned the word propaganda. It was a bad thing. It was what the Russians did when they constantly put out false information. The United States countered with information provided through media that were free and not manipulated, which included the official Voice of America broadcasts behind the Iron Curtain to describe events from our point of view.

Since then we have learned that propaganda is not just a tool that was used by the communists. Every government that ever existed has used it to one extent or another. In fact, the reliance of historians on written products from earlier civilizations meant buying into their forms of propaganda, which often glorified the actions of authoritarian monarchs.

Christians who are convinced that all of the Bible is directly from God will be shocked to hear that the Deuteronomistic history represents propaganda on behalf of the group that produced it. Once you become aware of this interpretation, evidence is easy to find. Kings are judged almost exclusively by religious standards important to the Deuteronomists. When the unified monarchy splits into northern and southern states, the Deuteronomists present every king of Israel as unpleasing to God. These rulers are consistently seen as supporting false gods through local shrines and at the royal court. Kings of Israel and Judah are criticized when they make accommodations with dominating empires that lead to foreign marriages or idols being placed in the temple. Little sympathy is shown for the diplomatic realities of the time, which required cooperation with dominant powers to avoid invasion.

The myopic nature of the Deuteronomistic interpretation is seen in the two kings of Judah that receive the most coverage and praise as another king of Judah is described as the worst of the Davidic dynasty. In the 720s BCE, Assyria was the dominant Mesopotamian power taking control of Palestine and threatening conquest of Egypt. The kingdom of Israel was considered more of a threat than Judah so that it was the focus of campaigns that resulted in deportations of population. The last, in 722, destroyed the capital Samaria and deported the elite of the society. Even after witnessing the power of Assyria, Hezekiah, king of Judah, began plotting his own revolt. His religious reforms brought an invasion so that Lachish was destroyed and Jerusalem was besieged in 701. According to 2 Kings 19:32–34, an angel of God struck the Assyrians so that they broke off the siege, bringing victory to Hezekiah. The temple, Jerusalem, and the monarchy were preserved, indicating the approval of God and a great victory through righteousness.[195]

Archaeology supports a more wide-ranging interpretation. The Assyrians wiped out cities and villages as they approached Jerusalem, which is acknowledged in 2 Kings 18:13–14. Lachish, the most important city after Jerusalem, was taken, and its leaders were executed or deported. Most of the country was devastated. Jerusalem did survive a siege, apparently resulting in a negotiated settlement by which tribute to Assyria was resumed. The account in 2 Kings focused primarily on the threat to Jerusalem so that when the capital survived it was God's victory. The account of the siege of Jerusalem illustrated how a king pleased God and brought about vindication of righteousness—that was how the Deuteronomists saw the situation even though most of the kingdom was laid waste.

After Hezekiah came Manasseh who received little attention in 2 Kings 21:1–17. He was acknowledged to rule for fifty-five years, the longest of anyone in the Davidic dynasty. His were years of peace and growing prosperity as the nation recovered from the havoc brought about by Hezekiah's revolt; yet Manasseh is regarded as so bad that his sins were responsible for the Babylonian conquest (21:10–15, 24:3–4). The explanation is given that Josiah served God better than other kings of Judah but even that did not turn away the anger of God because of the transgressions of Manasseh (23:25–27).

Following the stability and peace of Manasseh was a period of assassinations and dynastic uncertainty. A group made the child Josiah king, apparently so they could rule through him. As Josiah reached maturity, he resumed policies of Hezekiah by centralizing national rites exclusively in the temple and rejecting foreign gods. During his reign the high priest claimed to find a lost book of the Law in the temple. When it was read to Josiah, he made it the basis of national religious reform. Most scholars agree the scroll that was found was part but not all of what we know today as the book of Deuteronomy.

The result of Josiah's reform was military conflict with Egypt and Assyria. Josiah was killed in a battle with armies of Egypt, bringing about another period of dynastic instability as Egypt worked with internal factions. When apparent stability returned, Judah's neighbors allied with forces of Babylon. In the first invasion, Judah surrendered so that Jerusalem, temple, and monarchy were spared. But a subsequent uprising under a young king just placed on the throne led to a siege that brought destruction and deportation of the elite to Babylon.

Conservative regard for the Bible has meant accepting religious views and historical interpretation of the Deuteronomists as the viewpoint of God rather than self-serving propaganda of a religious group. This continues even when it is obvious that exclusively religious interpretations are no longer credible. For example, the ideal candidate for president of the United States, according to the standards I learned at church when I was a child, would be a pious Christian who had a genuine born-again experience. The three presidents of my lifetime who met that standard were Jimmy Carter, Bill Clinton, and George W. Bush. Today Carter and Bush are not considered successful presidents because of economic problems that haunted their terms. Clinton, in spite of moral scandals, is highly regarded and still popular in large part because of his economic success. Exclusively religious interpretations are not accepted in our time.

Much of the religious viewpoint of the Deuteronomists was shared by leading prophets. Primary loyalty was to be given to a single God and prophets were critical of national regimes that compromised that standard. Their religious interpretation guided views of national and personal events, consistent with the general tendency in the Old Testament to see most problems as the result of sin. National calamities, from loss in a battle to conquest by a foreign power, are brought on by sins of kings. Generally in the Bible, personal misfortune is seen as the product of individual sin that displeases God. One of the characteristics seen in Jewish literature is the lack of medical study to relieve sickness and disease. The closest it comes is in the sacrificial rituals for sins, the purification rituals performed by priests when healing occurs, or the miraculous cures associated with prophets. This indicates the extent to which religious explanations rather than more secular or medical explanations were valued.

One result of this was what Geza Vermes calls charismatic prophecy.[196] A less emphasized aspect of popular prophets was their ability to heal or work wonders, as in the case of Elijah raising a dead child or Elisha healing leprosy. This was one of the aspects of prophecy that was seen in rivalry with the temple and that continued into the times of Jesus so that Jesus himself was seen as a prophet in part because he healed, exorcised, and performed wondrous actions. Jesus even claimed the ability to forgive sins as he healed.

Recognizing the Deuteronomistic history as a one-sided religious interpretation by one element in ancient Israelite society does not lead to rejecting their accounts as fraudulent. Biased accounts can be valuable but must be recognized as biased rather than beyond question. Insisting on the infallible truth of these biblical accounts is like trusting my mother when I had a childhood crisis. As I grew to maturity, I began to appreciate that life was more complicated than just relying on parents as the source of all solutions.

How should we regard these biblical accounts? First, I am grateful to have them. Even though far from complete, they provide historical information that would be lacking if they did not exist. The stories of Saul, David, and Solomon present interesting and moving human accounts. Even those favored by the Deuteronomists are not exempt from negative judgments based on their religious standards. Justice is an important standard for these historians as a practical result of religious beliefs. David himself was exposed as using power to cover up adultery and murder.

The attractiveness of the Deuteronomists is found in their willingness to criticize political leadership from a moral standpoint. Even favored leaders who are loyal to Yahweh, like David and Solomon, are described as causing troubles in the nation through injustice and pride. After Israel splits into two kingdoms, only Hezekiah and Josiah are given approval similar to David. The clear favoritism for Josiah tends to support those who think much of the work of the Deuteronomists was done or at least begun at that time. Douglas Knight and Amy-Jill Levine point out that such overt written criticism of monarchs was not usual, so they suggest that the Persian or Hellenistic periods may have been the time of final composition because the monarchy no longer existed to exercise censorship.[197]

The Deuteronomists illustrated a tendency seen throughout Jewish history of struggling to preserve the integrity of religious traditions and not just national survival. Their efforts to discern the hand of God in events, however flawed those views may have been, contributed to a tradition that insists on an all-powerful God as the source of meaning. I see their concept of God as limited because it portrays an arbitrary God too easy to anger; yet the tradition to which I belong builds on the beliefs of the Deuteronomists rather than demolishing them. Try as we might to understand the world and how God may be working, our efforts will inevitably be considered dated and limited by those who come after us.

CHAPTER THIRTY

MYTH, ARCHAEOLOGY, AND POLITICS

Previously I mentioned that the first eleven chapters of Genesis are mythical but that they are a good kind of myth. The stories appear historical but they are poetic in nature, explaining how the world came to be the way it is through accounts filled with symbolism. These chapters are comparable to tales of Greek and Roman gods, which have always been referred to as mythology. In fact, most early cultures produced similar poetic tales to explain the origin of things or the hidden forces behind the visible world. It was clear to many Greek and Roman writers that the symbolic truth of such stories was not meant to be mistaken for historical events.

In my view, this kind of mythology is positive by helping us express aspects of reality that are difficult to capture in any prose or nonfiction account. A different use of the word myth equates it with false information. This is the most common use of the term.

During my time as an employee of the state of Georgia, I spent over ten years working with the people in charge of public relations and publications. They were often called on to help programs overcome public misperceptions or biases against certain types of programs or recipients. The method they found most effective often involved a heading of "Myths versus Facts" featuring parallel columns listing false ideas on the left and accurate information on the right.

One also finds this use of myth in scholarly writing, as in the case of *The Mythic Past: Biblical Archaeology and the Myth of Israel* by Thomas L. Thompson. This book uses unforgettable language in its preface:

Today we no longer have a history of Israel. Not only have
Adam and Eve and the flood story passed over to mythology,
but we can no longer talk about a time of the patriarchs.
There never was a 'United Monarchy' in history and it is
meaningless to speak of pre-exilic prophets and their writings. The history of Iron Age Palestine today knows of Israel
only as a small highland patronate lying north of Jerusalem
and south of the Jezreel Valley. Nor has Yahweh, the deity
dominant in the cult of that Israel's people, much to do with
the Bible's understanding of God.[198]

It would be difficult to find a more thorough denial of the historical value of
the Bible.

Thompson's approach to the Old Testament found little support in the
United States for many years. He became a professor at the University of
Copenhagen, where his ideas began to influence European scholars. The title
of his book refers to the bad kind of myth—something that makes claims to
be a historical account that is in fact entirely fiction. Thompson could have
called the history of ancient Israel propaganda because it represents self-serving political, social, and religious views that met the needs of specific groups
trying to persuade others to accept their claims to authority. But such a charge
would only have amounted to an accusation of bias. Thompson preferred to
be more extreme by labeling all the information about the time prior to the
Exile as invention without historical foundation.

Thompson said that much of the Old Testament came about under the
Persian and Hellenistic regimes in Palestine so that historical accounts in the
Bible were developed to justify the rule of groups in those times who had little
or no connection to peoples who actually lived in Canaan in earlier periods. He
based his views on his study of ancient sources and the results of archaeology.

Biblical archaeology has produced results that alternately encouraged and
disturbed supporters of the Bible. In the middle decades of the twentieth century, the foundations of biblical archaeology were laid by William F. Albright
and Nelson Glueck, both of them biblical scholars and theologians as well as
pioneers of archaeology. Neither was a believer in literal interpretations of the
Bible, yet both were motivated by a desire to show the essential reliability of
Old Testament accounts. Their discoveries and interpretations supported their
beliefs about the Bible. After midcentury, the retired Israeli general turned ar-

chaeologist, Yigael Yadin, made astonishing discoveries of structures that he attributed to the building program of Solomon described in 2 Kings. Public interest in America increased as more and more news seemed to support biblical accuracy.

In the latter decades of the twentieth century, new generations of archaeologists emerged who were not ministers or biblical scholars. Their desire was to develop the science of their profession without tying it to theological interests. New methods were added to the digging associated with archaeology so that projects came to involve sizeable teams involving experts in many allied fields. A method called field survey was developed, which did not involve digging into the earth, and eventually satellite and drone technologies became involved. A new focus and newer methods also led to re-evaluation of previous findings.

For many years debate centered on the patriarchal period through the settlement of the land described in Joshua and Judges. Early discoveries seemed to verify destruction of sites mentioned in Joshua. Further evaluation produced contradictory results. There was destruction at those sites, but not in the right time period. Key sites, such as Jericho, were shown not to have been occupied when it was supposedly conquered.

The debate on this phase of biblical history seems to be over for now. There is no evidence supporting a patriarchal period, Exodus, wandering in Sinai, or conquest of Canaan. Destruction of specific locations at a specific time and military conquest of Canaan have been disproved, but not whether there was an Exodus event or whether a group of people wandered through Sinai to eventually settle as part of ancient Israel. There is no evidence to prove the existence of Abraham, Isaac, Jacob, Moses, or Aaron; but absence of supporting evidence is not proof they never existed.[199]

The major debate taking place in archaeology at present concerns the existence of a united monarchy under Saul, David, and Solomon. In fact, the existence of any political entity in the area later known as Judah has been doubted. How is that possible?

We begin by looking at how key evidence is missing. In spite of extensive digging in Jerusalem, structures built by David or Solomon have either not been found or claims of findings are in dispute. As yet no trace of Solomon's original temple or of the palace, which was more extensive and took more years to build, have been found. The key evidence supporting a building program by Solomon was the discoveries made by Yigael Yadin. One of Israel's leading archaeologists, Israel Finkelstein, shocked the public when he declared that Yadin's findings needed to be dated to a century later than Solomon, to the period of King Ahab of Israel. Finkelstein's method for dating is still controversial and others have announced results dating the same finds to later than Solomon but not as late as the period of Ahab. The result is that archaeological evidence for Saul, David, and Solomon is still being contested.[200]

A second part of the argument is based on clear data, but there are disagreements over how to interpret it. Field survey evidence indicates that Jerusalem was very small in the time periods for David and Solomon. In fact, all of Judah had a very low population while the area associated with the kingdom of Israel was more densely populated. Other archaeological evidence clearly shows that the kingdom of Israel was a power in the politics and wars of the Near East around the time of Ahab. Interpreters like Finkelstein and Thompson have drawn the conclusion that no united monarchy could have existed, so that Thompson can refer to David and Solomon as myths. Finkelstein doesn't go that far because he acknowledges there may have been a David, but he would have been no more than a leader of bandits.

Field surveys also indicated that the conquest of Israel by Assyria in 722 BCE resulted in a population shift into Judah, suggesting that the period of Hezekiah was the time when the kingdom of Judah emerged. Finkelstein argues that much of the story of David and Solomon represents backward projection from the period of Josiah using experiences based on the actual history of Israel under Ahab. Thompson prefers to find the originators of Davidic myths in the times of Persian and Hellenistic domination. Prominent archaeologists William Dever and Amihai Mazar are among those who question Finkelstein's dating and defend the united monarchy.

A legitimate question to be asked by historians and others is whether archaeology, as represented by Finkelstein, and biblical studies, as represented by Thompson, have been guilty of over-reach. Have these scholars gone beyond the limits of their expertise?

William Dever and Israel Finkelstein were among those arguing that archaeology in Palestine needed to separate itself from biblical studies and theology. In the debate over the united monarchy, Dever and Finkelstein are rivals as Dever defends the essential reliability of Old Testament accounts. The point I would like to make is that Finkelstein is an archaeologist who is asserting opinions as to when parts of the Old Testament were written. Thompson is a biblical scholar claiming invention of events in part because of his interpretation of archaeological evidence. Dever has challenged both as misrepresenting archaeological evidence as he too gives opinions on when parts of the Bible came about. Even when archaeological data are clear, how they are interpreted and used may be subject to misuse, especially as they are the basis for conclusions beyond the field of archaeology.[201]

The outcome of the archaeological debate hangs in the balance. More evidence will be found and other interpretations are bound to challenge those now being presented. A clearer picture is likely to emerge in the future as knowledge advances through more accurate interpretation of increasingly reliable data.

It is disturbing that radical denial of the Bible seems to be in fashion. Referring to Jesus as a myth has become a common feature of atheist attacks on religion such as those by Richard Dawkins and Christopher Hitchens. Challenges by scholars to the existence of Jesus led Bart Ehrman to expose their many fallacies as he defended the historical basis for the gospels.[202] Thompson was included in the analysis because he wrote a book claiming that Jesus too was an invention.[203]

Thompson's supporters have also become political supporters of Palestinian claims. Accounts in the Old Testament are important in political discussions because of the rivalry between the state of Israel and Palestinian groups. The state of Israel asserts a heritage based on biblical accounts that justify its existence and boundaries. The website for the Israel Ministry of Foreign Affairs features historical accounts based on the Old Testament. It also supports archaeology, using many discoveries to support Israeli claims and keeping the public aware of progress on a great number of archaeological projects.[204] Politics is also seen in a book by Keith Whitelam, a Thompson supporter, that claims ancient Israel is an invention intended to silence genuine Palestinian history.[205]

Most archaeologists and scholars of the Old Testament would agree that reliable truth lies somewhere between the extremes of biblical literalism and mythical invention. Archaeologists are still making important discoveries and developing improved methods. Even when clearly important discoveries are made, it is usually premature to jump to interpretations supporting or opposing biblical accounts. As new methods are developed, old discoveries can be shown to have been misinterpreted.

From a historical point of view, some conclusions are unavoidable. All of the Bible could be considered propaganda because it represents the views and interests of different groups responsible for each book. That means none of the Bible should be treated as eternal truth, but it doesn't mean that any of it is necessarily false or invented. No doubt there are cases in the Old Testament of scribes in one time projecting events to an earlier time as a way of justifying their views and practices. Even so, making the claim that the pre-exilic prophets and kings did not exist is too extreme to be credible.

Skeptical questioning can be taken too far, as was the case in the 1960s when a group of professors made reputations by proclaiming, "God is dead." The Judeo-Christian tradition survived that fad and the Bible will survive skepticism that becomes too extreme.

Chapter Thirty-One

Ancient Prophecy

A few years before ending my government career, I took a part-time job on weekends to make financial preparation for impending retirement. I was single and didn't have grandchildren to see on a regular basis. The job turned into a blessing because I made some very good friends, especially Doug, who was about my age. He made a living selling insurance through his own small agency and worked part-time to build savings toward retirement. Doug was a master of networking, a very good skill for someone who lives by selling. In the few years we worked together, he was promoted to lead supervisor for evenings and weekends and I supervised part of the weekend shift. Doug's handling of many situations showed a strong sense of ethics and fairness that earned my admiration.

He always took off Sunday afternoons when the Falcons played at home in the Georgia Dome. He joined with three friends to buy season tickets at a low price. When one of the friends was out of town, he offered the open ticket to other friends. Once I went to a game as the result of this arrangement.

I retired from government service in February of 2005 and by July made the transition to full retirement by giving up the part-time job, even though there was an opportunity to become Doug's assistant. Soon after I left, he called to say that one of his buddies had dropped out of the season ticket arrangement and they wanted me to join their group. I thanked him but declined. I enjoy watching football on television. Watching games at the top of the Georgia Dome with all kinds of noise reverberating made action in the game hard to follow. Right after hanging up the phone, I had an unusual feeling. It occurred to me that just being with Doug would make the experience worthwhile. A strange sense of urgency came over me to take the offer. Immediately I called back and he had not yet made the offer to anyone else.

Within two weeks, we went to the first preseason game and followed a routine of tailgating in the parking area half a mile downhill from the Georgia Dome. In September we attended the first home game, following the same tailgating routine. This time Doug could not speak above a whisper. He explained that somehow he inhaled a weed killing spray as he was using it and his doctor said the hoarseness would be temporary. As we ate in the parking lot, he began throwing a football with one of his buddies. After a few minutes of mild exercise, he slumped into a chair gasping for breath for nearly ten minutes. As we walked up the hill to the stadium, he found it increasingly hard to breathe and walked slower and slower.

In the following week, he developed heart palpitations and went to the emergency room where a physician detected fluid in his lungs. I visited him in the hospital room where his wife sat as they had just talked with a lung specialist. I remember the matter of fact look on their faces as they told me the diagnosis was advanced lung cancer. He would soon begin treatment. They tried to sound hopeful but it was clear they were trying to absorb the impact of a very negative diagnosis.

We attended three more Falcon games. Each time Doug had to stop several times as we went up hill from the parking lot and also up the escalator in the stadium. He had always been thin and was quickly losing weight in spite of the protein bars he kept eating. Before the end of the football season, he was gone. I was grateful for the feeling that warned me to accept his offer so that we spent golden time together in his last few months.

The feeling I had when the ticket was offered turned out to be a form of prophecy, an insight that told me to do something now to enjoy a friendship that was about to end. The real prophets in this story were the doctors. The first one heard a complaint about loss of voice and failed to detect fluid in the lungs. The emergency room doctor was flabbergasted that cancer had gone undetected in several visits to a primary doctor. Medical diagnosis and prognosis are modern variations of what the ancients knew as prophecy.

After the resurrection, the early Jesus Movement looked for scriptural justification for believing in a Messiah who was executed and resurrected. Paul's appeal to scriptural support in 1 Corinthians 15:3 and the story of the journey to Emmaus in Luke 24:13–35 indicate the importance that was given to interpreting what they saw as prophecy related to Jesus. Looking into the distant past for prophetic support became a feature of the Christian approach that distorted the role the ancient prophets played in their lifetimes. The result has been a popular notion that prophets see and predict the distant future. Actually, they were most concerned about what they believed was going to happen very soon. Their role, similar to modern physicians, was to diagnose current symptoms and issue a prognosis for the near future. For the most part they were concerned about how a nation was straying from the path God wanted followed. Sometimes they were concerned about binding up the wounds of a people or even performing wonders and cures that showed the power of God.

The popular approach to the ancient prophets takes them out of their historical context to look for enduring messages; however, they can't be truly understood until they are first placed in the settings that compelled their actions. The books of Samuel and Kings are considered prophetic books in the Tanakh. Samuel's narrative describes events connected with Samuel and Nathan at the origin of the "house of David." Kings tells of Elijah, and Elisha under Ahab and those following him in the northern kingdom. None of the remaining prophetic books are arranged in historical order in any of the biblical arrangements.

If the Old Testament prophetic books were arranged in chronological order, Kings would be followed by Amos and then Hosea, both of whom made their proclamations in the Kingdom of Israel during a long period of prosperity before the Assyrians became a threat in the 730s BCE. Micah in Judah would come next, for he lived about the time of Amos and Hosea and continued into the reign of Hezekiah. His prophecies against Jerusalem were intended to spur Hezekiah to resist the Assyrians in the years leading to the siege of 701. Isaiah was also active under Hezekiah, supporting his reforms.[206]

The next group of prophets were active around the time of Josiah (641–609 BCE). Nahum and Habakkuk prophesied about the fall of Assyria to the emerging dominance of the Babylonians. Zephaniah supported the reforms of Josiah as did Jeremiah, whose career extended through all of the attacks on Jerusalem by the Babylonians. Ezekiel was apparently among those taken to Babylon, where his prophesies occurred. Following the return to Jerusalem around 520, the prophets Haggai and Zechariah were active in urging the rebuilding of the temple.

All of the prophets who were active before the destruction of Jerusalem predicted disaster and conquest as punishment for violating the covenant with

God. Each was focused on their own time, even though Micah and Isaiah are often cited for messianic predictions. These prophets were preserved because their predictions seemed to come true. These books refer to other prophets—especially those at court—who gave more favorable advice but whose words have not been honored by following ages.

From Elijah until the fall of Jerusalem, prophets reacted to political and social as well as religious trends in the monarchies that were growing in strength. The society that developed reminds me of the political history in Georgia in my youth as rural areas fought the emerging power of cities with their northern ways leading away from old southern lifestyles. For decades governors were elected using the county unit system, which allowed rural counties to overcome the population majorities of the cities. It was not until the 1960s, as the Civil Rights Movement gained strength, that rural dominance was overthrown. The same city versus country struggle took place in the Israelite monarchies, as cities were centers of power where kings, their officials, priests, and other allies lived who constituted a small elite over the society of the time. Most people lived in villages that were self-governing based on traditional principles. The elite in the cities increasingly gained economic dominance over the country so that absentee landlords began to take over ancestral lands. This very tension between city and villages can also be seen in the days of Jesus and is reflected in his preference for village communities.

Amos, Hosea, and Micah are often quoted for their statements on social justice. Their comments were aimed against a prosperous society going through rapid development, which overwhelmingly benefitted the city elites. Priests were part of the elite, so temple rituals were denounced as insufficient when requirements for justice and fairness were ignored.

Their times were not very different from the dynamics of our own time. A period of deregulation by the federal government and substantial reduction of taxes on the wealthy generated a time of economic growth characterized by increasingly high compensation for those at the top in our society, while those in the middle and lower brackets have seen far less benefits. The power of the moneyed-elite through corporate groups has been dramatically increased by recent Supreme Court rulings. Televised religious programming features the showy prosperity of celebrity religious leaders. The three prophets from times of prosperity would have a field day with the American cult of getting rich and buying luxury goods for display as much as personal use.

Before the destruction of Jerusalem, prophets came from commoners and the elite. They were often called through visions, which they described. Like other prophets in the Near East, they were known for ecstatic behavior and sometimes working wonders and healing people. They were also known for strange public demonstrations as part of their proclamation as in examples in Hosea, Isaiah, and Ezekiel. Hosea says God commanded him to marry an unfaithful woman, have children, and give them names signifying rejection (1:2–9). Isaiah tells of having a son and giving him a name as a sign of God's intention to ruin Damascus and Samaria (8:1–4). Then he walked naked and barefoot for three years as a sign of the approaching conquest of Egypt and Ethiopia by Assyria (20:1–4). In Ezekiel, God tells him to lie on his left side for 360 days and then his right side for 40 days to represent punishment for the kingdoms of Israel and Judah (4:1–9). These prophets were popular figures who made their proclamations orally and in public. Only Jeremiah was known to use a scribe to record his oracles. They lived in an oral culture in which few people could write and read.

After returning from exile, prophecy continued but with significant differences. The names of prophets from bygone eras were used in writings that relied on visions and intricate imagery. Rather than being proclaimed in public by popular figures, these were books by scribal groups who set their visions in an earlier time. The commentary was still focused on the times in which they wrote so that the visions announced the fate of current world powers. Daniel, who supposedly lived under the Persians, had visions about the succession of empires following the conquest by Alexander the Great. The New Testament book of Revelation, which was not an anonymous work, used the strategy of a heavenly vision to forecast terrible consequences for the Roman Empire.

The recorded prophecy that we have after the fall of Jerusalem is no longer a popular phenomenon. It is not proclaimed in public settings and the prophets do not attract followers who record and honor their words. The literature that is described as apocalyptic was a scribal phenomenon. It became known among the public, as is evident from Jesus's knowledge of the Son of Man imagery from Daniel. No doubt popular prophecy continued in some form but there is no record of it until the movements of John the Baptist and Jesus. Outside the gospels, Flavius Josephus records information about John the Baptist and Jesus as well as other popular prophetic movements that followed. The gospels also make it clear that John and Jesus continued the tradition of focusing on current issues as they spoke of God's coming judgment.

Earlier I mentioned that doctors are like prophets in our time. They apply basic principles of medicine as they test and diagnose. Their job often is to figure out what is causing problems. When diagnosis is made, they recommend treatment. Very often they will be reluctant to give a prognosis because many factors can determine how long it takes a disease process to run its course. Too many people every day hear in their doctors the voice of doom that many people hear when they read the prophets.

Biblical prophets had much too simplistic a view of life, seeing in all national and personal misfortune the impact of sin and disobedience. They had little appreciation for the impersonal nature of disease and economic and weather processes. Yet behind everything, they saw a God who gave meaning to life. From their visions emerged true monotheism and a foundation that allowed the people of Israel to continue worship of their God without having a territory to call home. J.R. McNeill referred to this as the first development of portable religion, a belief system freed of connection with territorially limited power.[207] A God who did not protect his own people from conquest became acknowledged through their exile as the God of everyone.

Christians believe they continue the traditions of the ancient prophets. Meeting someone like Will Campbell, an incarnation in recent times of the spirits of Amos and Jeremiah, is not a comfortable experience for those in power. A political system based on tolerance and democratic compromise finds it difficult to accommodate an uncompromising dedication to a cause. That's why someone like Will Campbell was not likely to be invited to participate in presidential inaugurations.

Chapter Thirty-Two

Does God Want Praise?

Asking a favor of someone who doesn't know you can be very difficult. Not long ago I needed to ask a favor of a distinguished person I didn't know. She knew a good friend of mine and that provided an entrée. We met in her office at a time when it was clear she was extremely rushed yet was allowing me a few precious minutes. I began with light conversation on some topics in her specialty, establishing that I was acquainted with her field. There were opportunities to let it show that I was familiar with several of her books. Before long I sensed a need to bring up the request. As I made a transition in the conversation, her posture became straighter in the chair and tension began to show in her face. She was a very busy person overwhelmed with more requests than could be granted. People always detect when you are about to ask for something and leading up to it with praise can often warn them to get ready to say no.

One of the supervisory courses I taught for many years involved giving criticism to employees during performance reviews. A method I was expected to teach was called the sandwich because it advocated leading up to each criticism with praise and then following with praise. I never liked that technique because it sent mixed signals by trying to soften the impact of negative performance information you wanted to be taken seriously. When I saw interviews using that method, it became obvious that employees were never fooled by the praise. As soon as they heard the good things, they tensed up waiting for the other shoe to drop. Really serious criticism was often given away by excessive praise on very small things, signaling that something really bad was coming.

When you want something, buttering someone up doesn't always work. Some people take a different approach by handing out laurels in a way that reminds someone that they owe a favor. A variation on this approach is to dispense with the praise and do something you think someone needs to have done, then let the person know they need to do something for you in return. These are coercive approaches that can make enemies even though they do what you ask.

There are many strategies people use to get something they want from God as well. One example can be found in Psalm 86. The superscription says this was a prayer of David. It begins with a request to preserve the person's life because God is being called on in a time of trouble. Then verses 8–12 turn to praise to motivate God to grant the request:

> There is none like you among the gods, O Lord, nor are there any works like yours.
> All the nations you have made shall come and bow down before you, O Lord, and shall glorify your name.
> For you are great and do wondrous things; you alone are God.
> Teach me your way, O Lord, that I may walk in your truth; give me an undivided heart to revere your name.
> I give thanks to you, O Lord my God, with my whole heart, and I will glorify your name forever.

The language in this psalm is found in Christian worship services routinely. Have we stopped to think about what we are saying? If God answers our prayer, the reward will be that nations and individuals will "glorify your name." This suggests that God is motivated by praise from his human subjects.

The same way of thinking is found outside the Bible in the Westminster Shorter Catechism where it says the purpose of humanity is "to glorify God, and to enjoy him forever." It goes on to say that scriptures teach us the duty we owe to God, which in part is to glorify God.[208]

Why would God want to be glorified? Does that make sense for a power responsible for our vast universe? If it is true that God really wants people to praise and glorify him, it suggests divine egotism of the kind that was seen in Near Eastern monarchs in ancient times. Biblical imagery of the majesty of God seems to be modeled on political trappings of those times when kings and emperors sat on thrones and hosts of court attendants bowed before them, reciting praise as part of court etiquette. This appears to be a case of projecting the behavior of leading political figures, who used religious claims of divine status, onto a transcendent God who became an enlarged version of the egotism, jealousy, and wrath of the kings.

This kind of praise shows how culture shapes our religious efforts. People seek God in ways that make sense to them or seem to work in their time. Flattering authority figures with authoritarian power that was used arbitrarily made sense in those cultures. There may be some leaders in our time who expect the kind of fawning praise seen in early Near Eastern cultures, but elected democratic governments would see this use of praise as offensive. Why wouldn't God be offended by overt praise? Using praise as a way of manipulating authority figures is not publicly acceptable today. Why would God respond favorably to such an approach?

Not long ago I had a conversation with a charismatic Christian who told me about going through a crisis when his wife became suddenly ill. He told me that when he really needed something from God, he fasted for a week and increased his prayer and praise routine so that he would be sure to receive the desired blessing. A week of fasting and praise had not worked when his wife was rushed to the emergency room and needed immediate life-saving surgery. Her life hung in the balance for several weeks as she experienced severe pain. His response was to fast and increase the prayer routine until she improved. It took three weeks. He told me he was becoming nervous as time went by, but he knew God would eventually respond to a method that always worked for him. Without realizing it, he was describing a way to use praise to coerce God to do what he wanted done.

The problem with this outmoded use of praise is that we assume that God wants and even needs ego gratification through flattery. Thomas Merton described the error this way: "We seek Him as if He could not do without our sacrifices, as if He needed to be entertained by our affection and flattered by our praise. We cannot find Him unless we know we need Him."[209]

A different image of God is presented in the book of Isaiah. Carolyn Sharp points out that God is referred to as "the Holy One of Israel" twenty-five times in Isaiah but rarely in other books.[210] This title is reinforced by the vision described in Isaiah 6. The prophet saw God "sitting on a throne, high and lofty; and the hem of his robe filled the temple." Holiness is emphasized not by describing God but by telling of the behavior of the six-winged seraphs in attendance. Four of their wings were used to cover their faces and genitals because they were in the presence of holiness.[211] They recited praise as smoke filled the temple and it shook with the voices of the seraphs. Isaiah's response was a sense of unworthiness in the face of the awesome separateness of God. He was commissioned as a prophet as one of the seraphs brought a burning coal from the altar to remove sin by touching his lips.

The sense of God's separateness and otherness from creation is seen in Exodus as the people of Israel cringe at the base of the smoking mountain hearing thunder and seeing lightning to indicate the presence of God. They tell Moses to speak to them because they fear that death will follow if God speaks directly to them. The Holy of Holies in the tent and the temple also represented the separateness of God even when present among the people, for anyone who entered without being purified risked immediate death. The message was that humanity was not equal to the majesty and holiness of a transcendent God.

We are aware of the separateness, the otherness, of God and somehow that seems to increase human seeking for God's presence. Prayer, reading scripture, and worship services are methods we use for establishing and maintaining a sense of the presence of God in our lives. In all forms of religious expression, praise is an important aspect of our quest for relationship. As Bernhard Andersons explains, all of the psalms in the Bible, including the multitude outside the book of Psalms, are forms of praise, even the third of them that are complaints.[212] But in spite of all efforts, there come times when we feel an absence or silence of God. This is especially distressing when we go through personal crises, for then we may desperately seek God by turning up the praise as if that would guarantee a response.

Why is praise an important aspect of seeking God? The answer, it seems to me, lies in our need rather than in God's nature. Just as the desire for God is built into the human brain, the need for praise as part of relationship is a built-in human need. A God of holiness and separateness from all of creation is certainly beyond needing to be praised by his creatures. Desperate uses of praise to get God's attention are actions showing the extent of our anxiety.

People also need to complain as well as praise. The psalms in the Bible provide many examples of criticisms aimed at God, which are also turned into another form of praise. The laments in the Bible are requests that lead with gripes as a way of trying to get what they want. Believe it or not, that is often an effective way of asking for something from people in power today. Letters of complaint to elected officials at all levels often bring quick responses that try to solve problems or at least give the person something that will make them feel their representative pays attention to their concerns.

It is also important to note that a substantial percentage of the book of Psalms consists of thanksgiving as a form of praise that is focused on something good that happened rather than on asking for something. We need to express appreciation as well as complaints and requests for help. Rehearsing the story of Israel's past in psalms was an important ritual of worship as a community reminded itself through thanksgiving of its historic allegiance to God because of deliverance.

In my experience as a manager and professor, I have seen those under my authority use praise, complaint, and thanks to get what they want. Someone in authority today is always aware that they answer to someone else or are accountable under specific policies or laws, so any request has to be given fair consideration even if presented in ways that seem insulting. The person thanking you is not usually difficult to deal with but you have to be on your guard not to respond by offering things in return even though they haven't been requested. Personally, I preferred dealing with the complainer more than someone who started with praise. Most often the complainer is upset about something and doesn't realize that a request is being implied. When you listen and seriously address the concern, the person feels listened to and a positive relationship is built. The job of the person in responsibility is not to be manipulated by praise or angered by criticism as the issues are identified and addressed as constructively as possible.

Perhaps God also tolerates both complaint and praise as natural expressions of his creatures without being influenced one way or the other. A person in authority today finds it is often beneficial when you take the time to listen to someone. Allowing people to express their concerns in their own way is therapeutic so that they feel better no matter what action you take. People also find the same kind of therapy in expressing their feelings to God. Sometimes it is difficult for a manager or professor not to take offense when people are expressing themselves, but they are obligated to avoid that trap. Surely God is beyond holding grudges for anything negative that is aimed in his direction.

Does God want praise? I doubt it. I don't think that our purpose is to glorify God's name because the existence of the universe is what glorifies God. I think that God is tolerant and understanding of humanity living out the needs built into us. It is we who need to express praise in many different forms—and we should thank God for giving us this avenue for therapeutic interaction.

Chapter Thirty-Three

Formula Versus Risk

Because I was the oldest of four children, my mother put extra responsibility on a son who already was inclined to take things too seriously. A sense of moral obligation along with a drive to succeed were daily burdens. Rigidity, especially when combined with fundamentalist religion, made me extremely judgmental. Young people are known for taking foolish risks that ignore their mortality, but that was not true of this young puritan. There was constant fear that straying from the narrow path might bring failure that would irretrievably damage my future.

Getting older often brings a sense of freedom and it did for me. As I matured, life taught me to be less judgmental. My religious beliefs became more tolerant. Completing educational goals put me on the social and cultural path I wanted to follow. Surviving many of life's unexpected challenges led to confidence that overcame the fear of failure that haunted the early years. I was a stable, reliable, hardworking professional who worked at the same place for over thirty years. Within that protective shell, I found myself willing to take more risks through part-time ventures. I held to a rule of risk-taking learned when playing poker in college—never stake more on a hand than you can afford to lose. Absorbing some of life's hard knocks made me more willing to take risks because I learned that even when you lose, there can be strength to recover and forge ahead.

After a few inactive years following retirement, the penchant for risk-taking asserted itself. Having recovered from a divorce, I was ready to meet new women. I volunteered for the Atlanta Symphony and other groups, but the women I met were usually married. Then I decided to try online dating. Twice I found rewarding relationships with women in college towns about forty or fifty miles from where I lived. Each relationship lasted more than a year but ended due to issues that naturally come with being older. When the second relationship ended suddenly, I was very grief-stricken but went back to online dating rather than sit around being depressed.

Exactly a week after the breakup, I met Vickie and we quickly became serious even though I was still grieving a recent loss. Several close friends warned me that I was on the rebound and in no mental condition to make a long-term commitment. I knew what they said was true, but the situation developed quickly and they did not see it as completely as I did. Meeting Vickie was all it took to change the opinions of those closest to me.

My friends admired the woman who had just broken up with me. They were also experienced counselors who knew about the stages of grief and basic principles used in all types of therapy. As soon as they met Vickie, they saw the possibilities I saw as well as the challenge of getting over a previous relationship. All of us were aware of formulas that are applied to these situations most of the time. Those closest to me agreed this was a time to make an exception to normal rules.

One friend who prided himself on his skill as a marital counselor did not get to know Vickie and held tight to the formulas he was sure worked best. You must completely get over the past before you launch into a relationship, he urged. He felt so strongly that he declined to participate in our wedding, which happened three months after we first met. The other friends played roles in the wedding as one of them performed the ceremony.

Many people think that the wisdom that comes with education, experience, and age involves learning to apply formulas for success. I could easily name five motivational speakers who make lots of money with presentations on the five, or seven, or ten steps to happiness and success in whatever field you want to name. This is also the approach of those who preach the gospel of prosperity on television and in mega churches. My experience has been quite different. I am suspicious of inflexible formulas for success because life presents us with so many exceptions to most rules.

The wisdom literature in the Bible has been neglected in Protestant traditions, except for sermons on Mother's Day using the section in Proverbs on the good wife (31:10–31). Some of the wisdom tradition seems at odds with prophetic messages, or at least seems more focused on worldly experience than on covenant with God, so that it doesn't fit into the Christian preference for seeing the Old Testament as pointing to a coming Messiah.

Within the wisdom literature there is a dissonance not found in other parts of the Bible. Prophets and Deuteronomists may have been at odds over the importance of temple rituals, but they agreed that disloyalty to the Mosaic covenant was the explanation for personal and national disasters. Far more variety of opinion is found in the wisdom books.

Many people are unaware that the book of Psalms is part of the wisdom tradition. In its final version, Psalms is a compilation of different collections organized into five parts, mirroring the books of the Torah. The psalm that leads the entire collection is a product of the wisdom tradition, suggesting at the beginning that the entire book should be seen in that light.[213] The message of the first psalm is simple. There are two ways, one leading to happiness and prosperity and the other to disaster. Success and wisdom come through meditation on the Torah and making it the guide for life. The message is that there is a formula for successful living, what Douglas Knight and Amy-Jill Levine point to as an "act-consequence connection" or cause and effect relationship.[214] Yet within the book of Psalms there are strong voices of dissent, especially in the laments, just as there is also dissent in the books of Ecclesiastes and Job.

The connection between right living and success is something that the prophets, Deuteronomists, and the Chronicler wanted to believe in. Personal and national crises are the result of disobedience in some form. When God is honored and obeyed, things go right. Bad health, economic reverses, sudden deaths are all explained as punishment for sins. All forms of suffering and misfortune are products of attitudes and behaviors. The cure is repentance. This is a consistent formula in the Old Testament.

The books of Proverbs, Ecclesiastes, and the Wisdom of Jesus Ben Sira were products of a scribal class. This means they were relatively well-to-do members of the elite of their society who enjoyed education and leisure to pursue study. These males personified wisdom as a woman but most often used female imagery in negative ways, as did the prophets, or praised females only as they pleased their husbands as in the description of the good wife versus the contentious wife in Proverbs.

Ecclesiastes presents a mildly dissenting voice to the biblical formula. The book begins with the famous statement that all is vanity, which the *Jewish Study Bible* translates as:

> Utter futility!—All is futile!
> What real value is there for a man
> In all the gains he makes beneath the sun?[215]

I call this mild dissent because the preacher does not reject the usual formula for success but ignores it. The lesson of experience is that nothing endures and it is best to simply enjoy the life we have while we can. The speaker doesn't probe into the implications of his realizations to speculate about good and evil or the purpose of God. He seems resigned to the way things are. He doesn't deny the importance of obeying God, but doesn't imitate the zeal of the prophets and Deuteronomists as he advocates moderation in all things. In spite of futility, there is affirmation of life—but it is a lukewarm affirmation at best.

Job takes dissent from the wisdom, prophetic, and priestly traditions to the extreme. The prologue and conclusion (1:1–2:13, 42:7–17), which appear to have been a folk story to which the poetic middle section was added later, show a disturbing picture of God playing a game that involves arbitrarily destroying the life of a faithful servant. Those responsible for these segments wanted to reflect traditional values by showing that virtue that withstands testing is rewarded, but they actually made things worse by describing a God who appears to ignore the promise of the covenant for what amounts to a game at the expense of someone described as extremely faithful. Calling it testing rather than a game does not make things better.

The poetry making up the heart of the book shows Job maintaining his innocence as his friends tell him he is questioning the justice of God. They advise him to curse God so he will die, but Job responds by cursing the day of his birth and wishes he had been stillborn. Finally God confronts Job, overwhelming him with superiority to human limitations without addressing any of Job's complaints. This is an unusual version of a judgment scene. God does not appear in a judicial or any anthropomorphic role as power is demonstrated through a voice in a whirlwind (40:6–41:34). There is no review of Job's life. There is a divine challenge to justify how a human being can presume to question the ways of a God beyond human comprehension. The nature of good and evil has been raised in the book and left unresolved, yet the poetic section makes clear that the old formulas are not adequate.

The psalms also present a variety of opinions going beyond the interests of a scribal elite. Laments present extensive suffering in often demanding tones that are then modulated into praise. Words of praise and confidence in God do not mask the desperation and skepticism voiced in the statements of suffering.[216] This is not hypocrisy, but a reflection of the natural ambivalence we feel in times of crisis when we don't see the divine hand moving events in the direction we want. It is unrealistic to deny that even deep trust is untinged with doubt as people undergo trials.[217]

The wisdom parts of the Bible have been described as efforts to understand the meaning of life. Perhaps this reflects the fact that many of the proverbial sayings are from the vantage point of age reflecting on lessons learned in the course of sixty or more years. Many of the wise answers follow a clear formula, as in Psalm 1 and in the works of the prophets, Deuteronomists, and Chronicler. But there is also a dissonance pointing to unresolved issues and the ultimate incomprehensibility of the ways of God as seen in life events.

In our time, people who reach their fifties or sixties can find themselves taking more risks than when stability was needed for a growing family. They change careers, develop long neglected interests with a new passion, or even take a chance on new relationships when children and friends object. Age brings a willingness to discard old formulas such as the idea that someone is called to one vocation or marriage for life. Rather than resting in a homey rocking chair, they take on the role of Odysseus late in life.

Formulas that seemed to work earlier in life may not apply to later stages. The Bible does not provide safe answers for those who support or oppose the kind of change that permeates society in our times. Perhaps the riskier mentality of our times has something to add to the way meaning was perceived in biblical times—which implies that God continues to speak through experiences today rather than being frozen in old formulas.

CHAPTER THIRTY-FOUR

CAN GOD BE TRUSTED?

In the early 1960s, Stanley Milgram did a troubling study at Yale University to test how obedient people would be to recognized authority. A number of ordinary people were paid for participation in research they were told would substantially improve human welfare. They were in a room with a test subject who was to perform specific tasks. If the subject failed or messed up, electrical shock was administered. The director of the experiment wore a lab coat and gave all the instructions. The ordinary people were told to increase the level of shock administered if mistakes continued. The subject even began to express pain and plead with the person at the controls as the dosage was often increased to the maximum amount. People at the controls were often reluctant to continue administering shock, but the director gave firm instructions that most often were followed.[218]

To those who are familiar with World War II, this experiment will remind you of Nazi atrocities on Jews and other non-Aryans, all of which were conducted by ordinarily good people following orders. That indeed was the point of the experiment. Rather than the authority of a military uniform, participants responded to the authority and superior knowledge implied by the lab coat of a scientist. For good scientific reasons, people usually continued to inflict what they thought was horrible pain in order to do as they were told. The entire experiment was a set up. The subject was not in pain but was instructed to act as if he were. The point was to see how far ordinary people would go in doing something unreasonable and even horrible simply because someone in authority told them to do it.

Even more distressing is that the book of Job shows God participating in the same kind of experiment. The story begins with the extreme faithfulness of Job in abiding by the requirements of the Mosaic covenant. The expected response would be fidelity to that covenant by God as part of the deal. Yet when a servant, which is what Satan was in this case, more or less bet God that the good guy could be shaken, God took the bet. In the guise of testing, Job loses everything in wave after wave of bad fortune intended to see how much he could take. The story ends with restitution that was supposed to cover up the betrayal that happened within the story—but those first children were still dead, which indicates that Job's grief could not be completely reversed.

Think of the experience of Israel in the 700s and 500s BCE. Three separate invasions by Assyrians resulted in the elimination of the Kingdom of Israel as their elite were deported and apparently absorbed with no trace remaining—the ten lost tribes. Two or three conquests by Babylon led to Jerusalem and the temple being destroyed with leadership deported to Mesopotamia. This time the remnant were allowed to maintain their identity so that a community of Babylonian Jews became a significant force in the further development of the people of Israel. The final compilation of the Old Testament happened after the exile so that the viewpoint of the surviving remnant is reflected with its emphasis on Jerusalem and the temple. Restoration of the people to their native land and the rebuilding of Jerusalem and the temple bring the Jewish scripture to completion.

The Old Testament struggles with the issue of whether God is to be trusted in terms of events leading to the destruction and rebuilding of their center in Jerusalem. The persistent theme is that God is faithful to the covenant while the people stray and bring horrible events upon themselves. God's righteous anger is followed by mercy that allows the people to continue and return to their homeland. How that mercy was applied to those in the north who were lost is not discussed. The key is ultimate fidelity to those centered in Jerusalem.

Today we see world events in a different perspective. Israel and Judah were enmeshed in a political system dominated by imperial powers in Mesopotamia and Egypt without a chance of overcoming either. Finding a way to cooperate with whoever was on top at the time was important. Uncompromising attitudes on religion impacted diplomacy and brought unavoidable conquest.

Since the formation of the United Nations, the world has become aware of the human scourge of genocide. The exile of the nation of Judah has now been followed in Jewish awareness by the horror of the Holocaust, the incredibly methodical effort by Hitler to eliminate several groups in Europe but especially the Jews. This horrific experience raised even more issues about how trustworthy God is as a keeper of his special people. But there are others with experiences too similar. Native Americans have spoken against what they perceive as systematic efforts to eliminate them from North America since the arrival of Europeans. The last fifty years have seen numerous efforts in many parts of the world to exterminate entire peoples in the name of some cause. Unfortunately, there are parts of the Bible that can be used as support for genocidal campaigns.

The Bible presents the answer that ultimately God is faithful to the covenant and the fault lies in the sins of the people. Terrible events are the result of righteous anger that may last a long time but always returns to mercy and ultimate commitment that is seen across many generations rather than in things that happen to one or two generations during bad times. God also tests the loyalty of his people. The example of Job was supposed to show that God is faithful in spite of testing, but it really shows a God whose agreement to keep his end of the covenant doesn't rule out making bets that lead to horrible destruction and death as relatively unimportant collateral damage.

Let's take a closer look at the Mosaic covenant. Christians have historically expressed who they are through creeds, statements that begin with "I believe." Heresies have been defined in terms of variations in belief from precise wording that is considered acceptable or orthodox. This approach is not consistent with the Mosaic covenant. At Sinai or Horeb (it makes no difference which account is used) the people of Israel are told to be loyal to a single God who does not tolerate images and who requires honoring the seventh day. It is not a matter of believing this is the only God, rather of being faithful and obeying only this God and no other. The commandments themselves make no promises to those who follow them other than that they will be the people of this God and that long life will come to those who honor parents. The people are commanded to adopt certain behaviors and an uncompromising loyalty to a single God. They are called on to trust this God to stand by them as his adopted people. The people take on restrictions but get very few specific promises in return.

The formulas laid out by prophets, Deuteronomists, the Chronicler, and the wisdom writers are expressions of hope that obedience will be rewarded because it is backed by trust in the character, loyalty, and fidelity of God himself.

This is relying on an interpersonal relationship with a power beyond our comprehension. That hope is disappointed again and again, so explanations are sought in terms of human infidelity.

The post-Biblical experience of the Holocaust raised the issue of God's trustworthiness to an extent beyond any of the historical events in the Bible. For the Jews, the Holocaust approximated the destruction of Noah's flood, which is followed by a promise never again to try to wipe out humanity. The Mosaic covenant and the Noah covenant were called into question by events in the twentieth century.

Christians have tried to nail down the vulnerability of trust by emphasizing the importance of specific beliefs as the key to salvation. Belief in the resurrection, in the divinity of Jesus as Christ, in the complete accuracy of the Bible has been used as guarantees of God's reliability. This alternative has proved untenable in an ever-changing world in which no truth is invulnerable to the mutations of human culture and evolution of the universe.

Biblical faith is an expression of hope in the ultimate trustworthiness of God to the extent that we know him through human cultural experiences. The conviction of prophets, Deuteronomists, the Chronicler, and the wisdom writers is no guarantee. The experience of Job in the poetic sections of the book mirrors the emotional depths of the Holocaust, which is a universal human experience not limited to one people. The resolution is amazement and continued affirmation of a God beyond our knowing. The only hope we have for meaning in this universe is that God shares human traits to the extent that we can know something of this ultimately unknowable power and that God is fundamentally trustworthy even when events make no sense in human terms.

Our most appropriate response to life is best expressed by Job. The last lines of the poetic section conclude in 42:2–3 and 6:

> I know that you can do everything,
> That nothing you propose is impossible for you.
> Who is this who obscures counsel without knowledge?
> Indeed, I spoke without understanding
> Of things beyond me, which I did not know . . . .
> Therefore, I recant and relent,
> Being but dust and ashes. (JPS)

The end of Job refers us back to Job 1:21, which expresses the conclusion of the book at its beginning:

> He said, "Naked came I out of my mother's womb, and naked shall I return there; the Lord has given, and the Lord has taken away; blessed be the name of the Lord." (JPS)

There is no way to escape human vulnerability when it comes to trust, for trust represents intuitive knowledge rather than hard knowledge based on evidence. The Bible and individual experiences are based on convictions that people have experienced God through national and personal events, but convictions are beliefs that too often are unsubstantiated by concrete evidence. We fall back on personal insights, which ultimately are forms of revelation—of direct intuitive knowledge based on interactions with the divine. Newspapers, television, and the Internet are full of claims of experiences of revelation, many of which are fraudulent efforts to take advantage of human credulity, as demonstrated over and over by Michael Schermer in his *Skeptic* magazine.

Trusting God is unavoidably risky. Efforts to find security in infallible beliefs result in idolatry, which is alien to the foundation of the Judeo-Christian tradition. When it comes to historical evidence, the facts of history and the certainty that everyone experiences disease and death appear to undermine trust in God as one who delivers from all threats to survival. Yet the Bible and the entire history of the Judeo-Christian tradition is testimony to human conviction that the God known through the Bible is ultimately trustworthy as the source of meaning and purpose in the universe.

Trying to avoid the extreme riskiness of trust in God is almost always a wrong turn toward idolatry. Life is an exciting adventure and risk is essential to what makes the journey most invigorating. Joining with Job in affirming the goodness of God at a desperate moment is taking quite a risk—but that is what makes life really worthwhile.

Chapter Thirty-Five

Legitimacy, Prophecy, and Daniel

Legitimacy is a concept that governs human behavior more than we realize. When I was growing up, we used legitimacy primarily to talk about whether someone's parents were married when they were born. Children of legitimate marriages were considered entitled to more rights than illegitimate kids. More importantly, legitimacy guides our sense of what is just or deserves recognition.

Before democratic governments, political leadership came through dynastic birth, which was seen as being chosen by God for leadership. The Bible is emphatic that birth in the line of David was essential for leadership of Judah. Our political system rests on elections and American history is full of revolutions at the ballot box without subsequent violent outbreaks because our tradition accepts even electoral results we don't like.

Within families, certain responsibilities are a right of birth order. I resisted what my mother thought were the responsibilities of her oldest child when I left home for college, putting myself through school with minimal help from my family. I had to go my own way because higher education was not part of the family culture in which I was raised. Mother turned to my younger brother to manage her affairs as she grew older and made him the executor of her estate. When she died, my brother made funeral arrangements and probated the will. Everyone knew he was performing the role of family leader, yet there were public responsibilities the oldest was expected to play if things were to be done right. It was my responsibility to lead the family at the funeral by doing things such as call everyone together around the casket, join hands, lead a family prayer, and then order the casket closed.

Not long after that my paternal grandmother died. My father had four brothers and three sisters. They were a contentious group known for fistfights when the family gathered. Aunt Catherine, the oldest of the children, had become what my grandfather called a "holy-roller" and insisted that her mother had to be sent to eternity with the right kind of funeral conducted by a true believer. Her brothers and sisters were protesting and pulling on my grandfather for a decision. I was not the oldest grandchild, but I was the first member of the family to go to college and then graduate school. Uncles and aunts treated me with a special dignity, recognizing a level of achievement they never envisioned. Grandfather had turned to me before for help and bragged to everyone about his grandson who had influence in Atlanta. He turned to me again with a plaintive look, asking me to handle it so that everyone got along with whatever solution was reached. Being recognized by grandfather, aunts, and uncles as the family leader ended up satisfying everyone. It was a special moment for me.

Before the Babylonian conquest of Judah, the Bible describes three elements of society that depended on claims of legitimacy. The dynasty of David was rejected by the northern tribes of Israel, but Judah maintained Davidic stability until the Exile. Priests also claimed authority by right of descent and the role of high priest was based on lineage as several families competed for succession. The third pillar, the prophets, were legitimate by God's calling rather than by birth. Kings and priests would be anointed as part of inaugurating their role, but for prophets the call of God was the equivalent to anointing. Most often the call came through visions, such as the one described by Isaiah when he saw God enthroned while he was worshiping in the temple. Prophets were popular figures but also recognized at court. Their oracles were spoken but later written accounts were made of what they said. They were known for speaking with direct authority from God, often beginning with words equivalent to "Here is what God said to me."

The return from exile was marked by a determination to restore the temple more than the Davidic monarchy. A descendant of the line of David came home with a high priest but mysteriously vanished from all records along with his dynasty. Under the domination of Persia and the Hellenistic rulers who followed Alexander the Great, the area of Judah was under immediate political, military, and religious leadership of the high priest. Dynastic in-fighting usually seen among royal contenders took place among priestly claimants, leading to dissenting views about the legitimacy of the temple as well as the line of priests who presided over it. The group that took refuge at Qumran separated themselves from the temple, declaring it polluted. Illegitimate leadership meant that all the implements and rituals were polluted as well. Their messianic visions included a cleansed temple under the leadership of the correct priestly dynasty. The Hasmonean family, which led the revolt against the Seleucids, restored the monarchy but never achieved the kind of acceptance recorded for the Davidic line. When they combined the role of high priest and king, religious dissent became prominent so that their leadership was a source of ongoing division in the country.

There is a Jewish tradition that prophecy ceased with the restoration of the temple and that conviction may explain why, with the exception of Daniel, apocalyptic books written in the Hellenistic and Roman periods were not included in the Tanakh. What came to an end was the public role of popular prophets. No doubt there continued to be those known for performing wonders and healing people, but few were recorded until the gospels and Josephus noted the roles of John the Baptist and Jesus as popular prophets. There is also no record of prophets playing a role in official circles, as was the case with Isaiah and Jeremiah. It was the scribes who continued religious traditions that may have played a role at court. They expressed their criticisms in prophetic writings known as apocalypses.

It appears that in a period when the traditions of the past were compiled in writing to form the Bible, new prophecy was expressed in writing among select groups. As this trend took shape, the writers didn't reveal their identity or claim the same kind of authority that had been the habit of earlier prophets, for they used the names of reputed prophetic figures from the past, such as Daniel, Enoch, and Moses. Like the prophets of old, these writers were speaking about conditions of their own times but appealed to legitimacy of old prophetic voices as having foreseen the true dynamics of the current time.

The postexilic prophets made special use of visions. The pre-exilic prophets had used visions as part of their message from God, but angelic interpreters of visions became a distinctive characteristic of apocalyptic works. The term apocalypse is based on a Greek word meaning revelation. As a literary genre, the apocalypse became prominent around the middle of the first century CE. There are aspects of several prophetic books in the Bible that could be called apocalyptic, but Daniel is the only apocalypse in the Tanakh and Revelation is the only one in the New Testament. John Collins defined apocalyptic literature this way:

> The form of the apocalypse involves a narrative framework that describes the manner of revelation. The main means of revelation are visions and otherworldly journeys, supplemented by discourse or dialogue and occasionally by a heavenly book. The constant element is the presence of an angel who interprets the vision and serves as guide on the otherworldly journey. This figure indicates that the revelation is not intelligible without supernatural aid. It is out of this world. In all the Jewish apocalypses, the human recipient is a venerable figure from the distant past, whose name is used pseudonymously. This device adds to the remoteness and mystery of the revelation. The disposition of the seer before the revelation and his reaction to it typically emphasize human helplessness in the face of the supernatural.[219]

A great many of the writings considered apocalyptic developed after the Second Temple period, which means they came after Jesus. Richard Horsley describes important characteristics of those, such as Daniel, which originated during the Second Temple.

> Most of the second-temple Judean texts that have been classified as 'apocalyptic' take more or less the same form of 'vision-and-interpretation.' They consist largely of a review of previous history leading up to an acute historical crisis in Judea (that involves the composers). They conclude with a shorter future resolution of the crisis in God's judgment of the empire that is oppressing the people and renewal of the people of Judea and/or of all people.[220]

These definitions may seem confusing to those who are used to the popular concept of apocalyptic as involving the end of the world with a final judgment, especially as seen in the teachings of Jesus and the book of Revelation. One of the issues often discussed about Jesus is whether his vision of the kingdom of God involved an apocalyptic end time with universal resurrection and final judgment as opposed to transformation of ongoing existence. Richard Horsley, in the book just cited, is a leading proponent arguing that Jesus's teaching was not apocalyptic in the manner that has usually been presented.

Collins goes on to distinguish Jewish apocalypses into two general categories, those that are primarily otherworldly journeys and those, such as Daniel, that provide interpretations of historical events. Features distinguishing this literature from pre-exilic writings are that all of them involve judgment of the wicked, most of them envision an afterlife, and only some of them involve destruction or resurrection. Nearly all of them see some kind of "cosmic transformation" that does not necessarily involve destruction.[221] One thing that is clear is apocalyptic thought and literature saw the world as influenced by angels and demons, which Jesus also believed.

The only false claim to authorship that was allowed into the Tanakh was Daniel. Within the accepted Jewish canon there are compilations such as Isaiah that included at least two groupings from later prophets that were identified with the historical prophet. Psalms were traditionally attributed to David and the Torah to Moses, but there was no direct claim of authorship within those books. Apparently the compilers of the Tanakh were deceived in the case of Daniel because they rejected all other pseudonymous works such as those claimed for Enoch or Baruch.

Daniel is usually known for the stories of handwriting on a wall, three faithful believers thrown into a furnace without being burned, and Daniel in the den of lions. It is also known for a description of the Son of Man coming in clouds and for resurrection. Jesus made it clear he believed in resurrection and he used the term Son of Man in different ways, some of which reflected the use in Daniel.

The book of Daniel is actually made up of at least two separate works that have been combined. There appears to have been a cycle of works about the legendary Daniel, as indicated by three additional books that are in the Catholic and Orthodox Bibles and the Protestant Apocrypha, and that two books in the cycle were put together.[222] In chapters 1–6, Daniel is at the Babylonian and then the Persian court. Like Joseph in Egypt, he makes a reputation by interpreting dreams; but he does Joseph one better, because he has to know what the dream was without being told and then interpret it. Refusing to make a religious compromise leads to the effort to burn Shadrach, Meshach, and Abednego and then Daniel's victory over the lions. The stories in the first part continue with loyalty to prophetic traditions and manifest political resistance of a scribal group against Babylonian imperialism and the Hellenistic idolatry of Seleucid successors of Alexander the Great.

Chapters 7–12 describe heavenly visions that make the book apocalyptic. These chapters are a direct response to what was happening at the time because of Antiochus IV Epiphanes, the Seleucid king from 175–164 BCE. Most have heard the story of how Antiochus profaned the temple and demanded local observances that resulted in the revolt of a rural priest whose sons led the Jews to temporary independence and cleansing of the temple, which is celebrated as Hanukah. The story is more complicated because Antiochus had supporters among the high priestly families, resulting in a civil war that brought seizure of control by a family allied with Antiochus. They turned Jerusalem into a polis in the Greek manner. The scribes responsible for Daniel are protesting the actions of those priests and Antiochus prior to the events that led to the Maccabee uprising because the book of Daniel shows no awareness of the revolt. The context assumed by these visions is suffering by martyrs who have no hope of ordinary military victory so that their only hope for justice is beyond life through God's vindication.[223]

Christian interest has focused on the content of two chapters: the role of the Son of Man in chapter 7 and resurrection in chapter 12. A vision of four horrible beasts is described in chapter 7 with the worst of them representing Antiochus. This is happening in heaven so that thrones were set in place and God ("Ancient of Days" in the JPS and "Ancient One" in the NRSV, 7:9) took the seat of judgment. The beast representing Antiochus is killed and the power of other beasts is removed. Then appears "one like a human being," which is the translation of Son of Man, who comes in clouds and is given everlasting dominion by God. But that is not all. Daniel doesn't understand, so one of the angelic attendants provides an interpretation. Verses 26–28 appear to interpret the passage on the Son of Man by saying that dominion will be given to "the people of the holy ones of the Most High." The interpretation seems to tell us that the human-like figure that is such a contrast to the horrible beasts is not one person, but the Jews who have been faithful to God.

Beginning in the 10th chapter, Daniel describes yet another vision of the succession of empires which leads to defeat of the final ruler. In chapter 12 we are told that the angel Michael will arise after that defeat so that a time of trouble will follow, during which "many of those who sleep in the dust of the earth will awake, some to eternal life, others to reproaches, to everlasting abhorrence." This passage has been used to support belief in general resurrection as part of a last judgment, but the wording is not clear. "Many" does not necessarily imply a resurrection of everyone. It also is mentioned as part of a time of troubles following the defeat of the last terrible king and is not mentioned as part of giving dominion to the human figure who represents complete triumph over evil.

These visions represent a belief in final vindication as an act of God, but they use poetic symbols that do not give a consistent picture of what the judgment will be like. The ideas about the figure of the Son of Man and of resurrection are not clear, yet popular beliefs that gave a messianic role to the Son of Man and associated a general resurrection with the judgment seemed to emerge from these passages and from other apocalyptic writings. Jesus seemed to know Daniel and perhaps other writings so that his ideas about the Son of Man and resurrection were influenced. Such beliefs were considered legitimate prophecy, as indicated by comments of Josephus about Daniel as a great prophet.

The legitimacy of Daniel as divinely inspired was recognized when it was incorporated into the Tanakh, but popular recognition occurred long before the approval of a canon. Other prophetic works closer to the times of Jesus appear to have been considered legitimate in that period even though not recognized by later Jewish or Protestant canons. Even when the accounts are acknowledged as authoritative prophecy, the meaning of apparently contradictory imagery is still unclear because the divine interpretation within the text is not consistent or clear. No wonder it is difficult to grasp how Jesus understood and used this prophecy.

CHAPTER THIRTY-SIX

WHAT DOES GOD LOOK LIKE?

Three of the commandments received at Sinai are very clear. Jews are to worship only one God who does not tolerate images and who wants his name to be respected. Other religions of the Near East had multiple gods represented in images of people, animals, or imaginary creatures. Under domination by Hellenistic kings and Roman emperors, Jews were known for resisting efforts to place images in their temple. A compromise was made with the Romans so that a daily offering was made on behalf of the Roman emperor, at Roman expense, rather than to the emperor. They even refused to use coins with drawings of people on them, so that money changers were needed in the temple to provide worshipers from many nations with coinage suitable for buying animals to sacrifice and for making contributions to the temple. There were at least two riots when images of the emperor were brought into Jerusalem. This was also a time when Jews interpreted the commandment about respecting the name of God to mean that it should not be mentioned aloud.

Scholars and theologians agree on the significance of these three commandments. God is ineffable, beyond human comprehension and understanding. Respect for the transcendence of the divine is shown by refusing to represent it graphically. Yet the Bible includes stories in which God is described as human. There is abroad a mental picture of God as an elderly male with white hair and beard who is also clothed in flowing white robes. God is majestic and holy, as evidenced by sitting on a throne of power surrounded by hosts of attending angels singing "holy, holy, holy" or similar praises. This concept arises from the Bible and is perpetuated today in cartoons on television.

I have memories of sermons describing what it would be like to stand before God's judgment at the end of time. Most often the minister drew on the book of Revelation when describing that fearful experience. How did this imagery come to be associated with God? And is the biblical account of God's appearance consistent?

There are stories in the Old Testament in which God is encountered as an ordinary human being. This happens to Abraham, Lot, and Jacob. They realize they are speaking to either God or an angel, but the appearance of the divine characters seems like any ordinary male of the time.

This strand of interpretation begins with the two creation stories in Genesis. The first story tells of creative actions through verbal commands without describing the God who is acting, except for saying that humanity was created to look like him.

> So God created humankind in his image,
> in the image of God he created them;
> male and female he created them (1:27).

This implies that God looks like humans. The Hebrew term for humanity used here means that both male and female were created to look like God. Being in God's image also suggests that divine rule over creation is shared with humanity, which becomes God's representative.[224]

The second creation story describes God's actions and implies his appearance is like the humans. He makes a man and puts him in the garden to take care of it. Then he makes a woman out of the man. They are given charge of the garden with some limitations and then God leaves them alone. When God reappears to walk in the cool of the evening, he notices that the people are behaving oddly. With disobedience came a fear of God that had not existed, an alienation along with awareness of nakedness that causes embarrassment. The people are then excluded from the garden in part because this new awareness made them like God. It is not said directly, but the physical resemblance of God and people is assumed (2:4–3:22).

A second strand of tradition imagines God in connection with natural forces rather than in human shape. Thunderstorms, strong winds, fire, and earthquakes are associated with experiences of God.

Moses approaches a bush on fire to discover himself in the presence of God who spoke to him. He experienced the awesome holiness of nearness to God and had a conversation, but did not see anything beyond the bush itself (Exodus 3:1–4:18). When the commandments were given on Sinai, the people of Israel saw fire and smoke, heard thunder, and felt the earth shaking (19:16–25). They were at a distance but knew they were near God and begged Moses to speak to them because hearing directly from God might bring death (20:18–21).

A counterimpression is presented in Elijah's experience as he hid from Jezebel in a cave on Horeb, which apparently was another name for Sinai. God overcomes Elijah's depression by telling him to go to the mouth of the cave to experience God's passing by (2 Samuel 19:1–18). There came a wind that could break mountains, an earthquake, and then a fire; but we are told God was in none of them and was experienced afterward as "a sound of sheer silence."

Natural forces are also used in the climax of the poetic account in Job. Elihu, one of the friends of Job, ends his last speech with a description of the majesty of God as seen in thunderstorms, snow, and the clouds and sun in the sky (36:24–37:24). Then in a sudden transition, God answers Job out of a whirlwind and challenges him by describing the divine power to create natural forces as well as creatures (38:1–40:2). Except for the voice, God is not described. The power of God himself and the force of the words overwhelmed Job's complaints.

A third type of presentation found in Isaiah and Daniel combines the human shape and power of natural forces in describing a God who sits on a throne surrounded by hosts of attendants as was the case with kings in the ancient Near East. This imagery leads directly to the description in Revelation that is frequently used in Christian sermons.

Isaiah says he saw God enthroned but doesn't describe God except as a gigantic figure the hem of whose robe filled the temple (6:1–8). This implies he could not actually see God but saw enough to know there was a throne. It is the seraphs in attendance who communicate with Isaiah and this is taken as a message from God. The seraphs were animal-like creatures with six wings only two of which were used for flying. The majesty and holiness of God are suggested as they use wings to cover their face and genitals.[225] They also sing praises to God as a tribute to holiness. Isaiah does not talk with God directly, for it is a seraph who acts as intermediary to bring a coal that cleanses his lips and commissions him as a prophet. He interprets this contact through a court figure as a direct commission from God.

In Daniel 7:1–14, God is described in more detail as preparations are made for judgment. Thrones were set in place and on one of them was someone old with white hair in white clothing. The power of this figure is indicated by fire all around and issuing from him as he took the seat of judgment and was surrounded by thousands of attendants. It is not said that God is in human form, but the description of hair, clothing, and sitting in judgment seem to imply human appearance. After evil beasts representing oppressive kings are disposed of, the vision describes the arrival in clouds of another entity shaped like a human being, a Son of Man, to whom God gives power. What is implied is that evil imperial powers, which used beasts to symbolize their power, were actually terrible beasts in contrast to the more human appearance of God and God's agent.

Several visions are described in Daniel so that the picture of God and his agent becomes confusing. In chapter 10 he describes a personal vision that came to him beside the Tigris as someone appeared who was a man yet whose appearance was shiny like metals and jewels and fire and roaring sounds all at the same time. This may have been the human figure, the Son of Man, given dominion in chapter 7 but it is not entirely clear. Daniel calls this figure Lord and the words in the vision make it clear this person is an emissary of God separate from angels like Michael and who battles opposing forces in support of Michael. This is a contrast with the dominion that is given to the Son of Man following conquest in chapter 7. The vision ends in chapter 12 with Michael fighting on behalf of those who have been faithful with no mention of the Son of Man.

In Revelation 1:12–20, John describes a vision of the Son of Man, which seems to be Christ and which is a repetition of the description of the person in Daniel 10. After messages are given to seven churches, the vision describes God sitting on a throne, which combines the description in Daniel 10 with Isaiah's description of seraphs singing praises. Revelation adds twenty-four elders who join the praise.

What are the implications of these images of God?

Over the years I have experienced many sermons on heaven and the presence of God built around imagery from Isaiah, Daniel, and Revelation. All of these accounts rely on ancient mythology and political imagery of thrones and large courts of attendants in Near Eastern empires. In a world where everyone pictures important decisions being made in an oval office, people continue to imagine God sitting on a throne as hosts of attendants sing praises. It seems past the time when people should become aware of the dissonance of this imagery with realities of the modern world.

There are other ways in which this picture is outdated. The creator is seen as a person-like figure completely separate from the universe and located somewhere above or outside our normal experience. People still refer to heaven as up and hell as down, as if the three-story universe of ancient times were still the current view. As an entity outside the natural order, the actions of God become miracles that intervene and break the usual natural processes. People are aware of planetary systems and galaxies, along with natural processes that are explained by science; yet we continue to use religious language with outmoded imagery.

Paul Tillich undermined traditional imagery by referring to God as the Ground of Being. Some people embrace Being as the essence of God, sometimes using the term "Is-ness" in place of Being. Bishop John Shelby Spong, after retiring, attacked traditional views of God as "theism" with its projection of human qualities onto God. He argued for a non-theistic God, which rejects the projection of all human characteristics.[226] This causes difficulty because losing personality sacrifices the possibility of relationship. Marcus Borg has taken a different approach by rejecting "supernatural theism" in favor of seeing God as both transcending the world and immanent within it. He also argues that God can be perceived as personality without being turned into an idol.[227] The debate over God as outside or inside the universe, as personality or beyond personality, has gone on for millennia and will continue—but none of that debate has yet changed the popular image of God.[228]

In spite of this imagery taken from the Bible, most scholars would assert that the message of the Bible is that God is beyond human understanding. This is conveyed in the unflagging refusal to portray God in images. That standard was applied to things like statues used in worship, imagery on military insignia and coins, and other artistic products—but not in old folk stories or accounts of visions from which emerge the image of an old man on a throne.

It seems to me that we have a fundamental desire for relationship with God. This implies an interpersonal capacity that allows contact between humanity and divinity. We find ourselves assuming that God is another person. Calling God the Ground of Being or even Being itself sounds impersonal and unappealing. What we must always remember is that these images are approximations. They are the ones we need to use to make sense in our time and place, but they remain examples of the contrast mentioned by Paul when he said: "For now we see in a mirror, dimly, but then we will see face to face." (1 Corinthians 13:12) Later cultures will need different images in order to relate God to their perceptions of the world and their needs. Our knowledge is tentative and our understanding is fragmentary, yet we need to assume personal aspects of a God who can be trusted even if he can't be comprehended.

Chapter Thirty-Seven

Decisions and Encounters with God

When I was about ten years old, I had an experience in church one Sunday evening that shaped my expectations of what an experience of God was like. A devout female member of the church talked her non-believing husband into coming. The sermon, as best I can remember, featured the usual emphasis on personal salvation followed by pleas for commitment during the invitational hymn. Suddenly the woman's husband walked past the minister and fell on his knees before the pulpit. For several minutes he prayed earnestly. The minister knelt and spoke with him, then stood up and called on others to come pray with the man. About ten people came down and prayed on their knees as the man could be heard crying and pleading. Finally he stood up, turned around and joyously shouted that he was saved. I remember seeing him at church over the next several weeks, smiling and proclaiming how great it felt to be saved.

For years that experience was the model of what I thought it meant to become saved. We were taught the plan of salvation, which involved repentance and asking Jesus to "come into your heart," after which salvation was assured. This brought on a conversion experience, an unmistakable sign of salvation. The model, repeated often in sermons, was the experience of Paul on the road to Damascus when a confrontation with the risen Christ changed the direction of his life.

Not feeling the internal assurance of salvation, I thought that the usual process was not working for me. I prayed in tears many times, hoping for a shattering experience that would mark genuine salvation. This was not long after my maternal grandmother died, so it was a period of extreme emotional instability. I remember this period as a time when emotions, especially fear, dominated. Sermons on the Second Coming and Last Judgment led to fearful nightmares of standing before God to receive condemnation. This continued for about three years.

The tide was turned in an unexpected way. I felt so desperate one day that I decided to go to the extreme of praying in a downstairs closet to see if that made a difference. On my knees in that cramped space, I prayed tearfully for salvation and soon realized it made no difference at all. None of my pleading, crying, and kneeling brought the emotional confirmation I craved. As I slumped in frustration, it occurred to me that I had done everything possible but didn't believe that God had acted. It is pointless, I thought, to ask over and over if I don't believe God responds just because I asked. I decided to believe that God had answered my prayers even though I lacked internal conviction. This called for trust without a safety net. It was difficult, but I became more determined as I stood off anxiety attacks over the coming months. What I had decided was to make reason, not emotions, the guide for my life.

I did not think of that moment as an encounter with God. It all happened in my mind as I thought over the situation. Yet in retrospect it turned out to be a less intense version of other experiences that I consider personal encounters with God. All of them involved decisions that changed my life.

The experience that stands out most clearly happened in Monterrey, California, as I was studying North Vietnamese for the Air Force. In my first year after graduate school, while teaching at a university in North Carolina, I was drafted just before major revisions were made in the draft as Nixon claimed to be getting out of the Vietnam War. To avoid the war, I chose the Air Force and four years of enlisted service. I was selected for the intelligence branch and designated to learn Russian. Suddenly I was called in by a sergeant who overruled my orders because he said he needed another body on a plane leaving for Monterrey the next day. Thus I landed in a yearlong school for North Vietnamese, which brought an internal struggle over participating in a questionable war.

I spent that year reading almost every book on military history and strategy in the post library. It became clear that what we were doing in Vietnam ignored the lessons emphasized by all the leading military figures of World War II, even though Omar Bradley in his declining years had given his public support to it. Even worse, I decided our strategy was inherently immoral as it emphasized counting dead bodies, whether military or civilian, to determine progress. It seemed increasingly clear to me that I was heading for an assignment crucial for supporting immoral policies. I found myself unable to decide what to do.

With a month remaining before graduation, I was assigned kitchen duty for an entire day. Most of the work was done by lunchtime, so I was told to spend the afternoon waxing and buffing the dining room floor by myself. I didn't mind the assignment because it allowed time alone to think over my dilemma. There was something very soothing about mulling over a serious issue while pushing around a vibrating buffer. By the time I finished, I had decided. The moment of decision came upon me without willing it as I experienced what felt like God's intervention.

Barely able to contain my excitement and relief, I went home to talk it over with my wife. I knew I would tell my commanding officer I would not accept the current assignment because of moral objections. My wife and I discussed how this was a risky move that endangered the future for both of us, yet she supported me completely. What was extremely important to me was an internal conviction that God had directed my decision. There followed several months during which I constantly felt the presence and guidance of God. Officers in distant places who did not know me made decisions showing respect for my stand so that we landed in a far better situation for the remainder of military service. The feeling of God's presence in the afterglow of an important decision, sometimes lasting for months, has been the closest I have come to the emotional assurance I craved when younger.

Life-changing moments come in many different forms and are often perceived as religious experiences. Marcus Borg described three momentary experiences that changed his life.[229] He calls them mystical because they came upon him without anticipation, were very brief, and brought awareness and knowledge that was life-changing yet extremely difficult to put in words. In *The Varieties of Religious Experience*, William James described four characteristics of "mystical states of consciousness." They are ineffable because they are direct experiences that are almost impossible to put into words; noetic because they involve a sense of knowing as illumination or revelation; transient because the experience passes quickly; and passive because it comes without being caused by effort and brings with it a sense of being in the power of something beyond oneself.[230]

In an earlier book, Borg described mystical experiences as ecstatic awareness of God that happens in "eyes open" or "eyes closed" formats.[231] The second type occurs when one is meditating or participating in other religious exercises. Religious disciplines of study, prayer, and meditation are ways of seeking the eyes closed form of spirituality. Following practices that bring mindful spirituality into everyday life, such as those described by Barbara Brown Taylor in *An Altar in the World*, encourage mystical experiences of God's presence but can't guarantee results because mystical experiences often evade our seeking.[232] Borg's own experiences were of the first variety, for they happened in the ordinary course of events as a transformed awareness of reality came upon him unexpectedly. His momentary insights were life-changing as are many mystical experiences.

In reflecting on my experiences over the years, I never saw them as mystical or comparable to the conversion experience that I failed to achieve. Yet any feeling of the presence of God is mystical. What I have called the afterglow of important decisions lasted for as long as six months as follow up decisions were made with an attitude and confidence of God acting with and through me. For a long time I thought my experience was unique because I saw no biblical parallel. Now I see differently. When we look deeply into stories of calling, visions, or conversions, what stands out to me is that they all involved decisions by people who understood them as experiences of God's presence.

The Old Testament provides several descriptions of encounters with God as part of a decision-making process. Moses noticed a bush that seemed to be on fire yet was not being consumed. When he approached, he found himself talking with God. This was a commissioning experience in which God appears to coax a Moses who was resistant even when awestruck with an experience of holiness (Exodus 3:1–22). Elijah's experience on Horeb is another example. Running away from Jezebel, he hid in a cave, complaining that his efforts were failing and he was the only believer left. God said he would pass by, but was not in the powerful natural forces that happened. The impact of experiencing God in silence is not described, but God repeated his challenge to Elijah again and gave him a commission, which he carried out (1 Kings 19:9–18). Still another example was the vision of Isaiah in the temple, which led to a realization that he would speak on God's behalf (Isaiah 6:1–13). Most of the ancient prophets told of experiences in which God told them what to do. All of these could be seen as variations on how people came to decisions to do what they were convinced God was calling them to do.

Mark describes a similar time of decision for Jesus when he is baptized by John (1:9–11). After the baptism, as Jesus is emerging from the water, something happens that seems clearly to have been an internal experience more than something that was seen by others. Jesus saw the heavens opened, felt God's spirit descend in the form of a dove, and heard a voice adopting him into sonship. This appears to be the point at which he realized or decided that he had a special mission from God so that it launched his career. The stories of the temptations in the wilderness in Matthew and Luke also represent a decision-making process as they show Jesus wrestling with the nature of his calling after the baptism (Matthew 4:1–11 and Luke 4:1–13).

The most prominent decision experience in the New Testament is undoubtedly Paul's experience on the road to Damascus. Determined to apprehend followers of Jesus, he suddenly experiences a vision that is not witnessed by those with him. In his letters he describes this as an encounter with the risen Jesus equivalent to the experiences claimed by Peter and other disciples. The course of his life is changed but the direction it will take requires years to become clear to him (Acts 9:1–9). His experience is the paradigm of Christian conversion—a sudden turning of direction in life.

Evangelical Christians often emphasize the importance of conversion, usually seeing it as an emotional experience. Its essence is a decision. Cataclysmic decisions that coincide with an experience of God or Christ make good stories, but life is also shaped by multiple small decisions. My decision in the closet didn't seem cataclysmic, but it changed the direction of my life as a determination to abide by decisions made through reason combined with trust became my guide.

Encounters with God lead to decisions, as indicated by Moses, Jesus, and the commissioning stories of many prophets. Christians sometimes talk more about Christ experiences than God experiences. Evangelical Christians see Paul's Damascus road conversion as a model Christ experience.

My personal story was about failure to have a Christ experience. It has been God experiences that have most influenced my life. This arouses suspicion in some groups as to one's true salvation, as they focus on the statement in John that Jesus is the only way to God (14:6). My experience points to a different conclusion. In my defense, I would point to the Lord's Prayer where Jesus provided his disciples with direct access to God. This prayer is an example of how Jesus put God in first place and expected his disciples to do likewise. To put the kingdom of God first, as taught by Jesus, means seeking God as the key to truly following Jesus.

CHAPTER THIRTY-EIGHT

WHY DOESN'T GOD LAUGH?

In 1952, I was nine years old and my life changed unexpectedly. We were among the white poor in the South, but we had a black maid even though we didn't have many necessities. When many of their friends were buying televisions, my parents bought one too. It brought surprising things like wrestling and world news into our home. Mostly it brought comedy. I discovered Laurel and Hardy movies and then *I Love Lucy*.

I grew up in what was called the golden age of television. I enjoyed the comedy of Jack Benny, Milton Berle, and Syd Caesar with his incredible cast of young comics like Carl Reiner, Don Knotts, Tom Poston, and so many others. Before long I noticed that many of the comedians were Jewish and that they often told stories of the hardships in their lives. Over the years it became clear to me that most successful comedians made a living by telling very sad stories of their childhood in rhythms and punch lines that made people laugh. In private these people were often extremely introverted and emotionally flawed because of the experiences they made fun of so publicly. As an adult I appreciated the way that Woody Allen took his quirks and fears and Nora Ephron took very public stories of betrayal and turned them into one funny and wonderful movie after another.

A dear memory that was mentioned before was sitting at my maternal grandmother's big round table while eating and listening to my uncles talk. When I was about the age of seven, they began letting me sit at the men's table. The wives fed children at a separate table, served the men, and then gathered at their own long table to eat and talk. Mother had seven brothers and two sisters, so I sat with my father and nine uncles. All through the meal they told stories and afterward were joined by my aunts as they all sat around eating dessert, drinking iced tea, and telling more and more stories. Most of the stories were about their childhood years. Sometimes they told jokes as part of the stories, but even without jokes they laughed constantly and teased each other. Since then one of my greatest pleasures has been listening to adults talk over the past, laughing at the incredibly naïve or foolish things they managed to survive—and often of the love and effort of someone who helped them through bad decisions.

That grandmother also died in 1952 and the weight of death sank deep within me. I had nightmares and emotional outbursts. My mother was so worried that she took me to a doctor who told her to just ignore my problem because I would outgrow it. When I tried to talk to my mother about it, she shrugged me off. I didn't know she was following doctor's orders. All I knew was that I couldn't talk to the person closest to me about my deepest fears.

I have a nine-year-old grandson who is dealing with a lot of tension in his life that he is struggling to adjust to but is too young to understand. My wife and I are encouraging him to talk, even when he blames us. We laugh with him and help him talk about his feelings rather than explain as he tries to adjust. There is no guarantee, but talking openly about problems we can't understand and learning to laugh may help him through this without emotional scars.

I turned to my church for emotional support. Childhood memories are not reliable, so it is not fair to hold the pastor responsible for my reactions. I don't know how often he preached on the Second Coming or Last Judgment, but those ideas caught my imagination and set my fears aflame. I lived in a world of fear. When a storm approached, I feared it would turn into the Second Coming, which led to the very horrible experience of the Last Judgment. I had done everything I was told to do to win personal salvation, but instead of relief, I felt horror. It was the reality and permanence of death I dreaded and Christian reassurances of salvation and eternal justice didn't soften the blow of death.

Reading the Bible brought no comfort. At Christmas we heard Isaiah crying, "Comfort ye my people," but for the most part, Old Testament prophecy was gloom and doom. Amos, Hosea, and Jeremiah talked incessantly about human actions leading to divine rejection or condemnation. And many of the

Psalms graphically described the horrible suffering people can experience with no assurance that God cares.

Jesus also talked about judgment. In the parable of the virgins at the wedding, the groom arrives in the middle of the night and shuts out those who were unprepared because they didn't have enough oil for their lamps (Matthew 25:1–13). The steward in the story of the talents is called to account for how he used the money and is found wanting—his example is behind most examples people use when they refer to stewardship (Matthew 25:14–30). There is also the parable of the vineyard whose workers kill the owner's representatives so there is a promise the owner will come in judgment (Luke 20:9–19).

Most notably, in Matthew Jesus tells of the division of the lambs from the goats and God tells those who were judged harshly that they failed to treat others as if they were God himself (Matthew 25:31–48). That is a noble idea for human ethics, but still a frightening picture of how all of us will fall short if we have to step before God as presiding judge.

In an earlier conversation, I pointed to the parable of the Prodigal Son as an example of God blessing us with forgiveness without relieving us of the consequences of our actions. An irony of my life is that, as much as I have disliked the concept of a Last Judgment, I have made two careers of sitting in judgment of people. In one case, I was a consultant dealing with a variety of personnel problems as I helped managers figure out how to eliminate problem behaviors. Even efforts to use very impartial mediation processes often failed as the problem person insisted on seeing themselves as being persecuted rather than recognizing opportunity after opportunity for the closest an organization could come to offering forgiveness. If the problem had ceased, the person could have moved ahead and overcome the negative effects. All too often they insisted on seeing it as unfair judgment and made it necessary for extreme judgment to befall them.

As a college professor, I had comparable experiences. I learned it is always best to start out talking sternly so that by the end of the course you can add the empathy and gentleness that produce effective tough love. Starting with gentleness and cracking down on the inevitable violations just doesn't work. Students live in fear of the final exam and determination of the final grade—a very real Last Judgment situation. I know how much I am pulling for students to talk over issues with me and to make their best efforts on assignments; but too often they use negative images of the professor as an excuse for not making a legitimate effort. When students really try, every professor I know tries to give the benefit of every doubt when possible to soften harsh outcomes. However, there is no avoiding handing out grades that recognize that students have brought consequences on themselves. These very students often come pleading, when it is too late, for extra work, by which they mean something that calls for no work that gives them a higher grade they did not earn.

My experience of judgment in these situations is that compassion and a desire for justice are too often undermined by behavior that forces negative consequences. These are not times when you laugh, although in later years the stories of how these individuals kept undermining themselves can sound like slapstick comedy.

What will be the standard of God's judgment? In the book of Joshua there is a story of a defeat at the town of Ai (Joshua 7:1–26). Jericho had been taken and destroyed. There was a clear command from God to take valuable items and put them in God's treasury while everything else was destroyed. But one man kept something for himself. After the setback at Ai, Joshua prayed and learned the defeat was punishment of the entire people because of the violation of one man. He searched the entire encampment to find the guilty party who was stoned by everyone to appease the anger of God. That was judgment on a small scale. Something trivial done by one person brought death to many people because of God's anger, which could only be appeased when that person was found and judged.

Another example of judgment on a small scale is found in Job. According to the prologue, God had a contest with one of his servants over how faithful Job would be when pain was inflicted. Judgment in the form of game-playing by God is not a pleasant concept. The tidying up at the end of the book is supposed to make up for the collateral damage incurred by the game, but even God didn't tidy things up that completely. Job's first children were still gone and no parent will accept the end of the story as satisfaction for that loss.

At funeral after funeral, we are reminded of the 14th chapter of John. Don't let your hearts be troubled. There are many "mansions" and I go to prepare a place for you. Beyond judgment lies the bliss of heaven. How often do we hear someone say, "Your loved one is in a better place?" Hopeful as this assurance is, I have never known it to soften the permanence of the loss that has occurred.

The Bible is full of judgment. Perceptive studies of the Old Testament find humor here and there in small but interesting details. My complaint is there is no humor in the persistent judgment that is found. In prophetic literature, the Day of the Lord is mentioned as a hopeful time of judgment when things will be set right. Then other prophets come along and turn the Day of the Lord into a thing of dread because of misdeeds. There is ambivalence because Jews want God to set things right in the world through justice at judgment, but all too often the justice that is threatened comes in the form of horrible consequences across generations of sufferers. Even when the prophets offer hope, there is not one sign of humor I am aware of.

Why does God take everything so seriously in the Bible? Look at the heritage of comedy with one great Jewish humorist after another. Why didn't that get into the Bible?

Instead of laughing at human foibles, God seems to take everything so seriously. Look at Job. After all the suffering he experienced, he wanted to present his case to God. In the marvelous poetry of chapters 38–41, God responds from within a whirlwind. It is not what Job expected. No explanation is offered. Rather God challenges the arrogance of someone who thinks human beings can even put a case to God that is worth considering. God is the creator and sustainer of all things. This sounds like a God who is far above the petty games mentioned at the first of Job or the petty violations of someone when Jericho was burned. This is a God beyond human comprehension. All our lives we try to comprehend this incredibly marvelous universe God has placed us in and we fall very short in the course of a single lifetime. How is it possible that a God behind a universe like this can play games with the details of lives of single individuals or devote attention to what any of us would consider petty grievances? I am not saying that God is uninvolved or doesn't care. Why care about things that many of us laugh off?

My personal belief, which of course can't be proved, is that much of our thinking about what upsets or pleases God is a reflection of human arrogance. God was showing Job the ridiculousness of human arrogance and I think that is a biblical message that has been very much ignored.

I suspect that the whole idea of a Last Judgment is human arrogance. God would actually worry about many petty details of everyone's lives? If God actually did that, why would he not feel the compassion and frustration of managers and professors who witness people insisting on doing what is not in their best interest? Any parent looking over such details of their children's lives would shake their head at the absurdity and often break out in belly laughs as well as shedding tears of compassion. People like Woody Allen and Nora Ephron give us pleasure that comes with empathy and laughter by making fun of the tragedies and fears of their lives. How can God not have compassion and a sense of humor? That is my biggest criticism of the Bible—it talks about compassion but Jews didn't put enough humor into it.

When my time comes, if there is indeed a time of judgment, I suspect it will be far more like Job before the whirlwind than any other description in the Bible. God is beyond our comprehension. It is only arrogance that projects all the pettiness of human guilt onto a God beyond our ability to understand. We are not on God's level and can't be. We are the creature. God understands us through and through even though we can't possibly take in all that is God. If God gives us the ability to laugh at our pain and sorrow, why should God lack that capacity?

If there is a judgment, even the whirlwind image will be inadequate to describe what it will be like. You can bet we will not understand everything but, like Job, realize the folly of even expecting to understand things from God's point of view.

Why can't judgment be more like the Jewish hope for a messianic banquet, which is something disciples believed they experienced with Jesus who was known to enjoy parties and good conversation. To me, the heart of the idea is not eating food but the joy of the company. I picture it being like sitting at the big round table with my uncles and aunts all of whom are recounting their lives and breaking everyone up with laughter. If God turns out to have a sense of humor as well as compassion, then maybe judgment will involve a lot of laughing and sobbing together.

Conclusion

The Challenge of Relationship with God

We have seen that the Bible says a lot of important things that are significant for Christians and Jews. Not everything it says is consistent or without contradiction, as seen in two creation accounts in Genesis and four gospels giving rival accounts of similar events.

Is there a central message of the Bible? The focus of the Old Testament is on the God of Israel while the New Testament is primarily about the life and significance of Jesus. Underlying both is a conviction, hope, and trust that God stands behind all that happens in this world, giving it meaning and purpose. More than that, the Bible expresses the desire for relationship with a God who can be known through history and experience. Like other relationships, this one has its ups and downs, moments of joy along with times of sadness and even despair. There are times when God appears to break up the relationship or betray it, yet the message is that ultimately God is faithful and desires loyalty and fidelity in return. In spite of the inconsistent messages of historical experience, God can be trusted.

As an undergraduate at Mercer, I was very close to a history professor who was a second father to me. He was a Baptist but not a fundamentalist. He encouraged me to persist in the questioning and exploration that was reshaping my belief system, giving confidence that a person of faith should not fear entertaining ideas that some religious leaders considered taboo.

In one conversation near the end of my time at Mercer, I mentioned Harvey Cox's book *Secular City* and gave him the high points since he had not yet read it.[233] I remember being excited about the argument that our current idea of God needed to change to get in step with realities of modern secular society. My mentor looked at me and asked: "Don't you realize that if we change our ideas about God, it means we create God rather than God creating us?" This was the first time I became aware of the view that God is merely a projection of the human mind, a critique frequently mentioned since the Enlightenment as part of atheist rejections of God.

Those college years saw a great change in the fundamentalist beliefs that had guided my life. There were many internal struggles along the way with few leaps to extreme conclusions. Other students had different experiences. At church I heard parents express fear that new religious ideas were undermining the faith of those who had arrived at Mercer as good Christians. Some of my friends verified those concerns as they made drastic leaps by adopting sarcastic attitudes toward traditional beliefs or turning to outright rejection as they saw how infallible truths were products of historical processes and not direct revelation. The next forty years saw continued movement in my views as knowledge and experience increased, yet there was always a sense of continuity of essential beliefs. It never bothered me that God might be only a human projection.

A sudden change took place over a few weeks in my midfifties. As usual I was reading several books at one time, one of them Bishop Spong's *Why Christianity Must Change or Die* and two of them popular scientific writings on cosmology.[234] There was great pressure at work. The state of Georgia was installing a new computer system consolidating personnel, payroll, accounting, and training functions in preparation for the approaching year 2000. I was scheduling and coordinating training for over a thousand employees in the largest state agency, facing stressful deadlines that would make possible the work of others in completing the project on time. Health and welfare programs for every citizen in the state hinged on my ability to make training happen in time for technicians and multitudes of others in the project to accomplish their deadlines.

Sleep became a problem. At first there was no difficulty going to sleep, but after only one or at most two hours I would wake up, unable to go back to sleep. People must have seen that stress was affecting me, but the quality and timeliness of my work was not impaired. Off the job, I found myself uncommunicative with my family. Children were always around and had been a source of joy, yet I realized one day that they brought no pleasure. Nothing was enjoyable. I felt a sense of despair and passivity, as I was unable to respond to things I always loved.

One afternoon, I was reading a difficult science book while at home alone and thinking about the vastness of the universe. Suddenly I felt overwhelmed by the immense size and darkness of the universe. A sense of despair and the futility of life flooded over me. Reeling in the impact of these emotions, I realized there couldn't be a God in this kind of a universe. A decision had come upon me—I no longer believed in God. I felt utterly devastated for the next several hours. Even worse, I was locked in silence because this was something I could not share with my wife or anyone.

Over the next days, it came to me that I was experiencing depression. Everything I had gone through made sense in light of this diagnosis. Within a few days, I saw my internist and received a small dose of medicine for depression. He said I had a mild case. If the kind of despair I felt with mild depression could get worse, I understood how deeper problems could lead to acts of extreme desperation. Within a week, the gloom of depression receded and sleep problems improved. Energy returned to my life away from work. I discovered that, against my will, I had made a decision about God that was not changed by the medicine. The entire belief system on which my life was built was shattered and seemed beyond repair.

In an earlier conversation, I mentioned personal encounters with God that took the form of important decisions followed by an afterglow of sensing God's presence for several months. It soon became clear to me that now I was experiencing the reverse effect. A similar mystical experience had occurred in connection with a decision being made, but this time it was the devastating feeling of God's absence. Belief in God was the foundation on which all my convictions rested. I wanted to undo the decision that I had not willed, but could not.

In this process I confronted one of the deep mysteries of life. How is it that we believe what we believe? A person can explain all kinds of rational support for something, yet not be able to find it credible or trustworthy. Reasons are how we justify what we already believe; they are not the cause of our belief. Somehow within us, we make a leap of faith that accepts something. In my case, I knew reasons for believing in God and why that belief was important to me—but I could no longer bring something deep within me to embrace that belief. There were months of the reverse of afterglow, for they were times when I felt despair over the loss experienced and the absence of God.

As happened at other times in my life, this challenge turned into a research assignment. It was not information that was sought, but insights that would make it possible for me to believe in God once again.

One starting point was reading the classic Gifford Lectures of William James, *The Varieties of Religious Experience*.[235] The language of these lectures was not easy reading, but the large number of quotations of personal experiences was fascinating. From James I learned of Tolstoy's depression, which he described as a feeling of hanging from the side of a bottomless pit clutching a small bush, the roots of which were being gnawed away by a mouse. He described how he read everything he could find to help his depression but found no wisdom or knowledge that helped. It was a sudden experience of God leading to an enthusiastic conversion experience that broke the depression and turned his life into something meaningful.[236]

It wasn't long before I decided I was repeating Tolstoy's quest for knowledge, except my search was to find knowledge for overcoming loss of faith. I read several accounts of prominent individuals who experienced depression. The autobiographical account of John Stuart Mill was amazingly shallow, I thought. He described what must have been a disturbing experience as if it were a headache that is unpleasant for a while and passes. He recorded the experience, but showed little indication that it caused the kind of internal doubts and emotions that probably occurred.

I read the works of prominent atheists, attended a Unitarian Church where atheists were a substantial percentage of the membership, and attended some atheist organizations. What I found was an evangelistic enthusiasm that was a dark-side version of the fundamentalism of my youth. Many of the leaders had been evangelical ministers of one variety or another who had first a dramatic conversion and then an equally dramatic de-conversion experience. Now they were using the same old sales approaches for winning people to the cause of atheism. None of this ever felt right for me, but I stuck with it long enough to see if there was anything of value to be learned.

I spent a great deal of time pondering Bishop Spong's two books calling for a non-theistic belief in God as the salvation for Christianity. He vividly attacked the old concepts but the new alternative seemed to have no life to it. He rejected all anthropomorphism, which means that seeing personality in God was also rejected. This troubled me a great deal. I went to Oak Ridge, Tennessee, with some friends to hear Spong in person and ask a question about having a personal relationship with God. Much thought went into the question so it was phrased carefully and thoughtfully. As I asked it, I saw people in the audience responding favorably to a desire to find the possibility of relationship with God. It seemed to me that Spong himself implied that he felt a relationship with God. His answer was disappointing because it was a repetition of something he said in one of the books, that if horses had gods they would look like horses. The question of having a relationship with God was of paramount importance to me, so I was very disappointed by this encounter.

Reading efforts continued for a decade without producing satisfactory results for much of that time. At first I hoped to find a new outlook that would enable me to reach a more satisfactory decision about God. As it became clear that would not happen, I reached a decision like the one I made around the age of eleven in a closet when my prayers for conversion failed. I find life meaningful when I believe in a God I can trust. If God doesn't exist outside the imaginations of human beings, then the universe has no meaning or purpose. In that case, believing in God makes no difference, no matter how convinced we are of God's faithfulness. The truth is that all of us are agnostics about God because as a matter of fact we cannot know for sure there is a God. Recognizing the agnostic nature of reality, I decided that life is more meaningful for me when I believe in God and that if I am mistaken it doesn't make any difference. My decision was to live as if there were indeed a God who can be trusted. This decision reshaped my search. If I am to choose to believe in a God, what kind of God do I want to affirm?

Guided by that question, the search became more fruitful. I discovered Marcus Borg's *The God We Never Knew* and several writings by Bishop John A. T. Robinson.[237] Both of them spoke against old-fashioned views of God that conflicted with science and modern culture. Both used the term panentheism, a new concept for me, which sees God as part of the world yet separate. This became a positive explanation that made far more sense than the negative emphasis of Spong in attacking what he called theism. Still more progress was made when I discovered Hans Kung's *The Beginning of All Things*, on the relationship of God to science. Through him I learned of British scientists-turned-priests John Polkinghorne and Arthur Peacocke.[238] Reading their books related God's interaction with creation to systems theory as well as current ideas in physics and other sciences.

From all of these books emerged the kind of God I wanted to believe in and stake my life on. There was recognition that God is beyond human form or equation with human abilities, yet capable of relating to human beings in an interpersonal way without violating natural processes.

The result of this spiritual crisis and the decade-long search that followed has not been the kind of cocksure faith of earlier years. When we embrace important beliefs, we are taking risks even if we don't realize it. I am very aware that we can't know God in the way we think we know scientific truth, but I value a life that risks trusting in God whether God exists or not. If God does not exist, it will make no difference in the end whether one believes or disbelieves. In either case, this short life will have felt more meaningful and satisfying—and that can be reward enough if necessary.

I have realized that it is not the existence of God that is most important, but the possibility of relationship with God. All of us need relationships for survival and then for healthy living. Babies that are not held and talked to will die. Infants that do not bond with people are bound for lives of malfunction. We must have the capacity to form relationship based on interpersonal trust. This also extends to the force responsible for bringing about and sustaining the world as we know it. The most crucial question for humanity is not belief in God, but the ability to trust in God as something positive underlying reality that cares what happens to all of creation.

The Bible is a record of the Judeo-Christian tradition seeking relationship with God. What the Bible says is that members of that tradition found a relationship with God to be meaningful and essential through bright and dark moments in the past. Continued reliance on the Bible means incorporating the experiences it records along with others in this long tradition with experiences today. It is conversation with the Bible, an ongoing interaction with its contents based on current understanding, rather than obedience to authority that is the hallmark of the Judeo-Christian tradition.

NOTES

Introduction

[1] N. T. Wright, *The New Testament and the People of God: Christian Origins and the Question of God, Volume One* (Minneapolis: Fortress Press, 1992); *Jesus and the Victory of God: Christian Origins and the Question of God, Volume Two* (Minneapolis: Fortress Press, 1996); and *The Resurrection of the Son of God: Christian Origins and the Question of God, Volume Three* (Minneapolis: Fortress Press, 2003). John P. Meier, *A Marginal Jew: Rethinking the Historical Jesus. Volume One: The Roots of the Problem and Person* (New York: Doubleday, 1991); *A Marginal Jew: Rethinking the Historical Jesus, Volume Two: Mentor, Message, and Miracles* (New York: Doubleday, 1994); *A Marginal Jew: Rethinking the Historical Jesus, Volume Three: Companions and Competitors* (New Haven: Yale University Press, 2001); and *A Marginal Jew: Rethinking the Historical Jesus, Volume Four: Law and Love* (New Haven: Yale University Press, 2009).

[2] Albert Schweitzer, *The Quest of the Historical Jesus: A Critical Study of its Progress from Reimarus to Wrede* (New York: The Macmillan Company, 1961).

[3] Geza Vermes, *Jesus the Jew: A Historian's Reading of the Gospels* (Philadelphia: Fortress Press, 1981); *The Religion of Jesus the Jew* (Minneapolis: Fortress Press, 1993); *The Authentic Gospel of Jesus* (London: Penguin Books, 2003); and *Christian Beginning: From Nazareth to Nicaea* (New Haven: Yale University Press, 2012).

[4] Amy-Jill Levine, *The Misunderstood Jew: The Church and the Scandal of the Jewish Jesus* (New York: HarperOne, 2007); and *Short Stories by Jesus: The Enigmatic Parables of a Controversial Rabbi* (New York: HarperOne, 2014).

[5] Richard Horsley, *The Prophet Jesus and the Renewal of Israel: Moving Beyond a Diversionary Debate* (Grand Rapids, Michigan: William B. Eerdmans Publishing Company, 2012), 151.

[6] On the relationship of genetics and evolution, see Francis S. Collins, *The Language of God: A Scientist Presents Evidence for Belief* (New York: Free Press, 2006), 109–142. In that chapter, Collins describes conclusions from his experience directing the Human Genome Project.

Chapter 1

[7] For a somewhat different view of biblical reliability, see the article by Harold W. Attridge, "Can We Trust the Bible?" *Reflections: A Magazine of Theological and Ethical Inquiry* (Spring 2014), http://reflections.yale.edu/article/ end-times-and-end-gamesis-scripture-being-left-behind/can-we-trust-bible (accessed March 24, 2015).

[8] Marcus J. Borg, *Reading the Bible Again for the First Time: Taking the Bible Seriously but not Literally* (New York: HarperOne, 2001), 30.

Chapter 2

[9] For recent versions of these books, see Nikos Kazantzakis, *Zorba the Greek* (New York: Scribner Paperback Fiction, 1996); and Nikos Kazantzakis, *The Last Temptation of Christ*, trans. P. A. Bien (New York, Scribner Paperback Fiction, 1998).

[10] Bart D. Ehrman, *Did Jesus Exist? The Historical Argument for Jesus of Nazareth* (New York: HarperOne, 2012).

[11] Bart D. Ehrman, *How Jesus Became God: The Exaltation of a Jewish Preacher from Galilee* (New York: HarperOne, 2014).

[12] For interesting insights into the connection of the prologue of John to the wisdom tradition, see N. T. Wright, *Christian Origins and the Question of God. Volume One: The New Testament and the People of God* (Minneapolis: Fortress Press, 1992), 410–417.

[13] Three recent discussions of the historical evolution of sin are Gary A. Anderson, *Sin: A History* (New Haven: Yale University Press, 2009); Paula Fredriksen, *Sin: The Early History of an Idea* (Princeton: Princeton University Press, 2012); and John Portman, *A History of Sin: Its Evolution to Today and Beyond* (New York: Rowman and Littlefield Publishers, Inc., 2007).

[14] William James, *The Varieties of Religious Experience* (New York: New American Library, 1958), 391.

Chapter 3

[15] Notable works on the topic are James H. Charlesworth, *Jesus within Judaism: New Light from Exciting Archaeological Discoveries* (London: SPCK, 1988); Geza Vermes, *Jesus the Jew: A Historian's Reading of the Gospels* (Philadelphia: Fortress Press, 1981); and Amy-Jill Levine, *The Misunderstood Jew: The Church and the Scandal of the Jewish Jesus* (New York: HarperOne, 2006).

[16] See Matthew 10:5–6, where it is made specific that disciples were not to go to non-Jews; while in Mark 6:8–11 and Luke 9:2–5, they are told to go to the villages, which implies keeping to primarily Jewish rural areas as Jesus was doing.

[17] For a thorough examination of the many images of Jesus over centuries and their impacts, see Jaroslav Pelikan, *Jesus through the Centuries: His Place in the History of Culture* (New Haven: Yale University Press, 1985).

Chapter 4

[18] For a discussion of synagogues in Jesus's time, see William R. Herzog II, *Prophet and Teacher: An Introduction to the Historical Jesus* (Louisville: Westminster John Knox Press, 2005), 72–74.

[19] An explanation of frames is found in Marcus J. Borg and John Dominic Crossan, *The Last Week: What the Gospels Really Teach about Jesus's Final Days in Jerusalem* (New York: HarperOne, 2006), 32–36.

Chapter 5

[20] William Kang, "Mark 3 Commentary: Mark 3: 38–40," Gracepoint Devotions: Devotional Quiet Times and Bible Commentary, http://www.gracepointdevotions.org/2010/03/07/mark-3-commentary/#_ftn11 (accessed May 23, 2013).

[21] Kang, "Mark 3: 38–40."

[22] Marcus J. Borg, *Jesus: Uncovering the Life, Teachings, and Relevance of a Religious Revolutionary* (New York: HarperOne, 2006), 25.

[23] Marcus J. Borg, *Conversations with Scripture: The Gospel of Mark* (New York: Church Publishing Incorporated, 2009), 34. It should be noted this book is part of a series intended to illustrate the Anglican use of scripture.

Chapter 6

[24] Thomas Jefferson, *The Jefferson Bible: The Life and Morals of Jesus of Nazareth Extracted Textually from the Gospels in Greek, Latin, French and English* (Washington D.C: Smithsonian Books, Smithsonian Edition, 2011).

[25] See Rudolph Bultmann, *Jesus and the Word* (New York: Charles Scribner's Sons, 1958).

Chapter 7

[26] For a discussion of the special nature of poetic symbols, see Robert N. Bellah, *Religion in Human Evolution: From the Paleolithic Age to the Axial Age*, Kindle ed. (Cambridge, Massachusetts: Harvard University Press, 2011), locations 682–690. Bellah refers to Suzanne Langer's *Philosophy in a New Key* where she argues that poetry is untranslatable and cannot be fully explained by any interpretation. He also refers to Rimbaud's statement of how metaphor can change the world. In location 723, he says: "Religious language is often condensed, poetic, and, because of its involvement in ritual, performative. No more than any other kind of poetry can it be conceptually paraphrased without significant loss of meaning." Those statements apply to the parables and much of the teaching of Jesus as well as to Old Testament passages referring to the Messiah.

[27] William R. Herzog II discusses four possible meanings of Son of Man in *Prophet and Teacher: An Introduction to the Historical Jesus* (Louisville: Westminster John Knox Press, 2005), 86.

[28] For a brief introduction to messianic beliefs, see David B. Levinson, "Messianic Movements," in Amy-Jill Levine and Marc Zvi Brettler, eds., *The Jewish Annotated New Testament* (Oxford New York: Oxford University Press, 2011), 530–535. More information on the messianic and prophetic movements before and after Jesus is given in conversations 15 and 17.

[29] John J. Collins, *The Apocalyptic Imagination: An Introduction to Jewish Apocalyptic Literature* (Grand Rapids, Michigan: William B. Eerdman's Publishing Company, 1998), 262. See also Herzog's comments on the prophetic movements around the time of Jesus and what they had in common with his approach, in *Prophet and Teacher*, 99–109.

[30] For more insight into the concept of Messiah, see James H. Charlesworth, ed., *The Messiah: Developments in Earliest Judaism and Christianity* (Minneapolis: Fortress Press, 2010).

Chapter 8

[31] Robert W. Funk, Roy W. Hoover, and The Jesus Seminar, *The Five Gospels: The Search for the Authentic Words of Jesus* (San Francisco: HarperSanFrancisco, 1993), 133–134; Robert Funk and The Jesus Seminar, *The Acts of Jesus: The*

Search for the Authentic Deeds of Jesus (San Francisco: HarperSanFrancisco, 1998), 43–44.

[32] The responses come, respectively, from Deuteronomy 8:3, then he answers a quotation from Psalms 91:11–12 with Deuteronomy 6:16, and ends with Deuteronomy 6:13. The texts used by Jesus are all part of explicating the Ten Commandments given in Deuteronomy 5.

[33] W. Somerset Maugham, *The Razor's Edge* (New York: Vintage Books, 1944), 207.

[34] Maugham, 208.

Chapter 9

[35] A very thorough discussion of all these issues is found in John P. Meier, *A Marginal Jew: Rethinking the Historical Jesus. Volume I. The Roots of the Problem and the Person* (New York: Doubleday, 1991), 205–433.

[36] Luke includes three stories of meals with Pharisees in 7:36–51, 11:37–44, and 14:1–24. In John 3, Nicodemus does not eat with Jesus but comes at night for a long consultation. These stories, in my view, show an element of respect for Jesus and knowledge of proper behavior on his part that would not be expected of an ordinary peasant.

[37] Amy-Jill Levine, *The Misunderstood Jew: The Church and the Scandal of the Jewish Jesus* (New York: HarperOne, 2006), 55; and Amy-Jill Levine, "The Battle for Judaism—Archaeology and History versus the Social Sciences and Cultural Anthropology." Disk 1. *Jesus and the Second Temple*, a DVD of 5 lectures from the Biblical Archaeology Society's Bible and Archaeology Fest in San Diego, 2008. For a discussion of Jewish society at the time of Jesus that explains the retainer class as part of agrarian society, see William R. Herzog II, *Prophet and Teacher: An Introduction to the Historical Jesus* (Louisville: Westminster John Knox Press, 2005), 50–57.

[38] Among his many books, see especially Richard A. Horsley, *Scribes, Visionaries, and Politics of Second Temple Judea* (Louisville: Westminster John Knox Press, 2007); *Jesus in Context: People, Power, and Performance* (Minneapolis: Fortress Press, 2008); and *Jesus and the Powers: Conflict, Covenant, and the Hope of the Poor* (Minneapolis: Fortress Press, 2011).

[39] Herzog, 68.

[40] Meier, 253–315 provides detailed examination of the early education, literacy, and languages Jesus probably experienced.

[41] To understand Jewish patterns of family life in the time of Jesus, see Ross S.

Kraemer, "Jewish Family Life in the First Century CE," in Amy-Jill Levine and Marc Zvi Brettler, eds., *The Jewish Annotated New Testament* (Oxford New York: Oxford University Press, 2011), 537–540. Meier, 316–371 provides very detailed consideration of these questions.

[42] John Shelby Spong, *Jesus for the Non-Religious: Recovering the Divine at the Heart of the Human* (New York: HarperOne, 2007), 262.

Chapter 10

[43] John P. Meier, *A Marginal Jew: Rethinking the Historical Jesus. Volume I. The Roots of the Problem and the Person* (New York: Doubleday, 1991), 205–252 goes into great detail in examining birth narratives for any vestige of historically reliable information.

[44] Robert W. Funk, Roy W. Hoover, and The Jesus Seminar, *The Five Gospels: The Search for the Authentic Words of Jesus* (San Francisco: HarperSanFrancisco, 1993).

[45] Albert Schweitzer, *The Quest of the Historical Jesus: A Critical Study of its Progress from Reimarus to Wrede* (New York: MacMillan Company, 1961).

[46] See especially James H. Charlesworth, *The Historical Jesus: An Essential Guide* (Nashville: Abingdon Press, 2007); "Introduction: Why Evaluate Twenty-Five Years of Jesus Research?" in *Jesus Research: An International Perspective, The First Princeton-Prague Symposium on Jesus Research, Prague 2005*, ed. James H. Charlesworth and Petr Pokorny (Grand Rapids, Michigan: William B. Eerdmans Publishing Company, 2009), 1–15; and "Introduction: The Second Princeton-Prague Symposium: Jesus Research Methodologies," in *Jesus Research: New Methodologies and Perceptions, The Second Princeton-Prague Symposium on Jesus Research, Princeton 2007*, ed. James H. Charlesworth with Brian Rhea and Petr Pokorny (Grand Rapids. Michigan: William B. Eerdmans Publishing Company, 2014), 1–13. N T. Wright provides a thorough review of the various quests, their methods, and results in *Christian Origins and the Question of God. Volume Two: Jesus and the Victory of God* (Minneapolis: Fortress Press, 1996), 3–144. There are also two more recent descriptions of results of the quest for the historical Jesus and their implications. See William R. Herzog II, *Prophet and Teacher: An Introduction to the Historical Jesus* (Louisville: Westminster John Knox Press, 2005); and Richard Horsley, *The Prophet Jesus and the Renewal of Israel: Moving Beyond a Diversionary Debate* (Grand Rapids, Michigan: William B. Eerdmans Publishing Company, 2012).

[47] Rudolf Bultmann, *Jesus and the Word* (New York: Charles Scribner's Sons,

1958), 8–11.

[48] Funk, Hoover, and The Jesus Seminar, *The Five Gospels*; and Robert W. Funk and The Jesus Seminar, *The Acts of Jesus: The Search for the Authentic Deeds of Jesus* (San Francisco: HarperSanFrancisco, 1998).

[49] Werner H. Kelber, "Rethinking the Oral-Scribal Transmission Performance," in Charlesworth and Rhea, eds., *Jesus Research: New Methodologies and Perceptions. The Second Princeton-Prague Symposium on Jesus Research, Princeton 2007*, 500–530. See also Susan Niditch, *Oral World and Written Word: Ancient Israelite Literature* (Louisville, Kentucky: Westminster John Knox Press, 1996). For application to the gospels, see James D. G. Dunn, *Jesus, Paul, and the Gospels* (Grand Rapids, Michigan: William B. Eerdmans Publishing Company, 2011) and *The Oral Gospel Tradition* (Grand Rapids, Michigan: William B. Eerdmans Publishing Company, 2013); and also, among his many works, Richard A. Horsley, *Jesus in Context: Power, People and Performance* (Minneapolis: Fortress Press, 2008) for a discussion of the orality of the synoptic gospels; and Richard A. Horsley and Tom Thatcher, *John, Jesus, and the Renewal of Israel* (Grand Rapids, Michigan: William B. Eerdmans Publishing Company, 2013) for an examination of John in light of new approaches to oral traditions.

[50] Urban C. Wahlde, "Archaeology and John's Gospel," in *Jesus and Archaeology*, ed. James H. Charlesworth (Grand Rapids, Michigan: William B. Eerdmans Publishing Company, 2006), 523–586; and Paul N. Anderson, "Aspects of the Historicity of John: Implications for Investigations of Jesus and Archaeology," also in *Jesus and Archaeology*, 587–618.

[51] Dunn, *Jesus, Paul, and the Gospels*, 70–91.

Chapter 11

[52] Saint Augustine, "Sermon 112A," *Essential Sermons: The Works of Saint Augustine A Translation for the 21st Century*, ed. Boniface Ramsey, trans. Edmund Hill (Hyde Park, New York: New City Press, 2007), 184–185.

[53] Harold W. Attridge, gen. ed. with the Society of Biblical Literature, *The HarperCollins Study Bible* (New York: HarperOne, 2006), 2047.

[54] Amy-Jill Levine and Marc Zvi-Brettler, eds., *The Jewish Annotated New Testament* (Oxford New York: Oxford University Press, 2011), 420.

[55] Sigmund Freud, *The Future of an Illusion*, trans. James Strachey (New York: W. W. Norton and Company, 1989); and Richard Dawkins, *The God Delusion* (New York: Houghton Mifflin Company, 2006).

[56] Michael Shermer, *How We Believe: Science, Skepticism, and the Search for God*

(New York: Henry Holt and Company, 2000); and *The Believing Brain: From Ghosts and Gods to Politics and Conspiracies—How We Construct Beliefs and Reinforce Them as Truths* (New York: St. Martin's Griffin, 2011).

[57] G. G. Coulton, *From Saint Francis to Dante: Translations from the Chronicle of the Franciscan Salimbene (122–1288) with Notes and Illustrations from Other Medieval Sources*, trans. G. G. Coulton, 2nd ed. (University of Pennsylvania Press, 1972), 242.

[58] See Deborah Blum, *Love at Goon Park: Harry Harlow and the Science of Affection*. 2nd ed. (New York: Basic Books, 2011); and William T. McKinney, "Love at Goon Park: Harry Harlow and the Science of Affection," *The American Journal of Psychiatry* 160, no. 12 (Dec 2003), 2254–2255, http://ajp.psychiatryonline.org/doi/full/10.1176/appi.ajp.160.12.2254 (accessed December 20, 2014).

[59] Blum, *Love at Goon Park*, 31–60.

Chapter 12

[60] Marcus J. Borg, *The God We Never Knew: Beyond Dogmatic Religion to a More Authentic Contemporary Faith* (San Francisco: HarperSanFrancisco, 1998), 13–29.

[61] William R. Herzog II, *Prophet and Teacher: An Introduction to the Historical Jesus* (Louisville: Westminster John Knox Press, 2005), 82–91, 158–161.

[62] For discussion of this feature of biblical poetry, see Bernhard Anderson with Steven Bishop, *Out of the Depths: The Psalms Speak for us Today*, 3rd ed., (Louisville, Kentucky: Westminster John Knox Press, 2000), 21–26; and Adele Berlin, "Reading Biblical Poetry," in *The Jewish Study Bible: Jewish Publication Society TANAKH Translation*, eds. Adele Berlin and Marc Zvi Brettler (Oxford New York: Oxford University Press, 2004), 2098–2099.

[63] See the commentary on these verses in Amy-Jill Levine and Marc Zvi Brettler eds., *The Jewish Annotated New Testament* (Oxford New York: Oxford University Press, 2011), 13, 125.

[64] Marcus J. Borg, *Reading the Bible Again for the First Time: Taking the Bible Seriously but not Literally* (New York: HarperOne, 2002), 299–300.

Chapter 13

[65] Rabbi Harold S. Kushner addresses the problem of unmerited suffering in response to the death of a son in *When Bad Things Happen to Good People* (New York: Anchor Books, 1981). Bart D. Ehrman describes how the problem of suffering led to his transition to agnosticism in *God's Problem: How the Bible*

Fails to Answer Our Most Important Question—Why We Suffer (New York: HarperOne, 2008).

[66] *The Jazz Singer*, directed by Richard Fleischer, EMI Films, 1980.

[67] Amy-Jill Levine, *Short Stories by Jesus: The Enigmatic Parables of a Controversial Rabbi* (New York: HarperOne, 2014), 45–70.

[68] Levine, 69, where she gives a very different view of the prodigal: "What are we to make of that younger son? ... I neither like nor trust the younger son. I do not see him doing anything other than what he has always done—take advantage of his father's love. It's hard to get much work done when one is filled with fatted calf."

Chapter 14

[69] Saint Augustine, "Sermon 112A," *Essential Sermons. The Works of Saint Augustine: A Translation for the 21ˢᵗ Century*, ed. Boniface Ramsey, trans. Edmund Hill, O.P. (Hyde Park, New York: New City Press, 2007), 184, 188–189.

[70] Amy-Jill Levine, *Short Stories by Jesus: The Enigmatic Parables of a Controversial Rabbi* (New York: HarperOne, 2014), 45–46, 61–62.

[71] Levine, 9, 46–47.

[72] Levine, 94–95; and Amy-Jill Levine, "Bearing False Witness: Common Errors Made About Early Judaism," in Amy-Jill Levine and Marc Zvi Brettler, eds., *The Jewish Annotated New Testament* (Oxford New York: Oxford University Press, 2011), 502.

[73] Some Christian interpretations of the parable interpret it as Jesus expanding Jewish love requirements to Gentiles, but that is not what the context of the story does, although the implications of being a neighbor do extend beyond the bounds of ethnicity. As Michael Fagenblat points out: "It shows the Jewish questioner what a neighbor *does* but does not redefine what a neighbor *is*." Michael Fagenblat, "The Concept of Neighbor in Jewish Ethics," in Levine and Brettler, 543.

[74] See Benyamim Tsedaka and Sharon Sullivan, eds., *The Israelite Samaritan Version of the Torah: First English Translation, Compared with the Masoretic Version*, trans. Benyamim Tsedaka (Grand Rapids, Michigan: William B. Eerdmans Publishing Company, 2013).

[75] Levine, 90–95.

[76] The story of this student and of the integration of Mercer is in Will D. Campbell, *The Stem of Jesse: The Costs of Community at a 1960s Southern School* (Macon: Mercer University Press, 2005). The story of the pastor who fought

but failed to have Sam Oni welcomed at the church on Mercer's campus is told in Thomas J. Holmes, *Ashes for Breakfast: A Diary of Racism in an American Church* (Valley Forge: The Judson Press, 1969); and in Grace Bryan Holmes, *Time to Reconcile: The Odyssey of a Southern Baptist* (Athens: The University of Georgia Press, 2000), 224–241.

[77] Clarence Jordan, *Clarence Jordan's Cotton Patch Gospel: Luke and Acts* (Macon, Georgia: Smyth and Helwys Publishing, Inc., 2013), 37–38. My interpretation at that time may also have been influenced by the fact that Clarence's son Jim was a classmate and fellow member of Mercer Independent Men's Association where we often discussed the religious views by which members of the Koinonia community lived.

[78] Origen, "Homily 34.3," *Origen Homilies on Luke: Fragments on Luke* (1996), 138. See also discussions of Augustine's allegorical use of the parable in C. H. Dodd, *The Parables of the Kingdom* (London: Nisbet and Company Ltd., 1950), 11–12; and John Dominic Crossan, *The Power of Parable: How Fiction by Jesus Became Fiction about Jesus* (New York: HarperOne, 2012), 51–53.

[79] John W. Welch, "The Good Samaritan: Forgotten Symbols," *Liahona*, February 2007, http://www.lds.org/liahona/2007/02/the-good-samaritan-forgotten-symbols?lang=eng (accessed May 22, 2013). Welch developed his point about the cathedrals and included extensive graphic illustrations in: "The Good Samaritan: A Type and Shadow of the Plan of Salvation," *Brigham Young University Studies*, Spring 1999, 51–115.

[80] *The Godfather*, directed by Francis Ford Coppola, Alfran Productions, 1972. It is interesting to note that in the movie the sons and not the original Godfather speak of murder as business not personal.

[81] See Lisa Quast, "I hate 'Its business, not Personal,'" *Forbes* (September 23, 2010), http://www.forbes.com/sites/work-in-progress/2010/09/23/i-hate-its-business-not-personal/ (accessed January 1, 2015) for a reaction to this concept in business that illustrates the importance of listening and compassion at work.

[82] Charles Dickens, *Four Complete Novels: Great Expectations, Hard Times, A Christmas Carol, A Tale of Two Cities* (New York: Gramercy Books, 1982), 537.

[83] Dickens, 543.

Chapter 15

[84] *Butch Cassidy and the Sundance Kid*, directed by George Roy Hill, 20th Century Fox, 1969.

[85] See the discussion of Son of Man in William R. Herzog II, *Prophet and*

Teacher: An Introduction to the Historical Jesus (Louisville: Westminster John Knox Press, 2005), 86.

[86] Richard A. Horsley, *The Prophet Jesus and the Renewal of Israel: Moving Beyond a Diversionary Debate* (Grand Rapids, Michigan: William B. Eerdman's Publishing Company, 2012), 1–64 provides an excellent analysis of this debate and calls for going beyond it. I have already expressed a preference for going beyond this debate by focusing on Jesus Research, as advocated by James H. Charlesworth in *The Historical Jesus: An Essential Guide* (Nashville: Abingdon Press, 2007), xiii-xx; "Introduction: Why Evaluate Twenty-Five Years of Jesus Research?" in *Jesus Research: An International Perspective, The First Princeton-Prague Symposium on Jesus Research*, ed. James H. Charlesworth (Grand Rapids, Michigan: William B. Eerdmans Publishing Company, 2009), 1–15; and "Introduction: The Second Princeton-Prague Symposium: Jesus Research Methodologies," in *Jesus Research: New Methodologies and Perceptions, The Second Princeton-Prague Symposium on Jesus Research, Princeton 2007*, ed. James H. Charlesworth (Grand Rapids. Michigan: William B. Eerdmans Publishing Company, 2014), 1–13. See also Herzog, 1–24.

[87] Bart D. Ehrman provides an excellent description of the accepted rules for attestation of texts in *How Jesus Became God: The Exaltation of a Jewish Preacher from Galilee* (New York: HarperOne, 2014), 94–98. However, these are what I would call "rules of thumb" rather than truly reliable scientific rules, as they fail to insure the kind of reliability that textual scholars wish to find. The publications of the Jesus Seminar also show results of their application of those principles, but their consensus has not gained general acceptance within the scholarly community where many personal opinions are offered for differing translations of texts and for varying applications of the rules of attestation. See Herzog, 25–42 for a detailed discussion of the criteria, which includes those applied by the Jesus Seminar and variations made by N. T. Wright.

[88] Richard A, Horsley, *Jesus and the Powers: Conflict, Covenant, and the Hope of the Poor* (Minneapolis: Fortress Press, 2011); and *The Prophet Jesus and the Renewal of Israel*. See also Herzog, 11–24 for another endorsement of Jesus as a prophetic figure leading a renewal movement. N.T. Wright, *Christian Origins and the Question of God. Volume Two: Jesus and the Victory of God* (Minneapolis: Fortress Press, 1996), 147–197 provides another view of Jesus as prophet, concluding that he was perceived as a prophet and in fact "was *conscious* of a vocation to be a prophet (196)."

[89] N. T. Wright, *Christian Origins and the Question of God. Volume One: The New*

Testament and the People of God (Minneapolis: Fortress Press, 1992), 331–338.

[90] Wright, 333–334 points to agreement that Schweitzer was right about the importance of the apocalyptic but is now seen as misunderstanding the detailed nature of apocalyptic expectations.

[91] James H. Charlesworth (ed), *The Messiah: Developments in Earliest Judaism and Christianity* (Minneapolis: Fortress Press, 2010), 19.

[92] For a brief introduction to the variety of forms taken by messianism, see David B. Levenson, "Messianic Movements," in Amy-Jill Levine and Marc Zvi Brettler, eds., *The Jewish Annotated New Testament* (Oxford New York: Oxford University Press, 2011), 530–535. The ministry of Jesus can also be seen in the context of traditions of charismatic prophecy of which there were other examples in Jesus's own time along with his healing and exorcism activity. See the brief account by Geza Vermes, "Jewish Miracle Workers in the Late Second Temple Period," in Levine and Brettler, *Jewish Annotated New Testament*, 536–537; and also Geza Vermes, *Christian Beginnings: From Nazareth to Nicaea* (New Haven: Yale University Press, 2012), 1–60. See also the comments by Herzog on the role of prophecy around the time of Jesus and the conception of time among the peasantry, all of which call into question the notion that prophetic language was apocalyptic or eschatological in the sense usually applied to Jesus, 99–124.

[93] Albert Schweitzer, *The Psychiatric Study of Jesus: Exposition and Criticism* (Boston: The Beacon Press, 1948).

[94] See the obituary for Will D. Campbell in the *New York Times*, June 4, 2013, http://www.nytimes.com/2013/06/05/us/will-d-campbell-maverick-minister-and-civil-rights-stalwart-dies-at-88.html?pagewanted=all&_r=0

Chapter 16

[95] Craig A. Evans, *Jesus and His World: The Archaeological Evidence* (Louisville: Westminster John Knox Press, 2013), 20–30. See also Mark A. Chancey, *The Myth of a Gentile Galilee* (Cambridge: Cambridge University Press, 2002); James H, Charlesworth, ed. *Jesus and Archaeology* (Grand Rapids, Michigan: William B. Eerdmans Publishing Company, 2006); and Jodi Magness, *Stone and Dung, Oil and Spit: Jewish Daily Life in the Time of Jesus* (Grand Rapids, Michigan: William B. Eerdmans Publishing Company, 2011).

[96] James H. Charlesworth, "Jesus and the Temple," in *Jesus and the Temple: Textual and Archaeological Explorations*, James H. Charlesworth ed. (Minneapolis: Fortress Press, 2014), 159.

[97] For more detail on the temple state under Roman domination, see William R. Herzog II, *Prophet and Teacher: An Introduction to the Historical Jesus* (Louisville: Westminster John Knox Press, 2004), 43–50.

[98] See the description of the governmental environment in which Jesus lived in Herzog, 43–69. One of his very interesting observations on page 68 is: "It is also true that Jesus showed relatively little interest in Rome but focuses his attention on internal elites like Herod and the Herodians or the high priests. Even then, Jesus interacted with their proxies and retainers like the Pharisees or their scribes, rather than confronting the elites directly."

[99] Amy-Jill Levine, *Short Stories by Jesus: The Enigmatic Parables of a Controversial Rabbi* (New York: HarperOne, 2014), emphasizes that Pharisees were village based and not connected with the temple elite as a group; however, Richard Horsley, *The Prophet Jesus and the Renewal of Israel: Moving Beyond a Diversionary Debate* (Grand Rapids, Michigan: William B. Eerdmans Publishing Company, 2012), 60, says the Pharisees and scribes came from Jerusalem to Galilee "as representatives of the high priestly rulers and are closely associated with the high priests in Jerusalem." See also Herzog, 71–98.

[100] Herzog, 79–98, describes this conflict in terms of "honor challenge" as scribes, Pharisees, and local synagogue leaders challenged the status and authority of Jesus in contemporary society. The challenge to Jesus was to uphold the role of the temple and the "great tradition" of Torah interpretation against the more prophetic "little tradition" interpretations coming from Jesus. Herzog, 158–161, also describes Jesus as playing the role of broker in offering God's power through healing and exorcism in a way that challenged the authority of the temple as the main broker of the power of God.

[101] Levine, 280–281 suggests the tenants may have been political powers such as Rome rather than the high priest.

[102] Amy-Jill Levine, *The Misunderstood Jew: The Church and the Scandal of the Jewish Jesus* (New York: Harper One, 2006), 23–24. On pages 24–26, she argues Jesus kept kosher standards. The Jewishness of Jesus has also been presented in several works by Geza Vermes, including *Jesus the Jew: A Historian's Reading of the Gospels* (Philadelphia: Fortress Press, 1981); *The Religion of Jesus the Jew* (Minneapolis: Fortress Press, 1993); and *Christian Beginnings: From Nazareth to Nicaea* (New Haven: Yale University Press, 2012).

Chapter 17

[103] Richard A. Horsley with John S. Hanson, *Bandits, Prophets, and Messiahs:*

Popular Movements in the Time of Jesus (Harrisburg, Pennsylvania: Trinity Press International, 1999), 112–114. See *Josephus: The Complete Works*, trans. By William Whiston, A.M. (Nashville: Thomas Nelson, 1998). For Judas the Galilean, *The Antiquities of the Jews*, 17.271–272, page 563; and *The Wars of the Jews*, 2.56, page 657. For Simon, *Antiquities* 17.273–276, pages 563–564. For Anthronges, *Antiquities*, 17.278–285, page 564. See the distinction between prophetic, royal, and priestly movements in David B. Levinson, "Messianic Movements," Amy-Jill Levine and Marc Zvi Brettler, eds., *The Jewish Annotated New Testament* (Oxford New York: Oxford University Press, 2011), 530–535. See also the discussion of the types of prophetic movements in William R. Herzog II, *Prophet and Teacher: An Introduction to the Historical Jesus* (Louisville: Westminster John Knox Press, 2005), 99–124.

[104] Horsley and Hanson, *Bandits*, 161–187; and *Josephus*. For John the Baptist, *Antiquities*, 18.116–119, page 581. For the Samaritan, *Antiquities*, 18.85–87, page 578. For Theudas, *Antiquities*, 20.97–98, page 579. For the Egyptian, *Antiquities*, 20.169–171, pages 637–638, and *Wars*, 2.261–263, page 737.

[105] Horsely and Hanson distinguishes between popular messianic movements, such as those at Herod's death, and the popular and oracular prophetic movements that included Jesus and John the Baptist with the other popular movements until the revolt in 66. On messianic expectations, see also Levinson, "Messianic Movements," in Levine and Brettler, 530–535; and James H. Charlesworth, ed. *The Messiah: Development in Earliest Judaism and Christianity* (Minneapolis: Fortress Press, 2010).

[106] Richard A. Horsley, *Jesus and the Spiral of Violence: Popular Jewish Resistance in Roman Palestine* (Minneapolis; Fortress Press, 1993), 253–255; and *Jesus and the Powers: Conflict. Covenant, and the Hope of the Poor* (Minneapolis: Fortress Press, 2011), 101.

[107] Richard A. Horsley, *Jesus in Context: Power, People, and Performance* (Minneapolis: Fortress Press, 2008), 10.

Chapter 18

[108] Jack Kelley, "The Parable of the Workers in the Field," http://gracethru-faith.com/topical-studies/parables/the-parable-of-the-workers-in-the-field/ (accessed July 4, 2014).

[109] William R. Herzog II, *Prophet and Teacher: An Introduction to the Historical Jesus* (Louisville: Westminster John Knox Press, 2005), 145–151.

[110] See the analysis of Richard A. Horsely in *Christian Origins. A People's History*

of Christianity Volume I (Minneapolis: Fortress Press, 2010), 58–62. See also the analysis in Amy-Jill Levine, *Short Stories by Jesus: The Enigmatic Parables of a Controversial Rabbi* (New York: HarperOne, 2014), 247–273. Herzog, 121–124 gives a sobering description of the "familiar social script" explaining how Lazarus became a beggar and the life of rejection experienced by beggars.

[111] Horsley, 65–68. See also Levine, 280–281 for a somewhat different view.

[112] Horsley, 62–65; and Levine, 197–219. See also the description of Jewish society in Jesus's time in Herzog, *Prophet and Teacher*, 43–69.

[113] Sr. Rose Pacatte, "What the Parable of the Vineyard Workers Really Says," National Catholic Reporter, http://ncronline.org/blogs/ncr-today/what-parable-vineyard-workers-really-says (accessed July 4, 2014).

Chapter 19

[114] James H. Charlesworth (ed), The Messiah: Developments in Earliest Judaism and Christianity (Minneapolis: Fortress Press, 2010), xv.

[115] Charlesworth, 14.

[116] Charlesworth, 19.

[117] Charlesworth, 8–11.

[118] Charlesworth, 3, 35.

[119] See chapter 17 for more on these movements and for Horsley citations. Horsely presents his analysis of the movements recorded by Josephus most recently in *Jesus in Context: People, Power and Performance* (Minneapolis: Fortress press, 2008), 36–42; *Christian Origins. A People's History of Christianity, Volume I* (Minneapolis: Fortress Press, 2010), 24–30; and *Jesus and the Powers: Conflict, Covenant, and the Hope of the Poor* (Minneapolis: Fotress Press, 2011), 81–86.

[120] John J. Collins, *The Apocalyptic Imagination: An Introduction to Jewish Apocalyptic Literature* (Grand Rapids, Michigan: William B. Eerdmans Publishing Company, 1998), 261–264.

[121] Bart Ehrman, *How Jesus Became God: The Exaltation of a Jewish Preacher from Galilee* (New York: HarperOne, 2014), 118–124; Richard Horsley, *The Prophet Jesus and the Renewal of Israel: Moving Beyond a Diversionary Debate* (Grand Rapids, Michigan: William B. Eerdmans Publishing Company, 2012), 156–157.

Chapter 20

[122] Elisha A. Hoffman, "Are You Washed in the Blood of the Lamb," pub. 1878. The lyrics can be found online at the Timeless Truths Online Library,

http://library.timelesstruths.org/music/Are_You_Washed_in_the_Blood/ (accessed January 10, 2015).

[123] Fanny Crosby, "Though Yours Since be as Scarlet," pub. 1887. Lyrics can be found online through Cyberhymnal.org, http://www.cyberhymnal.org/htm/t/h/thoyours.htm (accessed January 10, 2015).

[124] *The Passion of the Christ*, directed by Mel Gibson, Newmarket Films, 2004.

[125] See Adele Berlin and Marc Zvi Brertler, eds., *The Jewish Study Bible: Jewish Publication Society TANAKH Translation* (Oxford, New York: Oxford University Press, 2004), 243–247, especially the commentary on 243–244 on the chapter as a whole, followed by commentary verse by verse. See also the text and commentary in Harold W. Attridge, ed., *The HarperColllins Study Bible* (New York: HarperOne, 2006), 174–176.

[126] Jonathan Klawans, "Concepts of Purity in the Bible," in *The Jewish Study Bible*, 2042.

[127] Klawans, 2043.

[128] Klawans, 2045.

[129] Klawans, 2045.

[130] Attredge, 1947.

Chapter 21

[131] William R. Herzog III compares this process to archaeology as it digs into a hill revealing later developments first and eventually reaching earlier features much further underground. See *Prophet and Teacher: An Introduction to the Historical Jesus* (Louisville: Westminster John Knox Press, 2005), 25–42.

[132] James D. G. Dunn, *Jesus, Paul, and the Gospels* (Grand Rapids, Michigan: William B. Eerdmans Publishing Company, 2011), 3–44 is a good summary of information presented at greater length in *The Oral Gospel Tradition* (Grand Rapids, Michigan: William B. Eerdmans Publishing Company, 2013) and *Jesus Remembered, Christianity in the Making, Volume I* (Grand Rapids, Michigan: William B. Eerdmans Publishing Company, 2003). John P. Meier, *A Marginal Jew: Rethinking the Historical Jesus. Volume One: The Roots of the Problem and the Person* (New York: Doubleday, 1991), 26–31 rejects a distinction between the historical and historic Jesus as a wrong turn, evident in scholars like Bultmann, because it involves developments in Christianity well past the time of Jesus. Dunn's use of the term is helpful, I think, to point to the distinction between the externals of what Jesus may have said and done (historical information) as opposed to the impact it made, which resulted in its incorporation in oral tra-

ditions. Both of these uses concern the lifetime of Jesus and the memory of what happened in that lifetime rather than later developments in Christianity.
[133] See Robert W. Funk, Roy W. Hoover, and The Jesus Seminar, *The Five Gospels: The Search for the Authentic Words of Jesus* (San Francisco: HarperSanFrancisco, 1997), 1–38; Robert W. Funk and The Jesus Seminar, *The Acts of Jesus: The Search for the Authentic Deeds of Jesus* (San Francisco: HarperSanFrancisco, 1998), 1–40.
[134] Ronald J. Allen, *The Life of Jesus for Today* (Louisville: Westminster John Knox Press, 2008), x.
[135] James H. Charlesworth, *The Historical Jesus: An Essential Guide* (Nashville: Abingdon Press, 2008), xiii–xx.
[136] Craig A. Evans, *Jesus and His World: The Archaeological Evidence* (Louisville: Westminster John Knox Press, 2012), 1, 9–10. Richard Horsley and Tom Thatcher, *John, Jesus, and the Renewal of Israel* (Grand Rapids, Michigan: William B. Eerdmans Publishing Company, 2013), 120–134 apply verisimilitude to the gospel of John.
[137] For insight into the oral tradition and how it produced gospels, see Horsley and Thatcher; and Dunn, *Jesus, Paul, and the Gospels*.
[138] Dunn, *Jesus, Paul, and the Gospels*, 51–83.

Chapter 22
[139] James D. G. Dunn, *Jesus, Paul, and the Gospels* (Grand Rapids, Michigan: William B. Eerdmans Publishing Company, 2011), 80–83, notes that John's approach appears to be an effort to fill gaps left by the synoptic versions. In this respect, John was writing later and apparently was aware of the synoptic versions. This could be taken as support for harmonization for some, but Dunn's point was that the four gospels draw on common oral traditions and John may have included some aspects he knew better from contacts in Jerusalem.
[140] Dunn, 70–91, attributes the differences in how Jesus spoke in John to the compiler of the gospel as his distinctive interpretation of elements in the oral tradition (and not as reliance on Greek philosophy as earlier scholarship had contended). His view lends support to the traditional interpretation of John as a more spiritual version of what was in the synoptics.
[141] For the application of verisimilitude to the gospel of John, see Richard Horsley and Tom Thatcher, *John, Jesus, and the Renewal of Israel* (Grand Rapids, Michigan: William B. Eerdmans Publishing Company, 2013), 120–134. John

P. Meier, *A Marginal Jew: Rethinking the Historical Jesus. Volume I. The Roots of the Problem and the Person* (New York: Doubleday, 1991), 372–433 is a thorough discussion of the probable chronology of Jesus's life.

Chapter 23

[142] Bart D. Ehrman, *How Jesus Became God: The Exaltation of a Jewish Preacher from Galilee* (New York: Harper One, 2014), 118–124.

[143] N. T. Wright, *Christian Origins and the Question of God. Volume Two: Jesus and the Victory of God* (Minneapolis: Fortress Press, 1996), stated succinctly in the second paragraph on page 522 and at greater length 540–552.

[144] John Shelby Spong, *Jesus for the Non-Religious: Recovering the Divine at the Heart of the Human* (New York: Harper One, 2007), 44–46.

[145] Amy-Jill Levine and Marc Zvi Brettler (eds), *The Jewish Annotated New Testament: New Revised Standard Version Translation* (New York: Oxford University Press, 2011), notes on page 50. Wright, 540–552 includes a thorough discussion of whether there was a trial.

[146] John Dominic Crossan, *Jesus: A Revolutionary Biography* (San Francisco: Harper San Francisco, 1994), 121–127, 154–158.

[147] Ehrman, 136–143, 151–169.

[148] Craig A. Evans, *Jesus and His World: The Archaeological Evidence* (Louisville: Westminster John Knox Press, 2013), 113–140.

[149] Ehrman, 189–192.

[150] N. T. Wright, *Christian Origins and the Question of God. Volume Three: The Resurrection of the Son of God* (Minneapolis: Fortress Press, 2003), 587–615 discusses the debate over resurrection and emphasizes the importance of embodiment but with a previously unknown form of body.

[151] Ehrman, 147–149; Bart D. Ehrman, *Jesus, Interrupted: Revealing the Hidden Contradictions in the Bible (and Why We Don't Know About Them)* (New York: Harper One, 2009), 171–179.

[152] N.T. Wright, *The Resurrection of the Son of God*, especially 553–738; and Craig A. Evans and N.T. Wright, *Jesus, the Final Days: What Really Happened* (Louisville: Westminster John Know Press, 2009), 81–107.

[153] [154] N. T. Wright, *Surprised by Scripture: Engaging Contemporary Issues*, Kindle ed. (New York: HarperOne, 2014), 54; "If there really is a new creation on the loose, the historian wouldn't have any analogies for it, and the scientist wouldn't be able to rank its characteristic events with other events that might otherwise have been open to inspection," 58.

[155] Amy-Jill Levine, *The Misunderstood Jew: The Church and the Scandal of the Jewish Jesus* (New York: Harper One, 2006), 58.

[156] Wright, *The Resurrection of the Son of God*, 326, 607–615; Evans and Wright, *Jesus, the Final Days*, 97.

[157] Wright, *The Resurrection of the Son of God*, 726–731.

Chapter 24

[158] Ralph Waldo Emerson, *Self-Reliance and Other Essays* (New York: Dover Publications, 1993), 24.

[159] Colin Harris, "Our Need to Be Right Undercuts Theological Process," at EthicsDaily.com, http://ethicsdaily.com/our-need-to-be-right-undercuts-theological-process-cms-21796 (accessed June 11, 2014).

[160] Colin Harris in a private email to the author.

[161] Marcus J. Borg, Reading the Bible Again for the First Time: Taking the Bible Seriously but Not Literally *(New York: Harper One, 2002)*, 205–218 applies his metaphorical approach to multiple accounts in the gospels.

[162] Marcus J. Borg, *Jesus: Understanding the Life, Teachings, and Relevance of a Religious Revolutionary* (New York: Harper One, 2006), 274–276.

[163] Marcus J. Borg, *Speaking Christian: Why Christian Words Have Lost Their Meaning and Power—And How They Can Be Restored* (New York: Harper One, 2011).

[164] Richard Rohr, *Falling Upward: A Spirituality for the Two Halves of Life* (San Francisco: Jossey-Bass, 2011).

[165] Erich Fromm, *The Art of Loving* (New York: Harper Collins Perennial Modern Classics, 2006); and M. Scott Peck, *The Road Less Traveled: A New Psychology of Love, Traditional Values and Spiritual Growth* (New York: Touchstone, 2003).

[166] Barbara Brown Taylor, *Learning to Walk in the Dark* (New York: Harper One, 2014), 43–47.

[167] Bernhard W. Anderson with Steven Bishop, *Out of the Depths: The Psalms Speak for us Today* (Louisville: Westminster John Knox Press, 2000), 5.

Chapter 25

[168] See David Christian, "The History of Our World in 18 Minutes," a TED presentation of May, 2011, at http://www.ted.com/talks/david_christian_big_history.

[169] See Michael Schermer's account of a 2001 Gallup poll in *How We Believe: Science. Skepticism, and the Search for God* (New York: Henry Holt and Com-

pany, 2002), 249.

[170] The Jewish Publishing Society translation begins: "When God began to create heaven and earth—the earth being unformed and void, with darkness over the surface of the deep and a wind from God sweeping over the water— God said, 'Let there be light'; and there was light." Adele Berlin and Marc Zvi Brettler, eds., *The Jewish Study Bible. Jewish Publication Society TANAKH Translation*, (Oxford New York: Oxford University Press, 2004). The introduction to the book of Genesis comments: "How much history lies behind the story in Genesis? Because the action of the primeval story is not represented as taking place on the plane of ordinary human history and has so many affinities with ancient mythology, it is very far-fetched to speak of its narratives as historical at all." Jon D. Levenson, "Genesis," *Jewish Study Bible*, 11.

[171] Steven Weinberg, *The First Three Minutes: A Modern View of the Origin of the Universe* (New York: Basic Books, 1993), 5.

[172] Weinberg, 6.

[173] Weinberg, 154.

[174] See Bernhard W. Anderson with Stephen Bishop, *Out of the Depths: The Psalms Speak for Us Today* (Louisville: Westminster John Knox Press, 2000), 121–146.

[175] William H. McNeill, *The Rise of the West: A History of the Human Community* (Chicago: University of Chicago Press, 1991).

[176] David Christian, *Maps of Time: An Introduction to Big History* (Berkeley: University of California Press, 2011).

[177] Cynthia Stokes Brown, "A Little Big History of Big History," in Richard B. Simon, Mojgan Behmand, and Thomas Burke, eds., *Teaching Big History* (Oakland, California: University of California Press, 2015), 296–308 tells a more complete story on the development of Big History. As usual, Christian was an innovator who built on the work of many predecessors.

[178] The site for the International Big History Association (www.ibhanet.org) has a link to a two-minute You Tube video featuring Bill Gates: http://www.youtube.com/watch?v=lyQiS-QGRc8&feature=related. Curriculum materials funded by the Gates Foundation are at: www.bighistory project.com. See also Andrew Ross Sorkin, "So Bill Gates Has This Idea for a History Class," *New York Times Magazine*, September 5, 2014. http://www.ny-times.com/2014/09/07/magazine/so-bill-gates-has-this-idea-for-a-history-class.html?_r=0 (accessed January 10, 2015). This article is a good introduction to some aspects of Big History and to David Christian. It is a shame that jour-

nalism so often increases sales by taking negative approaches, such as questioning whether Bill Gates should use his money to shape education in the way he likes, as new ideas such as Big History are presented to the public for the first time in a major newspaper.

[179] Cynthia Stokes Brown, "Constructing a Survey Big History Course," in Leonid Grinin, David Baker, Esther Quaedackers, and Andrey Korotyev eds., *Teaching and Researching Big History: Exploring a New Scholarly Field* (Volgograd: 'Uchitel', 2014), 328–335. Cynthia Stokes Brown was among the pioneers introducing the course at Dominican and the author of the widely used introduction *Big History: From The Big Bang to the Present*, 2nd ed. (New York: The New Press, 2012). See also a book compiling the experience at Dominican University in Simon, Behmand, and Burke, *Teaching Big History*.

[180] Harlan Stelmach, "Teaching Big History or Teaching about Big History?" in Simon, Behmand, and Burke, *Teaching Big History*, 318–335.

Chapter 26

[181] Douglas A. Knight and Amy-Jill Levine, *The Meaning of the Bible: What the Jewish Scriptures and Christian Old Testament Can Teach Us* (New York: Harper One, 2011), 197. See also Jon D. Levinson, "Genesis," in Adele Berlin and Marc Zvi Brettler, *The Jewish Study Bible, The Jewish Publication Society TANAKH Translation* (Oxford New York: Oxford University Press, 2004), 11.

[182] Amy-Jill Levine, *The Old Testament, Lecture 2 Adam and Eve* (Chantilly, Virginia: The Great Courses, 2001), 8.

[183] See a description of agrarian societies in William R. Herzog II, *Prophet and Teacher: An Introduction to the Historical Jesus* (Louisville: Westminster John Knox Press, 2005), 43–69.

Chapter 27

[184] Benyamin Tsedaka (ed), *The Israelite Samaritan Version of the Torah* (Grand Rapids, Michigan: William B. Eerdmans Publishing Company, 2013).

[185] Israel Finkelstein and Neil Asher Silberman, *The Bible Unearthed: Archaeology's New Vision of Ancient Israel and the Origin of its Sacred Texts* (New York: Simon and Schuster, 2001), 27–96.

[186] Finkelstein and Silberman, 58–62.

[187] William G. Dever, *Who Were the Early Israelites and Where Did They Come From?* (Grand Rapids, Michigan: William B. Eerdmans Publishing Company, 2003).

188 Dever, 229–232.

189 Harold W. Attridge (ed), *The HarperCollins Study Bible* (New York: Harper One, 2006), notes on page 109; and Bernhard W. Anderson, *Out of the Depths: The Psalms Speak for Us Today* (Louisville: Westminster John Knox Press, 2000), 36–37.

Chapter 28

190 The commentary on Exodus 20 in Adele Berlin and Marc Zvi Brettler, eds., *The Jewish Study Bible. Jewish Publication Society TANAKH Translation* (Oxford, New York: Oxford University Press, 2004), 148, divides the commandments into duties to God and "duties toward fellow humans."

191 There are interesting differences in interpretation among the commentators in the *Jewish Study Bible*. The commentary on Exodus 20:14 on page 151 notes that one's household is not to be coveted and that wives are among the belongings of the household, reflecting a nomadic period of Israelite history before there was fixed property. This commentator then says Deuteronomy 5:18 separates wife from other items that would have been property when the people settled in the land rather than living as nomads. The commentary on Deuteronomy 5:18, on pages 377–378, sees the change in wording as reflecting the separation of family and property law. The wording of Exodus is taken to include the wife among the "chattels" of the household while Deuteronomy "does not regard the woman as merely one commodity among others comprising a 'house.'" Thus we see in the two versions an evolution within Israelite legal attitudes toward the role of women that is not often appreciated in popular interpretations of the Ten Commandments.

192 Michael Fagenblat, "The Concept of Neighbor in Jewish and Christian Ethics," in Amy-Jill Levine and Marc Zvi Brettler, eds., *The Jewish Annotated New Testament*, 540–543, discusses the concept of neighbor through interpretations of Leviticus 19:18 to show that it applied to resident aliens but could be used to apply more generally to mean any human being or anyone in an intimate relationship with someone. He also points out this was meant to be national law of the community similar to United States law versus the law of another nation and should not be overgeneralized to show Jewish hostility to non-Jews. Fagenblat does not apply his analysis directly to the Ten Commandments. He emphasizes that Jesus's point in the story of the Good Samaritan shows "what a neighbor *does* but does not redefine what a neighbor *is*."

193 James H. Charlesworth, "Introduction: Devotion to and Worship in

Jerusalem's Temple," in *Jesus and the Temple: Textual and Archaeological Explorations* (Minneapolis: Fortress Press, 2014) 12–16 in which Charlesworth guides an imaginary virtual tour following Jesus in the temple. See also Leen and Kathleen Ritmeyer, *The Ritual of the Temple in the Time of Christ* (Jerusalem: Carta, 2002); and *Secrets of Jerusalem's Temple Mount* (Updated and enlarged edition, Washington, DC: Biblical Archaeology Society, 2006).

[194] See the account by Isabel Kirschner, "Israeli Girl, 8, at the Center of Tension over Religious Extremism," *New York Times* (December 27, 2011), http://www.nytimes.com/2011/12/28/world/middleeast/israeli-girl-at-center-of-tension-over-religious-extremism.html?pagewanted=all&module=Search&mabReward=r (accessed November 7, 2014).

[195] Amy-Jill Levine, *Short Stories by Jesus: The Enigmatic Parables of a Controversial Rabbi* (New York: HarperOne, 2014), 185–186 where she quotes the prayer and explains many interpretations to gloss over the apparent anti-female message. In this work, Levine also objects to flawed descriptions of the purity rules, which also would place women in prejudicial contexts. William R. Herzog II provides one such example that she would object to in *Prophet and Teacher: An Introduction to the Historical Jesus* (Louisville, Kentucky: Westminster John Knox Press, 2005), 125–126 as he discusses "purity maps" intended to separate incompatible pairs as God's holiness is separated from what is incompatible. This results in a hierarchy taken from Jerome Neyrey that begins by following the degrees of separation found in the temple (priests, then Levites, then Israelites), but lists converts, slaves, bastards, eunuchs and those with damaged testicles before coming to "those without a penis" as the last degree of separation.

Chapter 29

[196] Historians today often refer to Neo-Assyrians and Neo-Babylonians when referring to the people called Assyrians and Babylonians in the Bible. We will continue to use the terminology familiar from the Bible.

[197] Geza Vermes, *Christian Beginnings: From Nazareth to Nicaea* (New Haven: Yale University Press, 2013), 1–60. Douglas Knight and Amy-Jill Levine refer to ecstatic or frenzied aspects of prophecy found in other cultures of the Near East in *The Meaning of the Bible: What the Jewish Scriptures and Christian Old Testament Can Teach Us* (New York: Harper One, 2011), 416–417.

[198] Knight and Levine, 398.

Chapter 30

[199] Thomas L. Thompson, *The Mythic Past: Biblical Archaeology and the Myth of Israel* (New York: Basic Books, 1999), xv.

[200] See Israel Finkelstein and Neil Asher Silberman, *The Bible Unearthed: Archaeology's New Vision of Ancient Israel and the Origin of its Sacred Texts* (New York: Touchstone, 2001); and William G. Dever, *Who Were the Early Israelites and Where Did They Come From?* (Grand Rapids, Michigan: William B. Eerdmans Publishing Company, 2003).

[201] See Finkelstein and Silberman, *The Bible Unearthed: Archaeology's New Vision of Ancient Israel and the Origin of its Sacred Texts*; and *David and Solomon: In Search of the Bible's Sacred Kings and the Roots of the Western Tradition* (New York: Free Press, 2006). Also, Israel Finkelstein and Amihai Mazar, *The Quest for the Historical Israel: Debating Archaeology and the History of Early Israel* (Atlanta: Society of Biblical Literature, 2007). Eric M. Meyers, "The Bible and Archaeology," in *The HarperCollins Study Bible*, ed. by Harold Attridge (New York: Harper One, 2006), lxi, says that Finkelstein's views have been rejected but acknowledges continuing debate over the implications of calling the Bible a fictional narrative.

[202] Eric Meyers, "Bible and Archaeology," lxi, remarked: "Not everyone can be a good biblical scholar and an excellent field archaeologist at the same time."

[203] Bart D. Ehrman, *Did Jesus Exist? The Historical Argument for Jesus of Nazareth* (New York: Harper One, 2012).

[204] Thomas L. Thompson, *The Messiah Myth: The Near Eastern Roots of Jesus and David* (New York: Basic Books, 2005); and Thomas L. Thompson and Thomas S. Verenna, eds., *"Is This Not the Carpenter?" The Question of the Historicity of the Figure of Jesus* (Durham, UK: Acumen Publishing Limited, 2013).

[205] State of Israel, Ministry of Foreign Affairs, see the information under the tab for history at http://mfa.gov.il/MFA/AboutIsrael/Pages/default.aspx (accessed January 24, 2015).

[206] Keith W. Whitelam, *The Invention of Ancient Israel: The Silencing of Palestinian History* (New York: Routledge, 1996).

Chapter 31

[207] There are at least three collections represented in the current book of Isaiah. Chapters 1–39 are often identified as First Isaiah, produced by the historical Isaiah, but some chapters within that group appear to come from a later date.

[208] J. R. McNeill and William H. McNeill, *The Human Web: A Bird's-Eye View*

of World History (New York: W. W. Norton, 2003), 60–62.

Chapter 32

[209] Robert B. Balsinger (ed), *Westminster Shorter Catechism with Proof Texts (ESV): An Aid for Study of the Holy Bible* (Good News Publishers, 2010), 10.

[210] Thomas Merton, *No Man Is an Island* (New York: Harcourt, Inc., 1955), 235.

[211] Carolyn J. Sharp, *Old Testament Prophets for Today* (Louisville: Westminster John Knox Press, 2009), 60.

[212] The words of Isaiah 6:2 say they covered their feet. Douglas Knight and Amy-Jill Levine, *The Meaning of the Bible: What the Jewish Scriptures and Christian Old Testament Can Teach Us* (New York: HarperOne, 2011), 305–306, describes use of feet as a euphemism for genitals.

[213] Bernhard Anderson with Steven Bishop, *Out of the Depths: The Psalms Speak for us Today* (Louisville: Westminster John Knox Press, 2000).

Chapter 33

[214] See Bernhard W. Anderson with Steven Bishop, *Out of the Depths: The Psalms Speak to Us Today* (Westminster John Knox, 2000), 11–12, 187–198.

[215] Douglas A. Knight and Amy-Jill Levine, *The Meaning of the Bible: What the Jewish Scriptures and Christian Old Testament Can Teach Us* (New York: HarperOne, 2011), 429.

[216] Adele Berlin and Marc Zvi Brettler, eds., *The Jewish Study Bible. Jewish Publication Society TANAKH Translation* (New York: Oxford University Press, 2004), 1606

[217] Anderson and Bishop, *Out of the Depths*, 49–75.

[218] A more contemporary example is the combination of a very simple kind of faith with abysmal episodes of doubt and even despair that is seen in the private correspondence of Mother Teresa. See Mother Teresa with Brian Kolodiejchuk, *Mother Teresa: Come Be My Light. The Private Writings of the "Saint of Calcutta,"* ed. by Brian Kolodiejchuk (New York: Doubleday, 2007).

Chapter 34

[219] The experiment is described in Stanley Milgram, *Obedience to Authority: An Experimental View* (New York: Harper Perennial, 2009), 13–26.

Chapter 35

[220] John D. Collins, *The Apocalyptic Imagination: An Introduction to Jewish Apocalyptic Literature* (Grand Rapids, Michigan: William B. Eerdmans Publishing Company, 1984), 5–6.

[221] Richard Horsley, *The Prophet Jesus and the Renewal of Israel: Moving Beyond a Diversionary Debate* (Grand Rapids, Michigan: William B. Eerdmans Publishing Company, 2012) 57–58.

[222] See the table in Collins, 7.

[223] Other books about Daniel are The Prayer of Azariah and the Song of the Three Jews, Susanna, and Bel and the Dragon.

[224] See Collins, 85–115; Richard A. Horsley, *Scribes, Visionaries, and the Politics of the Second Temple* (Louisville: Westminster John Know Press, 2007), 173–191; and Richard A. Horsley, *Revolt of the Scribes: Resistance and Apocalyptic Origins* (Minneapolis: Fortress Press, 2010), 81–104

Chapter 36

[225] See the commentaries in Harold W. Attridge, ed., *The HarperCollins Study Bible* (New York: HarperOne, 2006), 6-7; and Adele Berlin and Marc Zvi Brettler, *The Jewish Study Bible. Jewish Publication Society TANAKH Translation* (Oxford, New York: Oxford University Press, 2004), 14.

[226] The text says they covered their feet. This is one of many examples in the Old Testament in which feet are used as a euphemism for genitals. See Douglas Knight and Amy-Jill Levine, *The Meaning of the Bible: What the Jewish Scriptures and Christian Old Testament Can Teach Us* (New York: HarperOne, 2011), 305–306.

[227] John Shelby Spong, *Why Christianity Must Change or Die: A Bishop Speaks to Believers in Exile* (New York: HarperSanFrancisco, 1998); and *A New Christianity for a New World: Why Traditional Faith Is Dying and How a New Faith Is Being Born* (New York: HarperSanFrancisco, 2001).

[228] Marcus J. Borg, *The God We Never Knew: Beyond Dogmatic Religion to a More Authentic Contemporary Faith* (New York: HarperSanFrancisco, 1997), 19–29.

[229] For the long history of thought about God in Judaism, Christianity, and Islam, see Karen Armstrong, *A History of God: The 4000-Year Quest of Judaism, Christianity and Islam* (New York: Alfred A. Knopf, 1994).

Chapter 37

[230] Marcus J. Borg, *Convictions: How I Learned What Matters Most* (New York:

HarperOne, 2014), 35–51.

[231] William James, *The Varieties of Religious Experience: A Study in Human Nature* (New York: The New American Library of World Literature, 1958), 292–293.

[232] Marcus J. Borg, *The God We Never Knew: Beyond Dogmatic Religion to a More Authentic Contemporary Faith* (New York: HarperSanFrancisco, 1997), 40.

[233] Barbara Brown Taylor, *An Altar in the World: A Geography of Faith* (New York: HarperOne, 2009).

Conclusion

[234] Harvey Cox, *The Secular City: Secularization and Urbanization in Theological Perspective* (New Jersey: Princeton University Press, 2013).

[235] John Shelby Spong, *Why Christianity Must Change or Die: A Bishop Speaks to Believers in Exile* (New York: HarperSanFrancisco, 1998).

[236] William James, *The Varieties of Religious Experience: A Study in Human Nature* (New York: New American Library of World Literature, 1958).

[237] Leo Tolstoy, *A Confession and Other Religious Writings* (Translated with an Introduction by Jane Kentish. New York: Penguin Books, 1987), 30, 34, 65.

[238] Marcus J. Borg, *The God We Never Knew: Beyond Dogmatic Religion to a More Authentic Contemporary Faith* (New York: HarperSanFrancisco, 1997); John A. T. Robinson, *The New Reformation?* (London: SCM Press, 1965); and *Exploration into God* (Stanford, California: Stanford University Press, 1967).

[239] Hans Kung, *The Beginning of All Things: Science and Religion* (Cambridge, UK: William B. Eerdmans Publishing Company, 2007); John C. Polkinghorne, *Faith, Science and Understanding* (New Haven: Yale University Press, 2000); and *The Faith of a Physicist* (Minneapolis: Fortress Press, 1996); and Arthur Peacocke, *Paths from Science Towards God: The End of All Our Exploring* (Oxford: Oneworld Publications, 2001).

CPSIA information can be obtained
at www.ICGtesting.com
Printed in the USA
BVOW06s0613181217
503094BV00012B/232/P